PUBLIC POLICY RESOURCES

Peter Knoepfel

Translated from French; first published in 2017 by Seismo-Verlag, Zurich
First published in Great Britain in 2018 by

Policy Press
University of Bristol
1-9 Old Park Hill
Bristol
BS2 8BB
UK
t: +44 (0)117 954 5940
pp-info@bristol.ac.uk
www.policypress.co.uk

North America office:
Policy Press
c/o The University of Chicago Press
1427 East 60th Street
Chicago, IL 60637, USA
t: +1 773 702 7700
f: +1 773-702-9756
sales@press.uchicago.edu
www.press.uchicago.edu

British Library Cataloguing in Publication Data
A catalogue record for this book is available from the British Library

Library of Congress Cataloging-in-Publication Data
A catalog record for this book has been requested

ISBN 978-1-4473-4505-3 hardcover
ISBN 978-1-4473-4507-7 ePub
ISBN 978-1-4473-4508-4 Mobi
ISBN 978-1-4473-4506-0 ePdf

Cover design by Hayes Design
Front cover image: istock
Printed and bound in Great Britain by CPI Group (UK) Ltd,
Croydon, CR0 4YY
Policy Press uses environmentally responsible print partners

Contents

List of tables and figures   iv
Preface   v
Introduction   1

Part I: Foundations and analytical dimensions   7
1   The foundations of public policy analysis   9
2   Definition of public action resources   43
3   Context: A survey of the literature   51

Part II: New conceptual developments: Resource-based approach and analytical dimensions   77
4   Conceptual development of the resource-based approach   81
5   The seven proposed analytical dimensions   91

Part III: The 10 public action resources   103
6   Force   109
7   Law   121
8   Personnel   133
9   Money   147
10   Property   161
11   Information   179
12   Organization   193
13   Consensus   213
14   Time   225
15   Political Support   237

Part IV: Outlook and advice for practical application   249
16   Public policy management by actors' endowment   251
17   Advice for practical application   259

Conclusion: Strengths and weaknesses of the proposed approach   277

References   283
Index   299

List of tables and figures

Tables

1.1   *Possession* rules governing the access of actors to public   35
action resources (using the example of Switzerland)

1.2   *Behavioural rules* governing the modalities of use of public   36
action resources (using the example of Switzerland)

1.3   *Decisional* rules governing the actual use of public action   36
resources in space and time (using the example of Switzerland)

3.1   Recap of the literature review   73

17.1   Units of measurement and suggested choice of indicators   265
for each of the 10 public action resources

17.2   Substantive and institutional content of the six public   270
policy products

Figures

2.1   Overview of the 10 public action resources   43

4.1   Actor groups of the resource information   86

4.2   Extent and coherence of regulations applicable to the   87
resource information

4.3   Summary of the gaps and incoherencies in the institutional   88
regime of the resource information

12.1   Simple and complex modes of circulation of identical   195
planning applications

12.2   The dilemma of divided loyalties   196

15.1   Ten important federal sectoral policy fields and their   240
representation by members of the federal chambers belonging
to the seven most important political parties in Switzerland

17.1   Inventory of public action resources   260

17.2   Template for identifying the exchange of resources between   266
public policy actors

17.3   (Classical) triangle of public policy actors   268

17.4   The six public policy products   268

Preface

This book sets out to demystify the idea of public power as it can be observed through public policy analysis, and to demonstrate it at work in everyday contexts. As part of this process it shows that it is possible to observe policy actors close up, and to pinpoint their share of the responsibility for the results obtained through their use of public action resources. Although this process involving the monitoring and management of the activities of public authorities remains a central issue for political science, and 'resources' are the focus of considerable attention these days, it is worrisome to note that fewer than two dozen authors throughout the world have attempted to provide a precise definition of this phenomenon, to identify its different categories, and to provide a sufficiently robust and operational typology for analysis of the policy actors' games that lead to everyday legislative decisions and the implementation of public policies.

This book proposes to fill this gap. I wrote it with my fellow citizens in mind who invest time and effort in public service. The text does not see itself as 'political' or as siding with one or other of the groups involved in the different public policy stages; rather, it aims to provide equal support to public sector collaborators and to the representatives of interest groups and policy beneficiaries to gain a better understanding of their own activities, and of the resource-related strategic and investment choices made by other actors involved in the public policy process.

The book reflects the fact that the 'people' are always more intelligent than the experts. For me, these 'people' include, among others, the communal council of my commune of Crissier (canton of Vaud), of which I was a member for 27 years, the hundreds of – doctoral and post-doctoral (*habillants*)[1] – students I had the pleasure of supporting in the development of their empirical studies, and the thousands of actors from a large number of communal, cantonal, federal and international policy fields whom I had the pleasure to observe over the course of my academic career from my earliest research in the 1970s. I would also like to acknowledge here my former and current collaborators (in chronological order): Corinne Larrue, Frédéric Varone, Stéphane Nahrath, Jean-David Gerber, Stéphane Boisseaux, Johann Dupuis and many others. I would like to dedicate this book to them as an expression of my gratitude. I would also like to note that, like this book, a considerable proportion of their work draws on our basic textbook entitled *Analyse et pilotage de politiques publiques*, which I wrote with Corrine Larrue and Frédéric Varone in 2006.[2]

I would also like to thank Linda Gubler for her work on the layout and finalising of this book, Stéphane Boisseaux for the final corrections and updates, Emmanuelle Buchard for copy-editing the French text, and last, but not least, Susan Cox[3] for translating the original French version into English.

Grignan, 18 October 2017

Notes

[1] IDHEAP, in chronological order: Serge Terribilini, Sonja Wälti, Chistophe Clivaz, Stéphane Nahrath, Jean-David Gerber, Tobias Hagmann, Jérôme Savary, Lee Nicol, Mirta Olgiati, Markus Rieder, Rémy Schweizer, Johann Dupuis, Guillaume de Buren, Melaine Laesslé, Vladimir Condo, Pablo Dussan. And external: Frédéric Varone, Helmut Weidner, Corinne Larrue, Jean Simos, Patrizia Baroni Cedro, Peter Glauser, Ingrid Kissling-Näf, Alexander Flückiger, Antonio Osada, Chloé Vlassopoulos, Emmanul Reynard, Lean-Marc Dziedzicki, Kurt Bisang, Tourane Corbière-Nicollier, David Aubin, Mathieu Bonnefond, Miritxell Costejà Florensa, Christian Brèthaut and Taras Tretiak.

[2] This book also provided the basis for a subsequent book on Swiss environmental policy (Knoepfel et al, 2010), which adopted most of the concepts presented in the earlier work and developed them in further detail. Versions of the 2006 book have been published in Spanish, English, German, Ukrainian and Canadian French. The English version is: Knoepfel, P., Larrue, C., Varone, F. and Hill, M. (2011) *Public policy analysis*, Bristol: Policy Press.

[3] Sadly, Susan Cox passed away before this book was published.

Introduction

Any observer of the public or private actors involved in the production of public action will encounter frequent complaints about the *lack of resources* available to these actors. A common statement likely to be heard in this context is: 'I would like to take action, but I do not have the necessary money, legal basis, people, time etc.' Surprisingly, such statements are made not only by marginal actors but also, and perhaps even more often, by individuals and groups that the observer would identify as powerful political-administrative, economic or social actors who enjoy a high degree of public visibility and a strong presence in a considerable number of policy contexts. Moreover, this observation is not limited to the development of new activities that may be initiated by these actors; it also concerns the implementation of follow-up interventions or inventions involving the production of public action in existing areas.

Aside from the fact that these complaints form part of the daily rituals of political-administrative actors and are made with a view to ensuring the maintenance or enlargement of their resource portfolios, the size of which is generally considered a reflection of their 'power' and political importance, in many cases they constitute a justified response to the budgetary cuts that affect the actors' scope for manoeuvre and, as a result, the effectiveness of 'their' policies.

The critical observer will confirm, however, that these complaints are frequently focused on *known action resources* that have been the subject of debate since time immemorial. The resources in question here are financial, legal, human and, of course, temporal in nature. One of the core messages of the concept of policy actors' resources consists, however, in the firm premise that there are at least *six other categories of resources*, which surprisingly receive little attention in the debates surrounding public policy resources. The resources in question here include Information,[1] Organization, Consensus, Property, Political Support and, one of the oldest resources of all, which I refer to as Force.

As discussed in detail in this book, in many cases a lack of traditional resources may be *compensated* for by the use of one or other of the other resources that tend to receive less attention but are nonetheless vital to the conduct of any policy that aims to be effective. It is worth recounting here the anecdote about a former director of a major federal agency in Switzerland who, having completed a course on the topic of resources, insisted that the cost of all measures suggested to him be verified not only in relation to the four primary traditional resources,

1

but also in relation to the six others and furthermore, in relation to the possible substitution of any potentially lacking traditional resources by one or more of the new resources he had discovered on the course.

Hence, given the scarcity of these resources across the entire community of public policy actors, the scientific focus on the resources available to these actors corresponds primarily to a practical and growing need. These resources are of *dual origin*: they come from *the state*, which supplies each of the substantive sectoral policies with the resources necessary for their successful functioning through its *institutional policies* (Knoepfel and Varone, 2009). Accordingly, public finance policies generate and accumulate financial resources that facilitate the levying of an entire series of taxes among taxpayers and then distribute this money to a large number of political-administrative actors, each of whom is responsible for the conduct of 'their' substantive public policies. Like the use made of it by the political-administrative actors, this distribution process is regulated by a large number of provisions defined in public finance policies (for example, budgets and accounting rules).

The selection criteria, based on which these institutional policies work, are only partly explained by the needs of the substantive policies. It is also necessary to consider the general economic framework of the state's budgetary policy (for example, state of the economy and public debt; see Soguel, 2011) and, for example, the rules governing the activation of the administrative assets that can lead, in accounting terms, to increases in the cost of producing the public action in question. The same applies to institutional policies governing the endowment of substantive policies with the public action resources Law (centralized justice services), Personnel (human resources policy shared by the entire administrative body in question) and Property (administrative bodies responsible for all of a public administration's buildings).

But that is not all. According to their categories, these resources at the disposal of public policy actors also originate, in part at least, from the *production of substantive policies by the actors themselves*. This applies equally to the financial resources that public actors generate through the deduction of charges, the levying of specific taxes and the generation of revenues from the 'sale' of services. The proportion of the public actors' portfolio of action resources that are 'self-generated' in this way is particularly high in the case of Information, Organization and Consensus, which a policy generates through the active maintenance of relations between the target groups, beneficiaries and political-administrative actors.

When it comes to the endowment of substantive policies with action resources, relations between the institutional policies, which are usually implemented at the level of centralized services (both within the administration and within major private and/or associative actors), and sectoral policies, which are managed by the political–administrative actors, are not without tensions. Particularly during times of increasing hardship, the resolution of such tensions necessitates the application of increasingly sophisticated accounting rules. This requires recognition on both sides of the *different action logics* at work in these two types of policies, and does not allow the attribution of absolute veto positions to the actors on either side. The intervention of a 'grand paymaster' who crushes operational services can be just as detrimental in its consequences as the intimidation by 'small paymasters' located at the level of each individual substantive policy who threaten to 'strike' if a budget that is considered adequate is not obtained. Hence it is necessary to avoid the emergence of 'resource wars' within the public sector.

In order to avoid such tensions in practice, it is necessary to avail oneself of the *theoretical conceptualizations* developed by the academic world. This recourse to theory will be limited to a strictly necessary level in this book as it does not aim to develop a new theory about the resources available to the actors involved in public action. In this regard, like the previous book I published with my colleagues on public policy analysis and management (see Knoepfel et al, 2006, 2011), this book simply proposes to situate the definition of the *concept of 'power'* in an *actorial*, *resource-based* and *institutional* context. Actorial, first and foremost, because I start from the theory that power is intrinsically linked with the actors involved in the production of the public action, which gives them the capacity to position themselves in relation to all other actors in the same policy action space. Thus an actor's power can only be defined in relative terms, that is, in relation to the power of other actors. The first use that an actor makes of what we refer to as their 'power' arises on their entry into or exit from this space, for example, by becoming – or avoiding becoming – the target group, beneficiary or one of the key public actors of a new policy or updated one. There is *no 'power' that is not attributed to an actor in one way or another*. Hence my premise is that the term 'actor' refers to a (natural or legal) person, individual or member of a body who is part of a (private or public) legal entity that acts as either a public actor or civil society actor in the context of a public policy through the mobilization or, conversely, non-mobilization of their resources.

Once established in the space of a policy in question, the actors position themselves in relation to the other actors by engaging in 'power games' with the aim of influencing the processes involved and leading to the production and final outcome of a stage in the policy cycle in accordance with their interests and/or values. In this way, they consolidate their power by using it. The latter consists of a *portfolio of public action resources* composed of one or more of the 10 action resources presented in this book. I start from the debatable premise (see Chapter 3 on the current status of the research) that there is a finite number of categories of resources for a given institutional constellation, that is, 10, and that there is no 11th category for the present. These resources are explored on a theoretical basis in this book, and this concept is compared with other conceptualizations of power based on public action resources.

The actors whose portfolio of resources exceeds that of the other actors are not always the ones who succeed in imposing themselves in terms of the content or products of a public policy. This empirical observation is based on a meta-rule of the game, which is acknowledged jointly by the actors and imposes a number of concrete *rules* (or 'institutions', in the language of the neo-institutionalists). These rules primarily govern the modalities of access available to the actors that make use of one of their resources, and these modalities of access can vary in terms of exclusivity. Given that these rules govern the modalities of possession linking a given resource to an actor, I refer to them as possession rules. In effect, the latter define the 'wealth' of each actor group. However, this wealth is merely theoretical because the actors in possession of the resources cannot use all of the resources in their portfolio in just any way or at any time. A second and third group of rules also limit the concrete uses that actors can make of 'their' resources. These involve, first, the behavioural rules governing the modalities of use that are commonly considered as 'acceptable', for example, the non-abusive use of Law and Force, and second, the modalities of use of a given resource in space and time. These rules, which are referred to as decisional, structure the decision-making process throughout the public policy cycle in a way that makes it accessible, predictable and calculable for all of the actors, irrespective of their different strategic objectives. This book revisits these categories of rules presented in our basic textbook and develops them further.

In accordance with the theories of neo-institutionalism and in line with various experiences and observations, these rules are not 'given' but are often the object of strategic games aimed at establishing a better position for one or more actors in relation to the others. Hence, just like the substantive content of the products in question, these institutions become *variables that are partly dependent* on the actors' games. I would suggest, therefore, that there are *no resources without institutions*. It can even be claimed that resources only exist thanks to the institutions, the ultimate purpose of which consists precisely in structuring the interactions between policy actors. These interactions manifest concretely as activities based on the exchange of resources.

This book presents a detailed re-examination of elements from previous publications on policy analysis, which is more systematic and enhanced by experience gained in the course of my teaching activities but does not aim to alter the *basic concepts*. It attempts to provide responses to the numerous questions posed by researchers and students on the positioning of the concept of resources in the scientific landscape and to the other attempts at theorizing this concept in the context of policy analysis. This engagement in dialogue with other conceptualizations defended in the scientific literature of the last 10 years – one of the truly new aspects of this book compared to my earlier works – will enable me to refine the analytical dimensions, among other things, and, based on this, apply them to each of the 10 resources.

The book is divided into *four parts*. Part I revisits the unchallenged constitutive basis of the policy analysis books (Knoepfel et al, 2006, 2010, 2011[2]) in the form of essential summaries and additions, that is, the actors, resources, institutions and products of the policy cycle (Chapter 1). It then proposes a (partly new) definition of public action resources (Chapter 2) and also contains the aforementioned chapter on the status of the literature and positioning of the proposed approach in the context of this scientific landscape (Chapter 3).

The second and entirely new part, Part II, proposes the extension of the public action resources approach to that of institutional resource regimes, in particular, natural resource regimes, which has been practised at my Institute for a good 20 years (Chapter 4), and presents the seven concrete analytical dimensions of public action resources in the field (Chapter 5). The latter provide the basis for the illustrations presented in Part III.

Part III represents the illustrative pièce de résistance of this publication. Following an introductory section, the 10 chapters contained in this part deal with each of the 10 public action resources identified in my policy analysis approach (Chapters 6-15), which are both structured on the basis of the three actor groups (political–administrative actors, target groups and beneficiary groups) and identify the modalities of mobilization based on the policy programming and implementation stages, and the interaction between these stages and the actors. This part of the book contains examples drawn mainly from everyday reality in Switzerland during the period in which the book was written (2012-

16); however, similar examples can be also be found in other countries and in other periods.

Part IV, entitled 'Outlook and advice for practical application', tackles new questions concerning current administrative practice, for example, in relation to the management of policies through their endowment with action resources. It concludes with a checklist for analysing the impacts of resource mobilization on public decisions (Chapter 17).

As required in an academic publication, however practice-oriented it may be, I conclude with a discussion of the strengths and weaknesses of the approach presented in this book. Among the latter I identify the analysis of the literature that is probably too sporadic and selective, and the fact that the book scarcely addresses the question of the capacity of actors to truly mobilize the action resources presented here.

Before moving on to the analysis, I would like to draw the reader's attention to a particular characteristic of this book. In presenting this *catalogue raisonné* of public action resources, I report on realities that are entirely observable but that in some cases remain under-analysed. Needless to say, the analysis of the resources Money and Personnel, for example, draws on a vast literature on public finances and human resources. More specifically, the research developed within our own research group makes an important contribution to the analysis of the resources Law, Property and Information. At the other end of the spectrum, the resources Time, Consensus and Organization remain 'pioneering territory'. It is my hope that future generations of researchers will enter this territory and gradually confirm – or invalidate – the ideas outlined here.

Notes

[1] When used to designate a 'resource' as defined in this book, these terms are written in significant capitals.

[2] Given that this book is a more recent publication and contains some changes to the definitions contained in Knoepfel et al (2006, 2011), a considerable number of the direct quotations are taken from it and translated into English.

Part I
Foundations and analytical dimensions[1]

1

The foundations of
public policy analysis[2]

Public policies

Definitions: Substantive and institutional policies (in particular, 'resource-based')

The definition of a substantive public policy adopted here is one that I have used since 2001 and formalized in our basic textbook that was published in 2006 [2011]. According to this text, a public policy is:

> ... a series of intentionally coherent decisions or activities taken or carried out by different public – and sometimes – private actors, whose resources, institutional links and interests vary, with a view to resolving in a targeted manner a problem that is politically defined as collective in nature. This group of decisions and activities gives rise to formalised actions of a more or less restrictive nature that are often aimed at modifying the behaviour of social groups presumed to be at the root of, or able to solve, the collective problem to be resolved (target groups) in the interest of the social groups who suffer the negative effects of the problem in question (final beneficiaries). (Knoepfel et al, 2006: 29 [2011: 24])

The same definition is adopted for *institutional policies*, which aim to tackle public problems involving the internal functioning of the state apparatus and whose target groups and beneficiaries are public actors in principle. These types of policies include institutional policies dealing with the allocation of action resources to the policy actors involved ('resource-based' institutional policies; see Knoepfel and Varone, 2009: 97ff). In contrast to the basic textbook, this publication also deals with these.

Distinction between the concept of a 'public policy' and the – analytically less relevant – concept of 'public action'

Our definition of public policies differs from the definitions of the 'public action' and 'collective action' type that tend to be used in France in particular (see, for example, Lascoume and Le Galès, 2012). In my view, these definitions are too vague; they include decisions, actors and resources without distinguishing clearly between them, and neglect the empirical fact that all public activity can be characterized very accurately based on its association with one of the *six products* that constitute a public policy cycle: the problem definition (PD), the political-administrative programme (PAP), the political-administrative arrangement for the implementation of the policy (PAA), the action plan (AP), the outputs and the evaluative statement (ES) (see later in this chapter). Moreover, these definitions do not differentiate sufficiently between the actors, the resources they mobilize throughout the policy process and the public decisions themselves. As I see it, public decisions are the result of the actors' activities that consist precisely in the mobilization of resources in accordance with a number of rules. The result must on no account be confused with the action that leads to it. The – intermediate or final – decision is a voluntary act that expresses the resolution reached by the actors and cannot, therefore, logically encompass them. This does not prevent this decision from having actors that participated in its production as its targets. Similarly a decision itself has as its object the allocation, redistribution and so on of public action resources (decisions of an institutional nature) for a subsequent stage of the cycle.

The programming decisions (problem definition, causality models and legislative programmes) place *action instruments* at the disposal of the actors, in particular, public actors, the content of which is often standardized for a given state on the basis of one of its preferred modes of action (regulatory, incentive-based, persuasive or constitutive). These instruments define the *modalities of use of the different categories of resources* at the disposal of the actors. They vary according to the 'intervention hypotheses' underlying a given public policy, which summarize the response shared by the majority of the actor-producers of a public policy to the following question: how can and should the authority succeed in changing the behaviour of the target groups believed to be responsible for the existence of the collective problem?

In contrast to the standard definitions of public action, the definition of a public policy as a cyclical set of decisions makes it possible to approach each of the decisions that constitute a policy while *differentiating between its 'before' and 'after'*. This distinction, which is important for different reasons (for example, rule of law, predictability, governability of complexity), will have a major consequence in my analysis of public action resources: in effect, it enables us to distinguish between *the mobilization of resources* prior to the decision-making (at the level of policy programming) and their mobilization *after* the decision (in particular, at the level of implementation). This decision can itself result in the redistribution of resources at a subsequent stage in the policy cycle to the advantage or disadvantage of specific actors in the target group (in the form of economic incentives), thereby facilitating or preventing a change in their behaviour.

Take, for example, the legislative process in relation to the conservation of soil and biodiversity in agriculture (*agro-environmental programmes*). In this case, *prior* to the enactment of the legislation, *the definition of the actual problem* (threat posed to natural resources by agricultural activity) and *the causality model* are still very general. This model includes what I refer to as the 'causal hypothesis': the need − or not − to intervene with farmers in the interests of other users of the natural resource in question. It also refers to the intervention hypothesis: whether the behaviour of farmers should be changed through regulatory-type instruments or conversely, through incentive-based ones. Once defined, these formulations define − in still rather vague terms − the constellation of actors that will dominate the process of legislative production by virtue of their belonging to the triangle of actors of the policy in question (target groups: farmers; beneficiaries: protectors of the resources in question; political-administrative actors; parliament, and the administration in charge of agricultural policy). This definition of the problem to be resolved by the policy, the first product of the agro-environmental policy cycle, essentially concerns the designation of actors 'legitimized' to produce the next product: the general and abstract agro-environmental legislation. Moreover, depending on the urgency of the problem, the level of media attention it receives and its political priority, this definition will influence the public action resources made available to these actors in the future. A declaration of urgency will reduce considerably the amount of 'Time' available to the farmers and the agricultural administration; the allocation of a high political priority will increase the availability of 'Political Support' available to the political-administrative actors and policy beneficiaries and the actors interested in ensuring the fast and effective protection of the natural resources in question.

Staying with the same example, the three actor groups will mobilize their own portfolios of resources, which will be modified in part based on the decision made in relation to the problem definition (see above), with a view to obtaining *legislative decisions* that reflect their interests and values. *During this process*, it is possible to observe multiple exchanges of resources between these actors that materialize in the form of cooperative or conflictive negotiations. These exchanges concern in particular the resources 'Information' (expert opinions, second opinions etc), 'Organization' (provision or blocking of access to development procedures and consultations for members of farming organizations, political-administrative actors outside of agricultural policy and non-governmental organizations [NGOs]), 'Time' (eventual modification of the duration of the official consultation period for the proposed legislation), 'Property' (use of identical computer programs by the three actor groups or conversely, of intentionally different programs) and 'Force' (organization of public demonstrations with tractors at the seat of parliament, for example, la Place fédérale in Bern).

Following the battle surrounding the legislation, the political-administrative programme enters into force. This product contains provisions for, among other things, the *payment of subsidies* to farmers who meet the minimum ecological requirements. Of course the aim of these subsidies is not to make farmers happy, otherwise it would be possible to award similarly large volumes of subsidies to other professions! The aim of these subsidies is to prompt the farmers to change their behaviour in the interests of maintaining the natural state of soil and its biodiversity. Once again, an exchange of resources occurs during this *stage 'after' the legislative decision*; moreover, this stage corresponds to the moment of the implementation arising *'before'* the production of the next policy products: the action plan and outputs.

Thanks to the law, the exchanges of resources that arise during this first stage of the implementation process (development of action plans) are better structured and the 'quantities' being exchanged are more accurately defined. By way of example here we can take an action plan, a mechanism involving *specific measures for the protection of waters* in a given location, according to Article 62, para 4, letter a of the Federal Act on the Protection of Waters of 24 January 1991. These plans usually concern several farms – their implementation is triggered by a proposal originating from a group of farmers from a single location. The final decision regarding the acceptance or rejection of such a plan proposed by the cantonal administration with responsibility for agriculture and/or actor-users of the natural resource in question (for example, industrial services for the distribution of drinking water) falls to the farmers. They must accept losses in yields on the plots involved as a result of the limitations placed on their right of ownership (Property).

In exchange, based on the relevant law (product of the preceding stage in the policy cycle), they receive subsidies from public actors that the latter can mobilize with the consent of the beneficiaries (Consensus: absence of open opposition on the part of the environmental protection groups).

This distinction between the mobilization of policy action resources 'before' (production process for a policy programming product) and 'after' (implementation) proves useful given that *the actors' games can change considerably from one stage in the cycle to the next.*

This distinction between policy decisions and actors applies, finally, to the third product of the programming process, that is, the *political-administrative arrangement (PAA).* This arrangement defines the structure of the administrative procedures and the public resources available for the implementation of the policy in question. Experience shows that the establishment of these arrangements is often as conflictive a process as that of creating legislation, as the corresponding decisions constitute eminently political public choices. There is a good reason why the task of implementing agro-environmental policies is assigned to the administration responsible for the environment, public health, spatial planning and construction or agriculture. As is the case with the process for the production of the PAP, in the course of setting up the PAA the actors mobilize and exchange their action resources. Again, the final decision not only concerns the actors involved in the decision-making; it establishes a structure enabling such actors (who may or not be identical to those involved in the production of the PAA) to position themselves in relation to the other actors. The same applies to the resources made available for these arrangements that are also the object of the decision-making despite not being an integral part of the administrative structure in question; the latter has an existence of its own that is not basically dependent on a specific endowment with resources. Neither does the decision itself create new resources. It merely allocates them or, possibly, establishes the organizational basis for their creation (in the form of taxes and fees).

Ultimately, therefore, a *policy (set of decision) exists* thanks to the actor-producers and their resources. In this sense it has an 'existence in itself', as each of its products is the result of the mobilization of resources by each of the three groups of actors involved. *Without actors, there are no policies, and without resources, there are no actors.* Furthermore, the content and scope of each of the six products of public policies depends on actors that are politically willing and capable of mobilizing their resources in the context of processes of cooperation or confrontation. This also applies to the processes of resource mobilization in the stage after the decision about the outputs. The change in behaviour on the part of the target groups is, by definition, a process of mobilization of public action resources (in many cases, the renunciation of Property in exchange for Money, Law, Force and Consensus). It should be noted that the provision for changing behaviour and subsequently, the fact of effectively changing behaviour, does not form part of a policy but is its result. *The state cannot create impacts but only produce outputs.* The output itself is the object of negotiations (sometimes with politically important stakes) other than the decisions regarding the political-administrative programmes; however, the changing of actual behaviour remains the consequence of the mobilization of resources in the stage 'after' the decision regarding the output (which the target groups may comply with or not). Thus the key resources are Law (right of opposition), Property and sometimes Force.

Causality models, actor triangles and resources

In accordance with the basic analytical model, as proposed, I suggest that every policy embodies a more or less explicit and concrete causality model in relation to each of its products that is composed of two types of hypotheses shared by the dominant actors: the *causal hypothesis or hypotheses* and the *intervention hypothesis or hypotheses* (see Knoepfel et al, 2001, 2006, 2011, updated in Knoepfel et al, 2010: 34). This model enables us, among other things, to identify a specific constellation of public and private actors for each policy, which we refer to as the 'basic triangle' of this policy.

In this section I suggest, moreover, that this causality model, in particular, that accompanying the first product (definition of the public problem), has significant *impacts on the distribution of the public action resources* and, above all, on the modalities of the exchange of resources between the actors. Causality models that differ considerably in time and space can exist for public problems that are defined in politically similar or identical terms. This is primarily due to *causal hypotheses regarding the causes of a public problem that can prove very different, depending on the actors that they identify as* 'target groups', that is, the social actors that are supposed to be at the root of the problem or at least capable of contributing to its resolution.

Hence the first-generation environmental policies defined the problem of pollution as a local problem associated with densely populated urban agglomerations and, as a result, designated the emitters of the pollution in these areas (households, trade, industry) as target groups (Knoepfel et al, 2011: 287ff). Similarly the first social policies designated all workers who pay social contributions and employers as the group 'responsible' for the poverty of particularly vulnerable people (principle of insurance based on the mutuality model; see Knoepfel, 2008). In these two cases, these hypotheses evolved while considerably extending *the circle of target groups*: environmental policies came to include all polluters whether located in the city or country (preventive principle), and social policies came to include the actual beneficiaries of social services in their target groups while also imposing obligations on them to reintegrate (into the primary labour market or society as a whole).

These changes contributed not only to the reconfiguration of the field of policy actors; they also *affected the availability of public action resources* and their exchange over the course of the processes preceding and following the production of their six products. The significance of the resources Information, Property and Organization at the disposition of the target groups grew considerably. These resources played a decisive role in the power relations between the target groups and political-administrative actors, as these three categories of resources strengthened the position of the target groups in negotiations with the state. The inclusion of the beneficiaries of social services in the target group of social policies probably contributed to the weakening of the position of the 'pure' beneficiaries ('very' vulnerable groups), as they remain unable to contribute to their own reintegration into society by making the required changes to their behaviour.

The causality model also includes *hypotheses on the state's interventions*. These constitute a response to the question regarding the modes of state action that are likely to change the behaviour of each of the specified target groups. Of course, changes at the level of these hypotheses will have a direct impact on the availability and extent of the action resources available to public actors and target groups. According to the principle of the rule of law, to be able to act in accordance with the regulatory mode of intervention and, increasingly also, the incentive-based mode, public actors must rely on legislative acts. Similarly, the beneficiary groups can only act against a policy output if they have a *right of appeal* (resource Law available to NGOs in relation to protection of work, consumers, the environment etc). In cases where the intervention hypothesis chooses incentive-based or persuasive instruments, the restrictive public action resources are more likely to be the resources Money, Information (authorized or non-authorized disclosure) and Organization (existence of all kinds of associations capable of spreading a message).

One final theory, adopted here from the basic concept, is that of the *cyclical unfolding of policies composed of the six products* listed above. In terms of practical policy analysis, it should be noted that:

- Products two (*political-administrative programmes*) and five (*outputs*) are easy to identify based on a public policy's constituent legal documents (laws, ordinances etc; administrative decisions, material acts[3] and the rulings of administrative tribunals). These products are constituents of the resource Law available to all actors.
- The *definition of the problem* (product one) features rarely in the legislative texts, but is found in the documents that accompany draft legislation (statements of reasons, other reports by the executive etc). Nevertheless, according to the guides to modern legislation (Mader, 2013), legislative texts increasingly contain concrete, objective definitions and evaluative elements that clarify the dimensions and indicators to be adopted for measuring the effectiveness (change in the behaviour of target groups) and efficacy (extent to which the targeted collective problem has been resolved). These objectives use the same dimensions as the definition of the problem and describe for the policy's area of intervention the desired state of problem resolution or, in other words, the 'state of play' to be attained following the implementation of the policy in question. Hence they are regularly used for measuring the efficacy of the policy in question. They should be distinguished from the action objectives relating to the modalities for changing the behaviour of the target groups (effectiveness) or, strictly speaking, the outputs to be produced (efficiency). The extent of the difference between the desired and actual states predetermines the extent of the need for public action resources, not only on the part of the public actors, but also on the part of the target groups.
- Products five (*action plan*) and six (*evaluative statement*) are relatively recent products, and it is still common for them not to feature in a given policy. The action plan is a product located between the actual political-administrative programme and the outputs. It combines all of the public decisions that prioritize or delay the future production of outputs in all policies whose implementation can only be carried out in stages. Like the policy product referred to here as the 'political-administrative arrangement for the implementation of the policy – PAA' (product three), it comprises important decisions relating to the *resources available to the political-administrative actors* in their interaction with the target and beneficiary groups through the outputs aimed at them during implementation. What is involved

here is not only the resource Money (incentive-based action mode), but also those of Organization (institutional and procedural embedding of the policy in question at the level of the different public actors), Property (infrastructure made available to the relevant authority; power conferred on the target group through ownership) and Force (availability of 'special' police to the authority).

- In the production of product six (*evaluative statement*), the public actors and beneficiaries essentially mobilize the Information and Consensus (in the sense of the credibility they enjoy among the other actors). In effect, this process requires the successive validation of information on the outputs, actual modification of the behaviour of the target groups (effectiveness) and changes in relation to the status of the problem targeted by the policy (efficacy). This information is regularly correlated with data on the use made of the resources Money, Personnel and Law (economic efficiency).

It should be noted that *the actors never 'quit'*. Thus a reduction in the intensity of the mobilization of resources may not be expected over the course of a policy cycle. In the case of controversial policies, it is likely that this mobilization will be even more intense in relation to the production of outputs than the definition of the problem or the parliamentary debates on a public policy's normative substance (legislation).

The actors

I would like to adopt the definition of actors formulated in a previous book:

> An actor is defined as such based on their known affiliation, their effective or theoretically probable mobilization in the social field that is defined as relevant to the policy in question. Hence, individuals, moral persons and social groups acquire the character of an actor when they are concerned with the collective problem that the policy seeks to resolve and, more specifically, by the issues addressed during one or more stage in the policy cycle. In this sense, an actor can very well remain on the sidelines (sometimes fully intentionally and strategically) during a particular stage in a public intervention (for example, the competitors of a shopping centre who do not emerge during the definition of the local land-use plan) but intervene significantly in

a subsequent stage in the process (for example, during the impact study that precedes the granting of planning permission for the shopping centre).

However, it is essential to take into consideration all of the actors affected by a public problem in the empirical analysis of a policy whether they manifest themselves or not; in effect, the content of the policy that is ultimately adopted and implemented will depend in particular on the fact that certain actors did not become aware of the issues and/or did not want to or were unable to influence the policy development and implementation process. For example, water quality standards that do not impose severe restrictions on polluters can result in the strong mobilization of polluters who will ultimately be subject to them and, at the same time, the absence of actors advocating the protection of the natural environment.

We consider actors to be essentially deliberate and rational in that they always aim for a more or less clearly defined outcome or objective and deliberately mobilize different action resources. In doing this they enjoy an – admittedly relative – margin for manoeuvre, both during the definition of the values and interests they defend and during the targeted investment of the resources available to them. Thus we suggest that the actors be considered as interested, endowed with resources and variable strategic calculation capacities, and, at the same time, motivated by the defence and promotion of collective values.

The behaviour of public policy actors is not entirely determined by the institutional and social context in which they evolve and interact, and they are not entirely autonomous and rational in the pursuit of the strategies they develop based on the objectives they seek to attain. Specifically, actors are limited in their action strategies for both institutional reasons (for example, the lack of a right of appeal for environmental organizations in relation to land-use planning), cognitive reasons (for example, the lack of knowledge about the natural phenomena associated with certain types of pollution) and cultural reasons (for example, the failure to consider the landscape value of the natural environment and of the local built heritage). These limits can also stem from an insufficient endowment with certain other action resources (financial, human, temporal etc).

Hence in our view, on the one hand, the successes or failures of the strategies adopted by the actors within a policy space can arise both from weaknesses in their intrinsic rationality, that is their own strategic intelligence (for example, due to internal differences and battles between farmers on the attitude to be adopted to GMOs), and from the existence of affinities or, conversely, contradictions between the defended values, pursued objectives and resources activated by different actors (for example, following the emergence of a coalition between certain producers, distributors and consumers demanding the energy labelling of household appliances, office electrical equipment and cars). On the other hand, the successes and failures may depend on the evolution of contextual characteristics (for example, changing institutional rules, economic events like a major industrial accident or new scientific discovery), the policy field in question, in which they are participants, and even the capacity of some actors to modify these contextual elements (for example, by extending or limiting the avenues of recourse offered to ideal associations). (Knoepfel et al, 2010: 31-3)

Beyond this general definition, more detailed *descriptions* of the three main actor groups that can have a direct or indirect impact on the public action resources that these groups can mobilize are presented below.

Political-administrative actors and their resources

A policy's political-administrative actors form the smallest entities (individuals or groups) responsible for making a supposedly necessary contribution to the production of one or other of the policy's products. Strictly speaking, political-administrative actors are considered to be 'indivisible' *administrative entities* (like atoms), and are usually referred to within the Swiss federal administration as *sections*. Hence, unlike in everyday language, a (main) division that includes several sections cannot be a policy actor as, in this case, the section or sections referred to in the requirements specifications that include the task in question is considered an actor. However, based on this understanding, the head of the division (as an individual) is also an actor if they are responsible for formulating a summarized decision through the coordination of the contributions of several sections and, if necessary, the elimination of eventual contradictions by imposing a hierarchical decision. If, in the case of politically difficult decisions, the division head's decision requires the explicit approval of the authority's director or management, these hierarchical superiors become actors of the policy in question and so forth.

Each of the aforementioned actors has an *(often annual) budget*[4] *of public action resources* at their disposal. *Institutional policy* actors, that are often organized on the basis of resource categories within centralized administrative bodies, are behind the allocation of these budgets. Thus the budgets come from institutional financial policies (ministries or departments of finance), legal policies (ministries or departments of justice), human resources policies (ministries or the Federal Personnel Office in Switzerland) and infrastructure policies (ministries responsible for state property, the Federal Office for Buildings and Logistics in Switzerland). The programming of these resource policies is primarily the responsibility of parliaments or governments. It should be remembered that increasing numbers of actors exist within substantive policies that produce their own resources, be they financial (generated in the traditional way through taxes or the sale of goods and/or services) or action resources, which were not really considered as real resources in the past. Examples of such resources include Consensus, Political Support and Organization ('networking').

As is the case with substantive policies, the production of the majority of institutional policy products involves a large number of political–administrative, national, regional and communal, political and administrative, operational and strategic actors. At sectoral level, these actors increasingly pool their resources and construct their own institutional policies that may accordingly be referred to as the *institutional policies of sectoral policies*. This phenomenon, which may be observed, for example, in the recent urban agglomeration policies, education and science policies and technology policies, give these emerging communities of public actors a certain degree of autonomy by allowing them, among other things, to engage in the exchange of resources with their 'partner' target or beneficiary groups.

This situation gives rise to the importance of the *exchange of resources 'within' the state apparatus* which, in Switzerland, sometimes crosses boundaries between the Confederation, cantons and communes in the context of arrangements referred to today as the *reconciliation of objectives, service-level agreements etc.* Even if the 'reconciled' actors originate from the private sector or should be considered as relatively autonomous public sector entities, nothing dictates that they should be considered in analytical terms as the target groups of the policies in question. Based on our definition, at least, the latter remain the social groups whose behaviour the policy proposes to change and who, for this reason, differ in status to the public or private actors responsible for producing services/outputs aimed at them. A good example of this is Swiss regional transport policy in which the cantons, with the support of the Confederation, conclude service-level agreements with the railway companies ('the operators'), based on which they specify a certain volume of traffic with a view to resolving the public ecological problem of the overuse of roads by motorists. In this case, the target groups remain the train users and car drivers who are expected to contribute to the resolution of the public problem by changing their behaviour. This applies despite the 'contracting' role of the transport companies that do not become target groups in the strict sense. Similarly, the organizations that offer their services in the area of disability policy do not constitute a target group simply by virtue of the fact that the state concludes a service mandate or service-level agreement with them. The key target group here remains (newly accountable) people with a disability, (public and/or private) companies and private service providers (disability assistance budgets).

Hence policy analyses should always distinguish between, first, the *exchange of resources between internal political-administrative actors* and second, *the exchange of resources between these political administrative actors and external actors originating from civil society (target groups, beneficiaries, third party winners and losers)*. In the case of public transport, the target groups are the users and the motorists who display varying degrees of reticence when it comes to using public transport and for this reason mobilize their public action resources that include, among others, Force (individual freedom and freedom of movement), Property (cars), Organization (motoring associations), Money (refusal to pay for railway tickets that are considered more expensive than the cost of an equivalent journey by car) and/or Political Support (for example, voting against the establishment of fare alliances in the context of referendums).

The same observation applies to the beneficiaries who, contrary to the common view, are not the operators who are paid all kinds of subsidies, despite their status as organizations that 'benefit' from these subsidies. According to the definition of the public problem, the beneficiaries are clearly those who suffer due to the existence of the problem. In the context of public transport policy they include, for example, commuters marooned on congested roads and residents exposed to the atmospheric and noise pollution generated by road transport.

Beyond the issue of the exchange of resources between public actors and 'bogus' target groups (which, in reality, belong to the public actors), situations also exist involving *exchanges between the political-administrative actors and the state itself, which is considered in this instance as the actual target group* of a public policy. This applies to cases in which the target groups are public actors whose behaviour is targeted by the public action in question. It is important to remember, nonetheless, that this change in behaviour cannot consist in the simple implementation of any unspecified policy but must include provisions in the areas in which these public actors have a similar freedom of choice to that of private actors based on a given legal or *de facto* situation.

A typical case for Switzerland in this context is that of the *communes that own land* (spatial planning), *forests* (forest policy) or *electricity generation utilities* (industrial services: energy policy). In effect, in such constellations, the substantive policies can impose obligations for behavioural changes on both the *owners* and *users*. In most cases, the users (for example, owners connected to the sewage network, people who walk in the forests, drivers and tenants) will be both the target groups that are subject to a specific regulation (tariff-based or other) and the beneficiaries (depending on the dominant definition of the public problem the policy sets out to resolve). The targeting of the state as owner (first/primary target group) can be justified by the fact that, like any private actor, it can dispose freely of its property – like other landowners, it is a holder of the resource Property. This is evident, moreover, in the fact that the state's property is considered part of its financial assets and not its administrative assets. It should be noted that in medium-sized and large public bodies, the political-administrative actor responsible for the management of these goods is usually the financial administration while the actor responsible for policies involving these goods is a specialized administrative body (housing, spatial planning, forest policy). Practice shows, furthermore, that these two public actors often maintain contradictory positions, with one attempting to make the most of the property and the other attempting to increase the pressure on the behaviour of the actor (in this instance, the state) in the direction desired by the policy in question, which often runs contrary to the commercial exploitation of the property.

Target groups and their resources

According to our basic concept, there are *no policies without target groups*. In effect, even the conception of a policy is borne of the encounter between the definition of an acknowledged public problem and an identified target group. As described below, this seed of a public policy is made up of one or more hypotheses relating to the causes of the problem shared by the dominant actors. These hypotheses identify the actors considered as being subjectively and/or objectively responsible and/or at least capable of contributing to the resolution of the identified problem. The ways in which they will be held responsible will only be defined at a later stage in one or more of the intervention hypotheses to be formulated for each of the target groups. Again, in accordance with our basic concept, whatever their degree of autonomy, public actors will not be considered as the *target group*; this applies, in particular, to *public authorities* (cantons and communes) and *public or private entities appointed to produce outputs* or services aimed at social actors for the purpose of changing their behaviour in the interests of primary and/ or secondary policy beneficiaries. The exception whereby *the state is an owner* that acts on an equal footing with other private owners (properties forming part of the financial assets of public bodies) has already been mentioned above.

A final definitive element arises from the fact that in social policies in particular, a target group (for example, employees obliged to pay contributions) is *regularly part of the group of beneficiaries* (for example, the recipients of services such as pensions, protected places of work, assistance services). In effect, the (future) beneficiaries form a usually much smaller sub-group of the contributors in all social insurance organized in accordance with the principle of mutuality (unemployment, retirement and survivors [AVS], and health insurance). Even in the case of invalidity insurance and social aid, which are not (entirely) based on the contribution principle, in accordance with a movement found at European level, the beneficiaries have become target groups to the extent that the delivery of services is associated with the fulfilment of certain obligations (for example, changes in behaviour such as attending training courses and applying for positions requiring lower qualifications than those held by the applicant = 'activation' policies; see Bonoli, 2013; Knoepfel, 2008).

The capacity to make a decisive contribution to the resolution of a public problem in accordance with the model adopted by the designers of a policy presupposes access to *significant (privately owned) economic, social and natural resources* (see Chapter 4, this volume). In effect, the target groups adopted by many policies have social influence and power that they can avail of to exert a positive or negative influence on the economic, social and environmental conditions of many other people. Depending on the use the former make of their (private) resources, the situation of the latter can improve or deteriorate. It is precisely because of their capacity to influence, control and dominate specific social fields that they are selected as target groups.

The capacity to dispose of these economic, social and environmental resources forms the basis for their allocations of public action resources, which must be distinguished systematically from the former type of resources as they must be recognized and related to the public action resources of the other actors in the triangle (*transformation of societal action resources into public action resources*).

As I have shown in a different context (see Knoepfel, 2006), the *economic, social and environmental* power drawn from the *ownership of resources based on natural, manufactured, social or human capital* (see The World Bank, 2006, 2011, 2014; Thalmann, 2016), *in particular, land ownership*, may be considered as a solid basis for the creation of public action resources in the form of Property. Similarly, the ownership of manufactured capital resources (means of production, infrastructure), which are constitutive of economic power, represents an undeniable basis for the constitution of the resources Property, Money, Personnel (engagement of specialists or professional lobbyists by large companies), Organization (at the level of umbrella branches of industry) and Information (financing of research or reports to promote the consideration of the interests of target groups). In the context of this book (for more details, see Knoepfel et al, 2009; Nahrath et al, 2009), we can content ourselves with the simple observation that for the target groups close to power, at the very least the material and immaterial resources that constitute their societal power can *easily transform themselves into important public action resources*. Without going into detail, it may be confirmed that similar processes may also be observed among actors from beneficiary groups with significant social and ecological power. In these cases, the societal power is more likely to transform itself into non-material public action resources such as Consensus, Political Support, Organization and Information, all of which may be painfully lacking among the target groups referred to here.

The target groups engage in an *exchange of resources* with the other two groups in the triangle. In effect, the relations they sometime maintain with the *beneficiary groups* prompt them to enter into negotiations with the latter with a view to avoiding the emergence of future policies that are likely to challenge autonomy and thus retain their societal power under the shelter of public policies. Hence, in order to claw back the confidence of victims of pollution or consumers and thus gain Consensus and avoid the mobilization of Political Support for a strict environmental policy, the latter may be willing to pay *compensation* to the victims of air pollution or environmental accidents. Such transactions often take the form of private law contracts that also involve the exchange of the resources Time (the victims agree to grant transitional periods to the polluters), Information (the polluters agree to be monitored by NGOs) and Force (renunciation of the occupation of sites or consumer strikes in exchange for use of property resources belonging to the polluters that are less harmful to the environment). Such contracts can also be found in other policy intervention fields, for example, the labour market, consumer protection, social and/or medical care.[5]

Of course, the target groups often find themselves in negotiations with the *political-administrative actors*, who, time and again, are propelled by the representatives of the beneficiaries towards the reinforcement of their interventions vis-à-vis the former. In these cases, the political-administrative actors mobilize their resources Law (while refraining from exhausting their intervention competencies or making different uses of them to the advantage of the target groups), Money (subsidies), Time (longer deadlines for adaptations) and Political Support to mitigate the reticence of target groups with regard to the altered uses of their Property or Money (investments). In this way the public actors bring about changes in the behaviour of the target groups that are indispensable to the resolution of the collective problem, the resolution of which is enshrined in their policy design specifications (regaining so-called secondary legitimation).

As in the case of the support of beneficiary groups by the third party winners (positively affected third parties), the target groups are often supported by *the third party losers* (negatively affected third parties). This observation, which is crucial in accordance with our basic concept, manifests in coalitions between these two groups under the aegis of common strategic objectives (rejection of an intervention that is perceived as too radical on the part of the state) and supported by the pooling of public action resources, in particular Money, Organization and Property. The pooling of public action resources by target groups and third party losers can considerably boost opposition to a policy that is perceived as a threat to the interests of numerically weak target groups.

Beneficiary groups and their resources

The consideration of the action resources of policy beneficiaries requires some conceptual clarification that goes beyond our basic concept. In effect, the beneficiary group is defined as all persons (physical and/or moral) who/which *are negatively affected by the existence of the public problem*, which, as we have seen, *is not dealt with explicitly in documents as precise as laws or ordinances.* Some mentions are found in the texts that accompany draft legislation, in statements produced by political parties, in official and/or unofficial reports compiled by the political-administrative actors and in the specialist scientific press. The term 'beneficiary' signifies that these groups of people can reasonably expect an *improvement in their situation* thanks to the provision of action mechanisms in a policy. This improvement can assume highly variable forms. It may consist in the reduction of a risk to a level considered 'acceptable', for example, in relation to food, health and public safety, or in better access to goods and/or services, for example, infrastructure, culture, education, health services and housing, that were previously inaccessible due to their non-existence or due to barriers to access that could not be overcome by the population in question.

However, a glance at political reality shows that this is merely one side of the coin. This improvement does not *solely concern these groups themselves*: in the majority of cases it includes the *interface between these (vulnerable) groups and 'the rest' of society.* To transform a societal problem into a true *public* problem and to succeed in putting it on the public agenda, it is necessary for these interfaces to be identified as posing a risk for other groups that do not suffer directly from the insufficient state. In a way, these other groups are the mouthpieces of the *primary beneficiaries* and suffer with the latter through solidarity ('good Samaritan motive': mobilization of universal human values) or through the simple fear of the eventual 'overflow' of the problem that might have a negative impact on their own situation ('selfish motive').

This second group is referred to as the *secondary beneficiaries* of the policy in question. Its existence and their capacity to mobilize public action resources are crucial, in my view. It should be remembered, for example, that Bismarck introduced the first social policies in the interest of affluent groups, whom he wished to protect against revolutionary riots led by disadvantaged sectors of the population. Similarly, the regulation of the financial market is demanded today not only by impoverished home owners but also by actors from the financial sector who fear the impacts of property bubbles on their business. And an intervention against air pollution not only protects residents exposed to clearly hazardous concentrations of pollutant substances but also residents who are (still) shielded from the impacts but who could become the next victims as they are positioned on the interface between those affected by the pollution and those who are not.

Given that the public policy, which is general and abstract at the level of the normative material that frames it, is also intended to give rise to impacts on the situation of these *secondary beneficiaries*, these *benefits are politically desirable*; hence, these secondary beneficiaries cannot be considered as third party winners (positively affected third parties) who are specifically defined as groups that profit from the implementation of a policy without this being the explicit aim of the legislature ('policy business'). The existence of this group of secondary beneficiaries is indispensable for the well-established consensus in the area of social policy today, where claims to the effect that unemployment is solely a matter for the unemployed or disability solely the concern of the disabled, for example, is firmly rejected. Such claims suggest, incorrectly, that these problems are not a matter of the public sphere, but the private one. When analysing policy beneficiaries whose mobilization is often the trigger for the inclusion of public problems in the public policy agenda, it is essential to examine these secondary beneficiaries, both at the level of scientific analysis and practical public action.

The *emergence* of collective and organized beneficiary actors endowed with public action resources resulted from the *advent of the major policies of the 1960s* (housing, spatial planning, public health, social and competition policies). These new policies clearly differed from earlier ones in that they successively transformed the definition of public problems, which had previously consisted in 'disturbances of the public order', that is, societal risks that did not simply threaten social peace and cohesion 'in general' (*general interest, public interest*) but affected specific civil society groups in a particular area of intervention (*specific public interest*). This transformation reflects the shift in the liberal policing policies, which limited public intervention to the guaranteeing of basic conditions for maintaining 'public order', towards the *welfare state*, whose action was aimed at precise objectives formulated in positive rather than negative terms. The latter defined *the politically desirable societal state* in an increasing number of areas of intervention that would be guaranteed through systematic action in relation to the target groups. These policies used the target groups as levers for resolving a problem that was not their problem but one that affected specific groups for whom new policies were created.

This new conception formed the basis for *the transformation of civil society organizations* (usually non-profit, often charitable or based on mutual support) *into groups for defending the interests of the (future) beneficiaries of new, entirely separate policies (and no longer merely the beneficiaries of organizational, corporatistic or private action strategies)*. In contrast to 50 years ago, policy beneficiary groups are a particularly tangible reality today. In their actions and strategies they refer to their statutory missions and their right to participate actively in the development and implementation of 'their' policies. This transformation of a previously poorly organized, passive and apolitical group into a partner that acts as a promoter or guardian of specific subjects of public action is expressed throughout the policy cycle in the right to be heard and to participate in an active and institutionally acknowledged manner and sometimes even in the right of appeal (for example, environment policies, consumer protection policies, work protection policies) accorded to these groups.

Without claiming that a clear cause-and-effect relationship exists between the emergence of the new sectoral policies and the transformation of the world of civil society organizations into groups of well-organized actors, it may be asserted that this process transformed these *civil society organizations* into a *partner* of the *powerful political-administrative actors* in that these actors acquired *considerable public action resources* over the last 50-year period. Depending on the area of activity involved, these resources include Personnel (political and technical professionalization at the level of the general secretariats), Information (accumulation of sometimes indispensable knowledge for the successful conduct of the policies in question by political-administrative actors, for example, in the areas of environment, health, labour market and nature and landscape conservation), Property (premises, IT equipment and real estate in the form of strategic assets for spatial planning or nature conservation), Money (contributions, donations, fundraising) and Law. These are obviously joined by the resource Consensus that is allocated to the organizations as a result of their often-considerable level of public credibility.

As in the case of political-administrative actors or target groups, the *mobilization of public action resources* is the result of an *internal decision-making process* that is sometimes complex, even conflictive, and unfolds between different organs of these beneficiary actors, which are often organized as associations or private law foundations in accordance with the Civil Code. Having originated from local or regional associations, today these groups are organized in the form of national and even international umbrella federations. Hence, in the context of policy decision-making processes they are present from the formulation of the political-administrative programmes to the production of outputs at local level. The fact that sections exist that can be 'rich' or 'poor' in terms of their endowment with public action resources means that the *mobilization of these resources* based on supra-local objective strategies is not always easy and sometimes requires heated *internal negotiations*. Based on such experiences, several such national beneficiary actors in Switzerland established quite detailed rules governing the competences of the various federal and local bodies in terms of decisions relating to the mobilization of the public action resources involved, for example, the requirement of a quorum for launch of a referendum or appeal.

Postscript 1: ... and the political parties?

Party-political militants who read this chapter on policy actors will probably be disappointed to discover they have only been mentioned once up to now, despite the fact that they see themselves as the main engineers of public policies. The observation of substantive policies reveals a relative absence of political parties, in particular in the stages that follow the decisions about political-administrative programmes in the form of parliamentary acts. This applies to the fine-tuning of the PAP at the level of federal and cantonal ordinances and directives, for the political battles around the distribution of the federal and cantonal departments and also for the processes of production of outputs within the political-administrative arrangements and action plans. Sometimes, however, the political parties intervene at the level of the production of particularly controversial outputs (for example, licences for mountain dams, extensions of airport runways, master plans for urban neighbourhoods). However, according to our model, which has been confirmed many times by empirical public policy reality, by definition, political parties *cannot be either target groups or end beneficiaries*. When we encountered them in the area of policy implementation, they effectively played the role of third party winners or losers, a role that, as highlighted in our basic concept, should not be neglected, and for which the parties sometimes invest significant public action resources.

This positioning of political parties as *negatively or positively affected third parties* can also be defended at the level of the production of the problem definition and legislation to the extent that, as hybrid organizations between the state and civil society, political parties intervene in a more obvious way in policy programming than implementation as actors that support the target groups and/or beneficiaries. Their gains or losses ultimately manifest in increases or decreases in their electorate. Having said that, the political parties obviously have their representatives among the *essential political-administrative actors*, that is, governments and parliaments. Just as no policy sees the light of day without an agreed definition of the public problem to be resolved and, without parliamentary legislation, government and opposition parties (referendum) have a considerable influence on the substantive and institutional content of all substantive policies in Switzerland. Remember, nevertheless, the fact that the substantive initiative for the creation of a new policy or modification of an existing one usually originates from the strategic operators within the agencies of the federal administration.

Postscript 2: ... and the capacity of actors to mobilize their resources?

As I will show later, in Chapter 3, several authors[6] also include the subjective capacities of actors to make more or less intelligent use of their resources in their lists of resources. While it is not disputed that these highly variable capacities significantly influence the results of the actors' games and hence the contents of the six policy products, I refuse to consider them on the same level as the resources presented here. The main reason for this is logical in nature. This capacity qualifies those who mobilize the resources, and this qualifier cannot simply be attributed equally and without distinction to the entities that they mobilize (*mobilans non est mobilatum*).

It is true to say that for certain public action resources (in particular, Information, Consensus and Organization), the actor in question must already have one or other of the public action resources presented here at their disposal, without which they would be unable to mobilize them. This know-how or knowledge can vary, however, from one person to another depending on highly variable characteristics, that is, empathy, charisma, position in the social, economic or political hierarchy etc. However, again, the variable capacities that arise from this and constitute a certain skill in terms of the use of public action resources must not be confused with the resources themselves.

Postscript 3: ... and the 'wealth' or 'poverty' of the actors?

I would like to stress again the difference between the power of an actor based on their portfolio of public action resources and their social status. In effect, every actor endowed with considerable financial assets, a strong social position and/or elevated ecological assets ('capital', according to Bourdieu, 2006: 29ff, and The World Bank, 2011, 2014) may one day risk being designated a target group if a policy's causal hypothesis designates the actor as being at the root of a (new) problem that has been acknowledged as a public issue (see above). It should be recalled, however, that the economic, social and/or environmental resources at the root of such 'wealth' or conversely (in the case of shortage), the 'poverty' of one of a policy's actors, must be distinguished from public action resources.

It is entirely conceivable that an actor that is 'poor' in terms of these societal resources will be endowed with a considerable portfolio of public action resources in a given policy context (for example, NGOs active in the area of consumer protection, trade unions active in the area of social policy, public health and environmental protection). The opposite situations also exist but are less common: the portfolio of public action resources of an actor that is 'rich' in economic capital can prove too weak to truly influence a public decision, for example, the granting of planning permission.

Hence the – empirically common – transformation of a public policy actor's economic, social or ecological capital into public action resources should not therefore be considered as a 'natural law'.

The institutions

Definitions

Our basic concept does not suffice entirely for detailed analysis of the role of the institutions that structure the relationship between actors and resources. For the purposes of this book, I adopt the *following basic premises*, according to which the institutions:

- are the rules that govern the game between the actors, which may be formal or informal in nature;
- facilitate or limit the political participation of the actors in the policy triangle;
- define the power relationships between these actors in time and space;
- present a sometimes high level of stability but are not, however, completely fixed or immutable;
- 'influence[s] a specific individual behaviour by increasing the information and knowledge available to actors, from a perspective of institutional transformation (strategic behaviour), and/or in suggesting a behaviour that is compatible with the conveyed social norms, from a perspective of cohesion and socialisation' (Knoepfel et al, 2010: 118).

As defined in our basic textbook, institutions are considered as rules that offer opportunities or, conversely, impose constraints on policy actors. It is possible to identify general institutional rules that govern all of a country's policies[7] and institutional rules that are associated with the conduct of specific policies.[8] Hence, within *each of the policy products*, it is possible to identify both *substantive elements and institutional elements* (revisited in Chapter 17 in the form of a reminder). The work of programming a policy does not solely consist in defining the process to be followed to resolve the problem involved, but also involves the identification of the political-administrative actors, procedural rules and public and/or private resources that will enable this resolution to be achieved. Each of the six policy products contain rules that structure the process of the production of the subsequent products (Knoepfel et al, 2006: 279; see Figure 17.2, Chapter 17. If necessary, these rules, which are themselves produced by the decision-making process, may differ considerably from the general rules in force.

These observations, which are drawn from our basic textbook, are not sufficient to accurately describe the relationship between actors, institutions and public action resources. This prompts me to *complete the conceptualization of institutional rules* from the specific perspective of interest here.

To do this, I propose comparing the games played by policy actors with *a game of cards*, an analogy that is clearly justified given that many authors working on public policies use the terms 'actors' games' and 'game theory' (*jeux, Spiele, Spieltheorie*). Three stages are often identified in these games: first, the definition of the groups of players (who plays with/against whom?), a stage that corresponds to the construction of a bi-, tri- or multi-lateral field of actors. Once these roles have been identified, a player distributes the cards (second stage). This process may be compared with that of the allocation of policy resources to the actors. Sometimes this distribution process is followed by all kinds of swapping of cards between the players. The next and final step is the declaration of the trumps and other rules that often involve an advantage for the caller and a disadvantage for the other players. For example, in Switzerland's national card game *Jass*, when it is decided to play 'bottoms-up', a 'minus' etc, the declaration corresponds to the, admittedly unilateral, definition of the rules of the game. This declaration may suddenly overturn the perhaps expected results of one or other of the players by the simple fact of practically devaluing or revaluing the cards.

To return to policy games, these rules can transform an actor that is well endowed with public action resources into a 'poor' actor by invalidating resources that were initially considered important. They may even prohibit the use of certain resources (in the card game the rule of depleting the cards of the suit played by the adversary before playing the trump cards) or deprive an actor of their turn, that is, the restructuring of 'windows of opportunity'.

This illustration is very useful, in my view, because it covers the *three categories of institutional rules* observed in public policy reality that affect the relationship between actors and resources. The rules in question are:

- *possession rules* that attribute rights to access and use resources (holder of the cards) to the (public and private) actors;
- *behavioural rules* that determine the modalities of their use in the interaction between the actors (rules concerning the permitted use of the cards);
- *decisional rules* that structure the public policy's decision-making process by identifying, among other things, the six products that emerge in the course of the policy cycle and thereby defining the admissible or non-admissible mobilization of resources by the actors (rules relating to the different rounds of the game) in space and time.

In this way, the institutional rules define the rules of the game so that their use ('activation') by one or other of the actors allows them to possess, more or less exclusively and in accordance with their objectives and strategies, public action resources, and to mobilize them in a given temporal and procedural space in the course of the production of one or other of the six policy products. These rules, defined as such, *often change in time and space* and, moreover, even within one and the same country. They are often based on *customary law, customs or 'habitus'* as transmitted by traditions or the education system, for example. As in the case of the rules of the Swiss card game *Jass*, the French *tarot* and German *Skat*, which vary from one region to the next, the rules of the public policy game can also change. Accordingly, a gift made to an official to the value of CHF 50 (Money) would be considered an illicit exchange of resources in Germany while the same gift could be considered an entirely normal expression of good wishes in Southern European countries. In some countries, the withdrawal of a parliamentary group from the plenum for the purpose of avoiding a vote is considered an entirely admissible use of the resource Force (behavioural rules) while it 'is not done' in the chambers of the Swiss Parliament. In French-speaking Switzerland, it is acceptable to arrive late to a meeting as long as one does not arrive later than the 'Vaud quarter of an hour' (behavioural rule relating to Force), while in German-speaking Switzerland the same behaviour would be considered a 'lack of respect' towards the other participants who arrived punctually for the meeting.

Examples

It is probably impossible to provide an *exhaustive list* of these rules (even the formal ones), and such an attempt would not make much sense in view of their variability in time and space. Moreover, actors are sufficiently astute to invent such rules depending on their needs, even the most unexpected ones, and to justify them through their advocates before all kinds of judicial bodies. To stimulate the imaginations of researchers and actual public policy actors, I have attempted nonetheless *to present some of these rules in the form of tables* based on a considerable number of empirical studies carried out by my Master's and doctoral students in public administration, among others (there is an explanation of Tables 1.1–1.3 in the text that follows).

General institutional versus special institutional rules

The three tables clearly show that, within each of these six products, each individual policy can devise its own institutional rules, which are known as 'special institutional rules' in my approach (the central column of the tables). In general, these even feature in the specific clauses of their political-administrative programmes (PAP). To recall, the rules are the product of the decision-making process, which may deviate strongly from the general rules if necessary. And this even applies to the political administrative arrangement (PAA) which, at first sight, is a purely institutional product but may give rise in reality to the crucial (re-)orientation of the substantive content of the policy in question (for example, allocation of responsibility of the policy to combat drug use to the department of the police, social affairs or public health).

The tables show that such specific institutional rules are becoming increasingly common. In effect, every substantive public policy now tends to weave its own institutional 'cloth'. This applies in particular to periods when the general frame of reference changes (for example, the advent of liberalization, globalization and the 'agencification' movement) and the actors involved in these policies set out to distinguish themselves from these general trends by opposing the frame of reference, adapting it to their own needs or circumventing it.

What we have here, therefore, is the break-up of institutional landscapes and, based on this, veritable battles between general institutional policies and the special rules that materialize either in the course of the struggle to maintain old institutional structures or in the widespread introduction of institutional reforms (such as New Public Management). The latter lead to a victory of (new) general rules over communities of actors of specific policies that are favourable to the old regimes ('policy-killing institutions') or conversely, to the political confirmation of the old institutions to the disadvantage of the

Table 1.1: *Possession* rules governing the access of actors to public action resources (using the example of Switzerland[a])

General institutions	Specific institutions: sectoral policies that are 'sensitive' for 'deviant' institutions	Main resource(s) involved
Equality – non-discrimination: origin, race, gender, age, language, social position, way of life etc (Cst. Article 8)	Aliens policy	All
Right to life, personal freedom (Cst. Article 10)	Public safety policy	Force/ Personnel
Freedom of religion and conscience (Cst. Article 15)	Social cohesion policy (religious policy)	Consensus, Organization
Freedom of expression and information (Cst. Article 16)	Public safety policy	Information, Consensus
Freedom of the media (Cst. Article 17)	Transparency policy	Information
Academic freedom (Cst. Article 20)	Research policy (codes of ethics)	Information
Freedom of assembly (Cst. Article 22)	Labour policy (prohibition of strikes in the public sector)	Organization, Force
Freedom of association (Cst. Article 23)	Anti-terrorism policy (prohibition of terrorist associations)	Organization
Guarantee of ownership (Cst. Article 26)	Spatial planning policy (limited land ownership)	Property, Money
Economic freedom (Cst. Article 27)	Competition policy (anti-trust legislation) etc	Property, Money, Information
Right to form professional associations – right to strike (Cst. Article 28)	Labour policy (prohibition of strikes in the public sector)	Organization, Force
General guarantee of judicial proceedings – right to have case heard by a court, right to be heard (Cst. Article 30)	Security policy	Law
Political rights (Cst. Article 34)	Aliens policy	Political Support

Note: [a] Cst = Federal Constitution of the Swiss Confederation of 18 April 1999, RS 101.

Table 1.2: *Behavioural* rules governing the modalities of use of public action resources (using the example of Switzerland)

General institutions	Specific institutions: Sectoral policies that are 'sensitive' for 'deviant' institutions	Main resource(s) involved
Equality before the law – exclusion of discrimination (Cst. Article 8)	Natural resource policies (combating scarcity, quotas)	All public actors' resources
State governed by principles of the rule of law (Cst. Article 5)	Technological security policies (precautionary principle)	All public actors' resources
Prohibition of strikes in the public sector	See above	Force (public actors)
Prohibition of corruption	Accepted practice of 'corruption' ('admissible' limit for spending on working meals, travel expenses, promotional gifts etc); commercial policies (eg, foreign trade)	Money
Professional, commercial, administrative etc secrecy	Security policy (lifting of secrecy); banking policy (contested 'banking secrecy')	Information
Prohibition of abuse of rights (Swiss Civil Code Article 2)	Policies with a high degree of juridification (family policies?)	All
Obligation for transparency in the public sector	Security policies (exceptions in the law on transparency)	Information (public actors)
Pacta sunt servanda	Transitional policies (retroactivity clauses allowed)	All
Principle of good faith (eg Swiss Civil Code Article 3)	?	All
Principle of proportionality (Cst. Article 5)	Policies with causal hypotheses that are poorly supported by empirical data	Law (public actors)
Principle of balance of sacrifices	Mono- or bi-causal policies (eg, water protection policy of the 1980s that excluded the targeting of farmers)	All public actors' resources
Principle of subsidiarity	Policies that do not respect communal autonomy (eg, increasingly education, social and/or spatial planning policies; policy to combat unemployment – catchment areas of regional employment agencies)	All
Principle of concordance between political parties in government	Policies in the process of being depoliticized (through the creation of 'independent' public actors in the form of technical 'regulators' (in particular, in so-called infrastructure or communication policies)	Political support
Safeguarding of the 'political culture'	'Globalized', 'Europeanized' policies that use their own technical language (often English), eg, higher education and research policy, the new technologies policies etc	All
Principle of neutrality of public service	'Mission' policies (public health, cultural identity policy)	All public actors' resources
Prohibition of retroactivity	See above (*pacta sunt servanda*)	Law (public actors)

Table 1.3: *Decisional* rules governing the actual use of public action resources in space and time (using the example of Switzerland)

General institutions	Specific institutions: Sectoral policies that are 'sensitive' for 'deviant' institutions	Main resource(s) involved
Structuring of policies in cycles (of six products)	'Grass-roots policies': public action starts at the level of outputs (eg, communal policies to combat drug use, injection rooms)	All (based on the policy stage involved)
Legislative federalism (legislative competence of the Confederation and cantons; Cst. Articles 42, 43)	'Intercantonal' policies (governed by intercantonal agreements, conventions, directives etc and formulated by the Conference of Cantonal Directors of security, spatial planning etc) [4th level of the Swiss federalist state, the Maison des cantons)	All, in particular, Law
Executive federalism (Cst. Article 46)	Customs, military, commercial etc policies with federal implementation competences or federal competences for giving notice of cantonal implementation acts (eg, mandatory notice of the Federal Commission for the Protection of Nature and Cultural Heritage)	Law, Personnel, Organization, Consensus
Collaboration between the Confederation and the cantons (Cst. Article 44)	Higher education policy (dominance of federal and intercantonal bodies compared to the actual competences of the cantons)	All
Principle of the precedence of federal law (Cst. Article 49)	Conflictive cases: sites for the disposal of nuclear waste, sectoral spatial planning plans (Spatial Planning Act Article 13) versus cantonal master plans (high-voltage power lines, airports and aerodromes etc)	Law, Political Support
Communal autonomy (Cst. Article 50)	See above	All, in particular, Law
Right of participation of the cantons in foreign policy decisions (Cst. Article 55)	Migration, public security policy (Schengen), higher education policy (Bologna process), asylum policy (planning permission for federal reception centres) etc	All
Objects of initiatives and referendums (Cst. Article 138ss)	Policies that are contested due to contradictions with international law (eg, human rights) or due to a lack of cohesion of subject matter (eg, use of income from road toll tags to finance old age and survivors insurance, AVS); possibility of cancellation of popular initiative by federal chambers (rule never activated)	Political Support
Competence of federal chambers and legislative procedures (Cst. Article 148ss)	Accelerated procedure for consultation of interested circles in urgent cases (exception clause of Consultation Procedure Act involved increasingly often)	All (for product two)
Form of federal assembly enactments (Cst. Article 163)	'Uncommon' forms (eg, 'parliamentary ordinance', in climate policy)	All (for product two)
Organization and procedures of the Federal Council and federal administration	'Specialist external agencies', 'regulators'	All (for products two and three)
Principles of administrative law (based on the principle of the rule of law), such as principle of legality, predictability etc	High rate of acceptance of appeals in the areas of spatial planning (planning permission), administrative transparency etc (areas to be identified based on the analysis of the jurisprudence of the Federal Administrative Court)	All, particularly Law (for product five)
Regulation of all kinds of mandatory deadlines (referendums, appeals against administrative decisions etc)	Environmental legislation (repeatedly) postponing the mandatory legal deadlines for remediation (eg, noise, minimum water flow rates); idem for remediation deadlines imposed at implementation level	Political Support, Law, Time
Regulation of the legislative process of the Confederation (including consultation procedure)	Urgent policies with exceptional regime justifying governmental competence (rather than that of the federal parliament); policies associated with foreign policies	Law, Information, Political Support (product two)
Regulation of administrative procedure (output)	So-called 'facilitated' procedure regarding the authorization of activities with impacts that are considered minimal ('minor authorizations' in construction law)	All, in particular, Information, Time, Consensus (product five)
Obligation for the evaluation of the effectiveness of federal policies (Cst. Article 170); principle behind the existence of product no six	Policies that are 'resistant' to evaluative procedures for empirical identification (hypothesis: security policy and national defence policy with weak evaluative elements at the level of their political-administrative programme)	All (product six)

general institutions, thereby evidencing the acknowledgement of the specificities of resistant sectoral policies ('institution killing policies'; see Knoepfel and Varone, 2009).

The very existence of these institutional games and their – at least partial – recognition by the actors who support a country's general institutional policies have prompted me to relativize the explanatory capacity of these general institutions (examples are provided in the three tables) with regard to the results of public policies. In effect, the detailed examination of a substantive policy advocating identical or similar objectives and action tools in two different countries, for example, Switzerland and France, will sometimes reveal that their specific institutional elements are far more similar than might be assumed based on a cursory glance at their very different general institutions. Hence, in such cases, the proponents of traditional 'comparative politics' risk assigning these two countries to two different groups precisely on the grounds of this apparent difference in their institutions and, based on this, to explain eventual differences on the level of dependent variable (results obtained at implementation level). However, these 'institutional differences' do not exist in this particular case.[9] Take, for example, the local 'microcosms' involving econeighbourhoods or groups for the management of food labels: be they in the UK, Germany, France or Switzerland, they need greater autonomy than the rest of society to function satisfactorily (see Knoepfel, 2016).

Moreover, it may be assumed that the Europeanization and globalization of substantive public policies have impacts not only on their substantive orientation, but also on their institutional 'garments' that begin to harmonize in the process of the globalization of their actors. Accordingly, international conventions increasingly impose the institutional rules that accompany the definitions of problems and the national public policy objectives to be adopted (for example, by specifying the professional skills to be provided by the required [new] agencies). While the substantive dynamics of internationalized public policies were already increasingly unpredictable, today at least, their communities of actors require common rules that they would like to define at the level of international treaties, conventions and protocols, and not solely at the level of their introduction into the national legislation. As this process involving the harmonization of the institutional landscape of internationalized substantive policies progresses, the general institutional rules governing all of the public policies of the countries involved will probably relinquish more and more of their explanatory capacity in terms of the differences in the results of the policies in question. In effect, these probably persistent differences are due to actor constellations and different power relations, not only in each country, but also during each of the programming and implementation stages of the policies in question.

Activation or non-activation of institutional rules

Another relativization of the role of general institutions as an explanatory variable of policy results resides in the fact that these institutions only govern part of the actual actor games. In effect, the activation of these rules facilitates or complicates the processes of resource exchange, but it does not in any way predetermine them entirely. An institutional rule remains a rule 'to take or leave'. Often, one or more actors of a public policy space invest their time, creativity and resources precisely to avoid applying these rules, to complement them or to circumvent them. My associates' recent research on local regulatory arrangements (LRA) conducted in an ad hoc and often informal basis in the areas of wine and cheese labelling, the management of forest ecosystems to the advantage of drinking water production, and the governance of water channels (*bisses*) in semi-arid mountain regions in Switzerland (Tippenhauer, 2014; Laesslé, 2015; Schweizer, 2015; de Buren 2015) confirms what our colleagues already observed and designated as 'bottom-up implementation' in the 1970s (Barret and Fudge, 1981; Hjern and Hull, 1982). In the real world, actors only activate institutional rules when they need it to impose their 'world view'. If they succeed in convincing their counterparts of the futility of activating this rule or if they succeed in simply 'cheating' unawares to the latter, they will do everything to avoid the activation of the rule in question.

Such observations themselves are obviously likely to relativize the explanatory contribution of general institutions in relation to the results of substantive public policies. They show that an actor often only activates institutional rules as a last resort. Hence a truly interesting research hypothesis should start from non-activation and focus on the specific conditions to be met so that activation arises nonetheless (Knoepfel, 2013).

The relationship between general and specific institutional policies: Research programme

Tables 1.1 to 1.3 about the general and specific possession, behavioural and decisional rules clearly demonstrate the existence of potential collision situations between general institutional rules and special rules forged on the basis of the particular requirements of substantive public policies. Such collisions become particularly noticeable in the case of changes in general institutional policies which, by definition, aim to be universal and applicable to all of a country's policies at the level of one or other of the products of the cycles involved. Today these changes are often borne by major shifts in frames of reference, such as the liberalization, globalization or economization of public policies, and manifest in movements of transformation of the entire public sector (for example, New Public Management, 'clientelization' of civil society by the public authorities, relativization of the needs of the rule of law in relation to the managerial flexibilization of the public service, contractualization). These reforms will produce very different reactions from the communities of actors of established substantive policies, which consider them as hindrances or conversely, as welcome help.

While such institutional reforms are generally welcome in the context of pilot policies, which are close to the 'first steps' of their conceptualization, they are often criticized by the actors that wish to maintain the old general frame of reference on which their policies are based (Knoepfel and Varone, 2009). Accordingly, the reference to sectoral areas in the second column of the tables labelled 'Specific institutions: Sensitive sectoral policies for "deviant" institutions' is based on the implicit hypothesis that these policies need an 'atypical' frame of reference that may be the one that was previously shared or the one that is likely to become established in the future as a new frame of reference. As already mentioned above, the policies in these areas will succeed in opposing the changes in general institutional policies (institution killers) by mobilizing the line of argument of a policy that sees itself as threatened and weakened by a (new) institutional policy that risks undermining it (policy-killing institutions).

The verification of the implicit hypotheses at the root of the references in the central columns of Tables 1.1 to 1.3 obviously requires detailed empirical research with both a diachronic and synchronic comparative design (international comparisons). Based on my observation regarding the similarity of the specific institutional rules of substantive policies that are in the process of being globalized, their capacity to resist changes in institutional policies and/or their capacity to absorb such changes without problems should also be similar if the institutional reform is identical in the compared countries.

This same phenomenon can be observed at the level of institutional policies whose objective is to allocate public action resources to public policy actors, particularly public actors. These institutional policies do not feature in the three tables because they combine possession, behavioural and decisional rules, which are separated in the tables. The target groups of these policies are the public actors of substantive policies' actor triangles and, in public authorities of a certain size at least, they are led by administrative entities referred to as 'support' or 'service' unites or in the terminology of our analysis by the actors of 'resource-related' policies. In effect, these organizations have personnel, finance, logistics and centralized statistical offices, whose triple task consists in allocating public action resources budgets to each substantive policy, regulating the use of these resources and monitoring these uses in minute detail.

It is well known that the actors associated with these resource-related institutional policies are not always popular with their substantive policy counterparts. In effect, collisions between them are often pre-programmed, and in many cases the substantive policies prepare to deal with possible changes at the level of these resource-based policies through the establishment of their own administrative units for the main resources (for example, legal, personnel, financial services of the individual federal offices in Switzerland). Apart from the fact that these resource-related 'squabbles' within the 'state apparatus' are themselves regulated by general institutional rules (for example, rules governing the budgeting process, public accounting rules, tendering rules, rules governing the appointment and professional training of employees, such as multilingualism), it may also be expected that sectoral policies exist here, too, that are more or less resilient compared to other more vulnerable policies and for which budgetary cuts, for example, are perceived as akin to a death sentence.

As with the other general institutional policies, we can also formulate hypotheses for these resource-related institutional policies regarding their capacity to resist the opposition of substantive policies or their vulnerability in the face of such pressures (for example, abandonment of the principle of annual budgets, shift from subvention to service mandates/service-level agreements, obligations to activate large[r] shares of the administrative assets and the analytical accounting of service costs).

Thus there is work to be done here. To my knowledge, the role of institutions – be they general, specific, activated or not – in explaining the different products of the public policy cycle and in interaction with the explanatory contribution of the actor configurations and their resources has never been the subject of systematic empirical research. One of the reasons for this deficit probably resides in the fact that, up to now, at the level of both teaching and academic research, the communities of researchers who study general institutions and their transformation rarely encountered the communities involved in the analysis of substantive public policies. My colleagues and I proposed research programmes dedicated to this question on several occasions, both at national level in Switzerland and at international level, but our applications were unsuccessful. We hope that such programmes could serve to finally eliminate this artificial division, which undoubtedly arose through the 'supremacy' of the institutionalists in the comparative public policy community and the over-estimation of the explanatory contribution of a country's general institutions in the analysis of the outcome of its substantive public policies.

Notes

[1] As is the case in the rest of the book, in Part I, significant capitals are used for terms that designate resources used as examples in the rest of the book (Force, Personnel, Law etc).

[2] This chapter is based on the basic textbook (Knoepfel et al, 2006, 2011), and the book dealing with the analysis of Swiss environmental policy (Knoepfel et al, 2010), which adopts these principles and applies them to this sectoral policy while providing greater detail on some of the definitions. Nonetheless, like the content of the other chapters, the 'specifications' provided in these texts are my sole responsibility and imply no obligation on the part of my former co-authors (Frédéric Varone, Corinne Larrue, Stéphane Nahrath, Jérôme Savary and Johann Dupuis), with whom I may have discussed the relevance of some of them.

[3] Even if they are not designated as 'decisions', these acts are recognized as appealable on the same grounds in the administrative courts (in accordance with the Federal Act on Administrative Procedures of 20 December 1968, Article 25a).

[4] The term 'budget' is used here to designate all resources and not only financial resources.

[5] For Japan, particularly in relation to environment policies, see Weidner (1989).

[6] See the authors mentioned in the last line of Table 3.1, Chapter 3.

[7] For Switzerland, for example, executive federalism, semi-direct democracy, the principle of the legality and equality of treatment and the constitutional guarantee of private property are general institutional rules described in our basic analysis of public policies. For more details, see Tables 1.1 to 1.3.

[8] For example, a greater degree of centrality than that provided for by executive federalism, thus enabling federal political-administrative actors to participate in specific implementation processes, 'deviations' from the precise legal basis for public policies that operate in areas of considerable incertitude and the rules that establish permanent and recognized contact between federal and communal actors. See Tables 1.1 to 1.3.

[9] This text is drawn entirely from Knoepfel (2013), which was presented at a workshop organized by Claudio Radaelli, Bruno Dente and Samuele Dossi, entitled 'The role of institutions in public policy outcomes should not be overestimated: A contribution to the ECPR International Conference in Grenoble, 26-28 June 2013'.

2

Definition of public action resources[1]

Overview (reminders)

Figure 2.1: Overview of the 10 public action resources

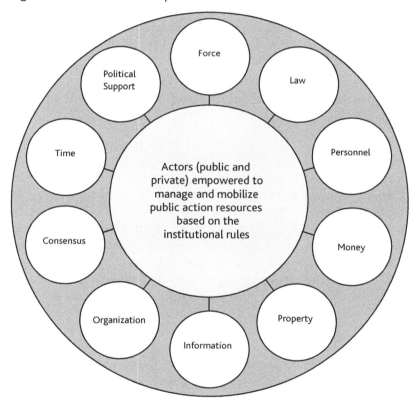

Source: Adapted from Knoepfel et al (2001: 73 [2011: 70])

The action resources of public policy actors[2] constitute the means of action available to each of the public and private actors affected by the collective problem to be resolved.

Throughout the policy cycle, the actors mobilize a number of resources that are available to them for the purpose of attaining their objectives. These resources enable them to act within this space, that is to position themselves in relation to the other actors, either on the basis of logics of cooperation (coalitions, apprenticeships) or logics of confrontation (conflicts, obstacles, opposition). The action resources constitute the actors' power which, according to the classical definition by Max Weber (Weber 1978), consists in the capacity of an actor to impose a particular behaviour on another actor that the latter would not have adopted if it had not been imposed by the former. Thus the resources available to an actor are fundamentally relational in that they constitute a lever of action for the latter in the context of the relationships it maintains with the other actors.... (Knoepfel et al, 2010: 61)

The specifics: 'Resource-related' definition of public action resources

The definition of a public action resource as presented in our basic textbook on the analysis of Swiss environmental policies aims to eliminate the ambiguity that continues to exist around the notion of power with the aim of enabling its more advanced application in empirical research and in the everyday management of resources. It is at the heart of this book, which adopts the finite number of these resources *hic et nunc* along with their qualifiers. However, I would like to extend its basis by referring to studies carried out over the last 20 years on institutional resource regimes (IRR) (see Gerber et al, 2009; de Buren, 2015) and concerning regimes for the management of natural resources. This research is based on a combination of approaches originating from institutional economics (particularly in relation to the environment) and public policy analysis. It focused initially on the area of renewable natural resources (water, air, climate, soil and forests) but progressively extended its interest to manufactured resources, both material (for example, water and aviation infrastructure) and immaterial (landscapes, documented information and labelled heritage).[3]

In the past we tended to differentiate strictly between the economic, social or ecological resources exploited for socio-economic or socio-cultural systems from the resources that constitute the power of public policy actors, sometimes even by using different terminology for the 'actors that exploit natural resources' by mobilizing their public action resources during struggles for the development of 'institutional regimes' and the 'local regulatory arrangements' created with a view to their sustainable exploitation (see, in particular, de Buren, 2015, who differentiates, for example, 'natural resources' from 'public action resources').

Today, we question whether these are, in fact, two different phenomena. Do these two phenomenological entities not share at least some common characteristics? Can we not find analogies or similarities between them on the conceptual level at least? It would appear that we can: in effect, in both cases we can differentiate between the resource, on the one hand, and a finite number of services (or goods and/or services) produced by it and made available to interested actor-users, on the other. In both cases, rival uses are likely to arise, and in both cases there are institutional rules governing access (possession rules), use (behavioural rules) and modalities of decision-making in relation to use (decisional rules). Other analogies reside in the fact that natural resources (natural capital), and also those constitutive of manufactured, social and human capital,[4] need reproduction processes (with or without human input), and this reproductive capacity is challenged by processes involving their over- and under-exploitation (non-use). A threat is likely to arise from unregulated rivalries between the (homogenous and heterogeneous) uses of public action resources, which may destroy the goods and services obtainable by one actor-user to the disadvantage of the others. Hence the basic premises of sustainable development are applicable to both resource types.

Another similarity concerns the distinction made by resource economics between a resource and a simple 'thing'. In effect, a thing can only be considered a resource if it is capable of producing goods and/or services beyond the basic elements that compose it. An actor exists that has an interest in the use of these goods and/or services and this validates them. Any reference to resources inevitably also includes the user-actors, and any reference to the user-actors also refers to actors who have or appropriate a right of use. Economically speaking, the actor-user is willing to pay a price to acquire the right of use. This indicates the *scarcity of this good and/or service*, based on which rivalries arise between the actors that may lead either to the overexploitation of the resource and hence its destruction or to the exclusion of another actor-user with an interest in the resource, or in the case of mutually exclusive heterogeneous uses, to the loss of a quantity of goods and/or services through 'contamination' (for example, drinking water vs wastewater).

In addition, as demonstrated for the resources of the four 'capitals' of our planet (based on the terminology proposed by The World Bank in relation to sustainable development; see The World Bank, 2006, 2011, 2014; Thalmann, 2016), all resources, even material ones, are a social construction (Gerber et al, 2009). This appears to be even more applicable to (material and immaterial) public action resources. Such resources only have a value if there are one or more other actors in addition to the holder that values the resource in question in a similar way. Strictly speaking, something that does not trigger the interest of a third party actor is not (yet) or no longer a public action resource. Even Money can lose its allure if the markets lose their faith in it. A software program purchased by the army at a cost of millions of francs can become obsolete from one day to the next if 'nobody wants it' – the Swiss army has an entire series of 'unsaleable objects' today, as no user is interested in them despite the sometimes enormous cost at which they were acquired.

What distinguishes these two types of resources from each other in my view is the fact that the value of public action resources is more relative than that of natural resources. In effect, the absolute quantity of the resources available to an actor proves to be far less important than its relation to the resources available to the other actors. As already stressed in the Introduction, power is a relative phenomenon that describes a relationship between two or more actors. In this relationship, the resource-related character of an actor's power manifests itself in the interest other actors have in being able to dispose of similar services provided by the same resource. A 'state secret' is truly a secret if actors interested in obtaining the information in question are excluded from it. Otherwise, the information formally covered by confidentiality requirements is no longer a valuable action resource for its holder.

We return to this 'resource-related' analysis of public action resources in the Part II of this book, in Chapter 4.

The role of the law[5]

We have already encountered the concept of law several times in this text. It is important to clarify the different meanings the term 'law' can have in the context of the relationship between actors, resources and institutions. First, as *objective law*, the law covers all of the general and specific substantive, organizational and procedural rules[6] that govern the games of the actors who mobilize resources in the process of the production of the six public policy products (*law = institutional rules = institutions*). According to the legal experts, these rules differ according to the characterization of their target groups (indeterminate vs determinate number: general vs individual) and according to the level of detail with which the behavioural changes imposed on them are described (abstract vs concrete). Along with other norms (for example, social, traditional, contractual norms), these rules are themselves the result of a process of production, as the public action composed of six public policy products culminates in decisions that form part of this objective law in the majority of cases. This obviously applies to the political-administrative programmes (PAP), but also to the rules governing the political-administrative arrangements (PAA), the mechanisms contained in the action plans (AP) and the administrative outputs,[7] as well as decisions governing the observation and interpretations of evaluative statements.

These examples show that these institutions (norms and decisions) differ on the basis of their different legal nature, that is, decisions of a general and abstract nature (= norms) contained in the PAAs, those of a *sui generis* nature (organizational decisions for the PAA), those of an abstract and individual nature (AP), those of a general and concrete nature (intermediate outcome: for example, zoning plan), and finally, the better known kind of an individual and concrete nature (outputs). The fact remains that what is involved here is objective law that in its entirety structures the game of the actors who mobilize their resources. In this sense, the objective law does not belong to anyone and cannot be considered as a public action resource in itself.

In our terminology, this objective law may be considered as the stock of a resource whose main service for an actor consists precisely in obliging another public or private actor to modify their behaviour. However, this use requires an act of mobilization, and this mobilization is only possible if the actor that wishes it has a *right of access to the objective law*; hence we refer here to a *subjective right* to mobilize the objective law and, as in the case of all other public action resources, this right is conferred by a possession rule. This gives the actor the right to mobilize the service that is potentially 'producible' by the stock of the resource Law.

It is this right that is considered here as a public action resource that is allocated to the public actors by means of an explicit legal competence (featuring in their mission statements) and to civil society actors by means of a general (target groups[8]) or exceptional (beneficiary groups and/or third party winners or losers) right of appeal. It should be noted that such rights to the mobilization of resources exist for all of the resources considered here; they are stipulated in the possession rules and grant rights of access to the resource in question (property, purchase agreements, human rights; see above). What differentiates the latter from the former is their selectivity and the fact that their allocation depends directly and solely on competent public actors.

Public actors have the monopoly on the production of objective law and its modification. Thus they enjoy this right of access almost automatically, and hence they can mobilize the resource Law at all times if they have the corresponding competency according to their mission statement (which, admittedly, can vary in terms of its detail). This right of mobilization is more limited for private actors despite the fact that the objective law can be invoked or activated (but not mobilized) by each of the public policy actors at any time in the public policy cycle.

To summarize, it is possible to identify the four following functions behind the notion of law that affect all public policy actors, albeit in considerably different ways:

1. The substantive and institutional rules (affecting all public policies), both general (affecting all public policies) and specific (concerning a particular public policy and normally featured in its PAP). These rules constitute the objective law, the mobilization of which requires a subjective right (private actors) or an explicit competency (public actors).
2. The *content of each of the six public policy products* often, but far from always,[9] assumes the legal form of legal rules.
3. The rules that confer (or not) *the right to use of one of the 10 resources* (among others, Law) on a public or private actor *thereby enabling them to mobilize it* as a resource (institutional rules governing possession) and defining the modalities of use (behavioural institutional rules) and the times and places (decisional rules) of when and where this mobilization is possible or not. These rules are referred to here as 'institutions'.
4. The rules that give an actor the *right to be able to impose a behaviour that complies with the objective law on another actor* based on their authority (political-administrative actor, including the courts). To be able to mobilize this service of the resource Law, the actor must have a right of use (opposable subjective right) that is conferred on them by a rule that features in the objective law. For the public actors, this law consists in an explicit norm of competence. It should be noted that the motif for the mobilization can vary considerably, and ranges from simple substantiation to misappropriation, circumvention or innovation (Schweizer, 2015: 80ff). For civil society actors, this right of use materializes in the form of the right of appeal.

Among these functions of the law, all four of which affect the public policy actors, only the latter concerns the Law as a public action resource in the sense under discussion here. It is the *(subjective) right to mobilize the objective law*. As function 3 above shows, the rules of law are obviously also decisive in terms of the recourse to all of the other public action resources. Even if everyone can invoke/activate the objective law at any time in the public policy cycle as an orientation guide, for example, the right to mobilize it as a true public action resource is reserved to those that hold this right (appeal against an administrative norm or decision or a precise material administrative act). Hence, Chapter 7, which is dedicated to the resource Law, returns to this fourth function of the law as a public action resource.

Notes

[1] The 10 public action resources are designated using significant capitals in this book.

[2] Newly designated as 'public action resources' in this book.

[3] Irrigation channels: Schweizer (2015); infrastructure: Nahrath et al (2011); landscape: Rodewald and Knoepfel (2005); Gerber (2006); documentary information: Olgiati Pelet (2011); the labelled heritage: Boisseaux (2012); Laesslé (2016); general (for so-called manufactured resources): Gerber et al (2009).

[4] The World Bank's concept of four forms of capital (2006, 2011, 2014); cf Thalmann (2016).

[5] See Moor (1997, 2016).

[6] Organizational and procedural = 'institutional' (in the sense of our definition of the content of public policy products).

[7] These products (*realisations*, terminology based on the French *Loi organique relative aux lois de finances*, LOLF [organic law on finance laws], 'outputs', in our terminology) also incorporate formal acts (Swiss terminology based on the Federal Act on Administrative Procedure [APA]: Article 5 B 'rulings'), the 'ruling[s] on real acts' (APA Article 25a), such as information, direct actions by agents of the state, arrests or warnings or recommendations by the state and the other activities of the administration that do not 'affect [the] rights or obligations' of citizens. For Switzerland, this definition (in particular, the article relating to the 'ruling on real acts', which is recognized as a legally appealable act), is based on the new constitutional provision (of 1999) relating to the guarantee of access to the courts (Federal Constitution, Article 29a) and to the jurisprudence of the European Court of Human Rights in relation to the Convention for the Protection of Human Rights and Fundamental Freedoms of 4 November 1950 (RS 0.101).

[8] The guarantee of the right of appeal of target groups ('targets of administrative decisions') is part of the constitutional principle of the rule of law (Federal Constitution Article 29a: Guarantee of access to the courts).

[9] Informal, intermediate decisions on reports, databases, contracts, conventions and so on.

3

Context: a survey of the literature

This chapter aims to provide an element missing from my approach hitherto by contextualizing it within the scientific literature that uses identical or similar dimensions to characterize the power of actors involved in public policies. The conceptualization developed with my colleagues in 2001 was initially based on the studies carried out by the Centre de Sociologie des Organisations (CSO) in the 1970s and in particular, the key contributions of Michel Crozier and Erhard Friedberg entitled *Actors and systems* (1981) and of Fritz Scharpf entitled *Games real actors play: Actor-centered institutionalism in public policy research* of 1997. For an analysis of these studies, I refer to our basic textbook (Knoepfel et al, 2006: 13ff, 69ff).

Hence the real purpose of this chapter is not to revisit the literature relating to the historical origins of our approach, but to examine other (complementary, competing or similar) conceptualizations of public policy actors' resources.

To do this I carried out a documentary survey with the help of the Google search engine using the terms 'resources' combined with the 10 qualifiers (force, law, personnel, money etc) and 'public policies' as keywords. This relatively time-consuming process, which was carried out twice – in 2013 and 2015 – enabled me to find a large number of documents and to identify around 500 that deal with phenomena that could be considered as public action resources in the sense of the definition used here of the power available to actors. With the help of further research, I sorted these documents on the basis of their relevance for the topic (elimination of around 450 irrelevant ones), and classified the remaining contributions in two groups based on whether they deal with an isolated resource (often: Time, Property, Money) or whether they cover all of the resources ranked on the basis of a given typology. Only the latter were ultimately included in the survey. Given that I wish to focus on more recent texts or texts explicitly dedicated to the question of resources, the classical contributions by Fritz Scharpf (1997) and Crozier and Friedberg (1981), which were already referred to in our basic textbook, are also excluded, as are those by Dahl (1957, 1961).

This process, which is admittedly open to criticism in several respects (in particular, nominalism, limitation to three languages – French, English, German – and sometimes arbitrary assessments of 'relevance') nonetheless provided me with a sample of quite varied texts, both in terms of the conceptual typologies involved and the specific resources dealt with. This chapter only reports on the latter, and the analyses of isolated resources are considered selectively in the chapters dedicated to the specific resources examined in this book (see Part III).

The presentation of the literature is followed by an analysis of the contributions involving attempts to typologize or combine several public action resources based on varied conceptual approaches. The texts are classified according to their authors and year of publication (from oldest to most recent). The focus of interest is the categories of resources adopted, the conceptualization based on a typology of a finite or infinite number of resources and the exchangeability of the resources. These criteria are adopted again in a summary table, Table 3.1, that facilitates the positioning of my approach in the context of the 19 contributions (4 of which are in French, 1 in German and 14 in English).

The 19 contributions

Arnold J. Meltsner (1972)

A typology of resources was developed by Arnold J. Meltsner (1972), which starts from the idea that resources are exchangeable. The non-exhaustive list proposed is based, *inter alia*, on Robert A. Dahl (1961) and Harold D. Lasswell and Abraham Kaplan (1950), three classical political scientists whose work is not included in this review of the literature. Under the heading of 'generic resources', the list includes material, symbolic and physical resources and also incorporates the individual characteristics of actors, for example, their position, information and 'skills': 'Skill is a special resource because it helps determine how effectively the other resources are deployed' (1972: 862). Nonetheless, the article refers to the exchange of resources: 'Actors will exchange specific resources to achieve specific outcomes, such as political support, and … much of the dynamics of politics is this simple notion of exchange. One can observe it in logrolling, bargaining and many of the sophisticated variants of interactions between actors' (Meltsner, 1972: 863).

Christopher Clapham (1978)

Christopher Clapham deals with the question of resources in the context of international comparisons (1978). His article shows how the concept of actors' resources was already used but in vague terms in the late 1970s. He presents these resources as the equivalent of production factors in the economic sense of the theory of rational choice (1978: 357). His text continues:

> So at the point where a social cleavage is recognized as politically relevant by a voter or party leader, where a gun becomes an instrument of political coercion, where an oil pipeline becomes a source of political contention, all of these become classifiable as resources, useful to those who manipulate or control them. In addition to setting a boundary to the requirements of political explanation, the concept of resources has two further advantages: it reduces all the disparate environmental influences on politics to a common category, which allows some comparison between them; and it integrates them into political explanation through the behaviour of actors, thus averting the problems which arise from trying to combine forms of explanation which arise at different conceptual levels. (Clapham, 1978: 358)

Clapham highlights the link between institutions and resources, confirming that:

> One of the most important functions of rules for the political scientist is indeed that they assign weights to different resources, and thus permit a degree of comparability which resources do not possess in themselves…, [resources] derive from the application of actors' skills and ambitions to the resources available in a given social setting, and they can only survive so long as the resources exist to maintain them, whether these resources be accepted social values, or economic bargaining power, or military force. (Clapham, 1978: 360)

> So, to summarize, a successful explanation in comparative politics must show how the behaviour to be explained derives from a combination of environmental resources, personality and rules, integrated into a common framework through the activities of actors who use resources within such constrains as the rules under which they operate place on them.… Resources, rules and personality are not only

about as general as explanatory concepts can get, but are also extremely easy to apply. (Clapham, 1978: 362)

Clapham pleads for not starting from a finite number of public activity resources. Nonetheless, he considers that this number is relatively low in practice:

> The available forms of resource may in principle be infinite, since there is no limit to the aspects of the social and physical environment which may be mobilized for political purposes, but in practice the perennially important ones are few and familiar enough: the means of the producing wealth and the social formations arising from them; the discontinuities of social identity induced by nationality, tribe, race, sex and so forth; and the technologies of communication and control in relation to physical constraints on their operation. (Clapham, 1978: 363)

This quote is included here, particularly because it supports my conceptualization of the relationship between resources and institutions which, according to Christopher Clapham, has the advantage of being simple and applicable in the area of international comparisons.

Didier Lapeyronnie (1988)

Another attempt at defining resources can be found in an article by Didier Lapeyronnie entitled 'Mouvements sociaux et action politique. Existe-t-il une théorie de la mobilisation des ressources?' ('Social movements and political action. Is there a theory of the mobilization of resources?') (1988). Citing Oberschall (1973), Lapeyronnie explains that, 'Mobilization designates the process by which a discontented group assembles and invests resources in the pursuit of its own ends.' He continues:

> Hence, mobilization is an instrumental activity that arises once the objective is defined; the resources are defined as the object of this activity. From this perspective, through its opposition to the field of action, society is defined as the environment that supplies the political actors and social movements with the resources necessary for action. (1988: 603)

He also quotes McCarthy and Zald's (1977) statement to the effect that: 'Society provides the infrastructure which social movement industries and other industries utilize' (pp 12-17).

According to Lapeyronnie, resources enable groups to create the action. Accordingly, they are conceived in the relationship they uphold with the social movements or political action. According to the author, resources are never defined as anything other than the different elements necessary for action. Each author provides a list of resources that they adopt for their approach: 'anything from material resources – jobs, incomes, savings, and the right to material goods and services – to nonmaterial resources – authority, moral commitment, trust, friendship, skills …' (Oberschall, 1973: 28). Hence, there is no shared conceptual definition of resources; each author uses this generic term to designate the social elements, the 'things' they deem as determining to explain or analyse a given action. Anything can be a resource – time, beauty, energy, hope. As Gamson puts it in an expression quoted by Lapeyronnie, it is the 'soft underbelly of the theory' (Gamson, 1987).

Thus, according to Lapeyronnie, resources are 'goods', 'things', akin to exchangeable values or more precisely, money or currency, so what is involved here is less a definition than an analogy. Society is conceived as an economic market where goods are exchanged and invested to produce power. Rare goods, in other words, resources, have one remarkable property: 'They are independent of the constitutive social and political resources of the situation' (Lapeyronnie, 1988: 604). He continues: 'Resources are goods belonging to the actors, intangible and fungible things, instruments placed at the service of a power or political action and constituting the object of the power or the action.... They are instruments at the service of political actors and which they fight over' (1988: 605). In contrast to the approach defended in this book and by other authors presented below, Lapeyronnie is opposed to the idea of a finite number of public action resources, and does not differentiate between the resources, instruments and the (subjective) capacities of actors.

Jean-Patrice Lacam (1988)

With the help of a politician considered a political entrepreneur (Maurice Faure, Senator for the Lot Department in France between 1951 and 1987), and with his own concepts drawn from economics, Jean-Patrice Lacam (1988) presents an 'inventory of political resources and activation processes.' He adopts the following definition to identify what he refers to as 'the political resource': 'All means at the disposal of a political entrepreneur, whose activation pushes back the limits of his constraints, extends the boundaries of what is possible for them, that is increases their initial autonomy and facilitates the development of their strategies' (1988: 27). Drawing on Robert A. Dahl (1973), he includes money, information, food distribution, the threat of physical force, employment, friendship, social rank, the right to legislate, votes and an entire series of other phenomena in his list of political resources. His own proposition consists in declining these phenomena on the basis of their institutional, contextual and personal nature.

Lacam defines three types of resources based on their function: 'coercive, redistributive and, finally, persuasive' resources (1988: 27). This declension gives a 'matrix of nine types which has a certain degree of exhaustiveness in itself.' The nine resource types defined by Lacam (1988: 28) are: coercive personal resources (for example, the ability to maintain order at meetings, 'henchmen' and 'guerrillas'); redistributive personal resources (a person's ability to provide financial aid to some of their clients); persuasive personal resources (art of the dialectic and eloquence in the media); coercive contextual resources (sanctioning adversaries, exploitation of a scandal); redistributive contextual resources (charging or relieving large companies of taxes and exempting constituents of a considerable tax effort); persuasive contextual resources (ability to be elected); coercive institutional resources (capacity to utilize legitimate violence); redistributive institutional resources (holding 'the keys to hiring in municipal services'); and persuasive institutional resources (capacity to publish a municipal journal that acts as a 'propaganda organ for the elected representatives').

This complete quote from the typology proposed by Jean-Patrice Lacam is a counter-example of the notion of public actors' resources used in this book because it conceives of these resources as constitutive qualifiers of the personalities of public policy actors. Lacam does not differentiate between actors and resources, and this excludes the objectification of resources and their exchange. According to this conceptualization, by definition, the powerful actor holds a wide variety of these nine resources that they can mobilize according to the opportunities that arise:

> The political entrepreneur should have a correct and exhaustive perception of the extent of the limitations and of their matrix of resources: the entrepreneur should be capable of combining in the most judicious way the resources of their matrix.... But they are expected to

constantly undertake to maintain their capacities while increasing the volume of the resources ("accumulation") and avoiding their aging through attrition and obsolescence. (Lacam, 1988: 31, 32)

What is interesting about this text is that the author arrives at similar conclusions to mine regarding the management of these resources by the politician. Accordingly, it is obvious for the author that 'all resources have a more or less limited lifespan. Attrition and obsolescence ... affect ... the stock of policy resources' (Lacam, 1988: 33). In addition, these resources are 'rare' (1988: 35), available ('acquired resource' already in stock) or 'to be acquired'. 'One expansion strategy consists in developing the variety of the permanent stock which makes it possible to overcome the lack of resources' (Lacam, 1988: 37).

Erik-Has Kiun (1996)

In his review of political processes in complex networks (1996), Erik-Has Kiun demonstrates the importance of resources and their exchange, and the interdependence generated by these exchanges in terms of the action capacity of these resources. He stresses that, to this end, the networks develop mechanisms of coordination that also aim 'to secure the functioning of individual organizations and to secure the necessary resource flow' (1996: 93). Referring to Crozier and Friedman (1981) and Scharpf (1978), he also highlights the fact that 'the power of each actor depends mainly on the resources that the actor possesses and the importance of these resources in the policy process' (1996: 93). However, he does not develop either a real typology or a conceptualization of these resources.

Michael Davern (2001)

In his article 'Social networks and economic sociology: A proposed research agenda for a more complete social science' (2001), Michael Davern highlights the role of resources in networks in considerable detail. According to Davern, resources are one of the four basic components of networks, the others being the 'structural component', the 'normative component' and the 'dynamic component': 'The resource focus is on the distribution within networks of various characteristics that differentiate among actors within society. Examples of these characteristics are ability, knowledge, ethnicity, estate, gender and class' (2001: 289). Davern characterizes resources as: 'Something that actors can turn to for help or support in order to achieve their goals' (2001: 290). Actors receive these resources from a network that is endowed with 'network capital'. The processes are governed by 'normative rules governing exchange between actors ...' (2001: 291).

Vincent Lemieux (2002)

Also included in my list is the typology developed by Vincent Lemieux in the second edition of his book on public policies, *L'étude des politiques publiques. Les acteurs et leur pouvoir* (2002), which, according to the author himself, is based on the spirit of the classical definition of power by K.W. Deutsch (1963), B. Walliser (1977) and French and Raven (1959). Wiender (1954) and Mackay (1964) are also cited as the godfathers of his typology. In this work, Lemieux outlines seven categories of resources considered 'as public policy instruments, whether they are the means or objects of the decisions, based on which the policies are made' (Lemieux, 2002: 25). The resources listed are: normative resources, that is, norms consisting of 'the values and rules which the actors avail of as assets or which they seek to control as challenges'; statutory resources or posts that refer to 'the official or effective positions occupied by the actors'; action resources or orders, that is, 'levers of action considered as assets of power'; relational resources or links consisting of 'positive relations established with other actors'; material resources or supports are 'material means, including financial means'; and finally, human resources, or staff, and information resources or information refer to 'the content of different messages' (2002: 24). Lemieux stresses that 'resources are analytical in nature and overlap with each other. In concrete situations there are always several resources that are used or targeted by the actors.... Finally, an actor's resources are always relative to those of the other actors who are party to a decision' (2002: 25).

Lemieux does not specify whether this catalogue is exhaustive, and we learn nothing about its genesis. It should be noted that my conceptualization differs from that presented here in that I specifically do not consider the actual characteristics of the actors as resources (the 'statutory' resources, that is, posts occupied by the actors, and 'action' resources, the levers of action). The five other resources correspond more or less to my definitions (material resources = Money; norms = Law; relational resources = Organization; human resources = Personnel; information resources = Information). However, this list does not include the four other resources, that is, Consensus, Property, Time and Political Support, which I have characterized above (see the Introduction to this volume) as relatively unknown.

Jens Newig (2005)

An interesting attempt at a relatively detailed conceptualization of public action resources can be found in Jens Newig (2005), whose article on public participation in the implementation of environmental measures examines the factors that affect the capacity of actors to participate in public decision-making processes. He refers to financial resources:

> ...and other resources, including personal social capital.... With increasing educational attainment, citizens claim the possibility to participate in decisions that influence their lives.... Conversely, missing resources – time and costs, in particular, for individual actors – are considered a reason that hinders participation. (2005: 13)

He also mentions collective resources based on social capital in the sense of 'generalized trust and social cohesion.... Social or moral norms and institutions, which are not included here in social capital, can also have a positive influence on the tendency to participate' (2005: 14; author's translation). This contribution refers explicitly to the resources Property and Time and above all to Consensus (trust), which Newig relates to social cohesion.

Peter J. Söderlund (2005)

Although Peter J. Söderlund is interested in the resources of political actors (and not those of public policy actors), in his article entitled 'Electoral success and federal-level influence of Russian regional executives' (2005), the nomenclature he uses, which is based on Dahl's (1957) famous terminology, lists 'time, wealth, popularity, intelligence, control over information, the rights pertaining to public office, charisma, legitimacy, legality, status and solidarity' (2005: 524) as resources. He continues: 'the term power denotes the capability of an actor to take advantage of available political resources, which can also be termed assets or values, in order to exercise power and influence over others' (2005: 524). Further on, he stresses the importance of the resource Time that covers 'different aspects of leadership skills and political resources available to a leader' (2005: 525). Dahl's famous definition of resources, which is referred to by Söderlund, features in particular the resources Time, Property ('wealth'), Information,

Political Support ('charisma legitimacy'), Law ('legality, status') and, in a manner of speaking, Consensus ('solidarity').

Thierry Blin (2005)

In his contribution entitled 'Ressources, stratégies et régulation d'un espace d'action collective: Le cas des "réfugiés" de Saint-Ambroise' ('Resources, strategies and regulation of a collective action space: The case of the Saint-Ambroise "refugees"'), Thierry Blin sets out to examine 'the paradigm of the mobilization of resources ... in its totality' (Blin, 2005: 174). He begins by asking whether it is possible to clarify the omnipresent concept of 'resources'. The sociologist confirms that the applications of the theory of the mobilization of resources advance as a shared generational principle 'the action capacities that are likely to be mobilized with a view to promoting an outcome. It is more about the capacities that the actors can mobilize in the context of a series of interactions and which enable them to influence a person or a group' (2005: 173).

Referring to C.J. Jenkins (1983, p 533), Blin then shows that:

> ... there is no founding agreement on this subject. Some content themselves with an *enumerated catalogue*, in which McCarthy and Zald (1977) include money, infrastructure, work and legitimacy, while Tilly (1978) lists land, work, capital and technical expertise. Others approach resources on the basis of their *use*. Hence, Rogers differentiates between *instrumental resources* (that is the *means of influence* used to "reward, punish or persuade") and *infra resources* which condition the use of instrumental resources. (Blin, 2005: 173)

Referring to J. Freeman (1979), Blin recalls the distinction between available resources (tangible and intangible resources). The tangible resources include:

> ... money, space, the means that make it possible to make the existence of the movement and its ideas public. Regarding the primary intangible resources, they are created by "persons"; with the understanding that these maintain distinctive relations to the control of resources.... The two other categories of resources are not specifically attributed to a specific type of person. These are time and

engagement (in the sense of the acceptance of risks and eventual disagreements). (Blin, 2005: 174)

At the end of this survey of the literature, in an effort to obtain 'operational' categories, Thierry Blin proposes five types of resources:

> ...the material resources (financial resources, premises...), symbolic resources (a number of demonstrators, the images associated with a movement, the demonstration of a position of weakness, the convocation of registers of legitimacy...), the authority resources (understood in the sense of capacities based on acquired skills, generally professional or arising from education: legal skills..., capacities based on an institutional distribution of statutes, on "charisma"...), social resources (networks, address books) and coercive resources (force, and, particularly "public force", but also all "powers of sanction": salary reduction, exclusion of a member...). (2005: 174)

According to Blin, this typology has 'the triple advantage of not being an enumerative catalogue, of not being constituted on the basis of a reading of the "nature" of resources, and of incorporating symbolic dimensions. It should, therefore, be more "manageable"' (2005: 174).

While this catalogue is interesting, Like Lemieux, it appears to confuse the characteristics of actors (non-exchangeable and non 'objectivable') with action resources that are precisely exchangeable and exist relatively independently of their concrete uses and can be accessed, in principle, by each of the three groups of public policy actors (and not only by political-administrative actors).

Paul Sabatier and Christopher Weible (2007)

The authors of 'The Advocacy Coalition Framework' (ACF), Paul Sabatier and Christopher Weible, proposed another complete catalogue of resources in an article published in 2007. They identify beliefs and resources in every *policy coalition*, and present '... a typology of policy-relevant resources that policy participants can use in their attempts to influence public policy. It overlaps about 40% with the Kilman and Sewell set of resources and somewhat more with Weible (2006)' (Sabatier and Weible, 2007: 201). The six proposed categories are: 'A. formal legal authority to make policy decisions.... B. Public opinion.... C. Information regarding the problem severity and causes and the costs and benefits of policy authorities.... D. Mobilizable troops.... E. Financial resources.... F. skilful leadership' (2007: 202). The choice of these six resources is not explained, and the list appears to have been compiled in a relatively inductive and arbitrary fashion.

Christopher Hood and Helen Margetts (2007)

Christopher Hood and Helen Margetts' book entitled *The tools of government in the digital age* (2007) starts from a simple distinction between two types of everyday 'government tools' that are used for detection and active intervention in civil society. Based on cyber-detection, the authors differentiate between four types of activities (communicate, determine, exchange and produce direct acts), each of which uses four main resources called 'NATO', 'nodality, authority, treasure, organization'. The simple criterion behind the choice of these resources, which is presented in a single sentence, alludes to an established fact: '... basic resources that governments tend to possess by virtue of *being* governments, and upon which they can draw for detecting and effecting tools' (2007: 5).

Each of these resources gives the government different capacities and can be allocated in different ways and subject to clear limits. 'Nodality denotes the property of being in the middle of an information or social network.... Strictly, a "node" is a junction of information channels....' Based on these nodes, the government 'may constitute a central presence in the form of a "figurehead". They may constitute a central presence in a more narrowly informational sense – seeing many different cases and thus building up a store of information not available to others' (Hood and Margetts, 2007: 5).

> Authority denotes the possession of legal or official power.... That is the power officially to demand, forbid, guarantee, and adjudicate.... Treasure denotes the possession of a stock of moneys or "fungible chattels". That means not only ... money in the common, every day sense of banknotes or coins, but anything which has the money-like property of "fungibility" ... that is, the capacity to be freely exchanged.... Organization denotes the possession of stock of people with whatever skills they may have (soldiers, workers, bureaucrats), land, buildings, materials, computers and equipment, somehow arranged.... [Organization] is not a simple derivative of [the other three basic resources],

in that it is logically possible to possess organization in this sense without (say) treasure or authority....

Nodality gives government the ability to traffic in information on the basis of "figureheadedness" or of having the "whole picture" ... the limiting factor is credibility and the 'coin' – how government spends this resource – is messages sent and received. *Authority* gives government the ability to "determine" in a legal or official sense, using tokens of official authority as the coin, and subject to a limit of legal standing. *Treasure* gives government the ability to exchange, using the coin of "moneys" and subject to a limit of "fungibility". Government may use its treasure as a means of trying to influence outsiders or as a way of buying "mercenaries" of various kinds, or buying information, subject to a limit of solvency. *Organization* gives government the physical ability to act directly, using its own forces rather than mercenaries. The coin is "treatments" or physical processing, and the limiting factor is *capacity*. (Hood and Margetts, 2007: 6)

What the authors refer to as 'coins' corresponds to the government's ways of spending or utilizing resources (Hood and Margetts, 2007: 9).

Keith Dowding (2008)

Counter to a current philosophy that claims that the notion of power cannot be reduced to something else, in his article entitled 'Power, capability and ableness: The fallacy of the vehicle fallacy' (2008), Keith Dowding claims 'that we can analyse power as ableness by reducing it to agents' resources' (2008: 239). He argues that: 'The resource account of power suggests that we can understand actors' power by looking at their resources ... all evidence of power is resource-based' (2008: 240). However, he remains cautious with regard to empirical work, and confirms that even if it were possible to measure all of an actor's resources precisely, 'we could still not predict precisely what the outcomes of their interactions would be' (2008: 240). This is due, among other things, to the fact that 'what counts as an actors' resources can only be understood in terms of how others view them' (2008: 240).

Dowding proposes four categories of resources based on game theory: information, legitimacy, the abilities of an actor to change the incentive structures of others and reputation. In the case of the latter:

... people may respond differently to an actor because they believe to have other resources (that he may not in fact have) or because they may predict his actions based on his (or others similarly situated) past behaviour. With the exception of information none of these sets of resources explicitly mention the many attributes of people that might be thought to be resources – money, charisma, a standing army – and so on. Any such list of physical attributes one could produce would almost certainly be incomplete, for many things might be used as a resource in this sense. Rather the four sets of resources provide an organizing principle around which we may study how actors respond to each other in different environments. (Dowding, 2008: 245-6)

It should be noted that this philosophical contribution, which is written in the form of a response to a colleague, Peter Morriss (Morriss, 2012), starts from a finite number of resources that are capable of explaining the phenomenon of power. In addition, Dowding stresses the relativity of resources: 'Power undoubtedly is a resource of actors, but we can only analyse that resource in relationship to resources of other actors' (2008: 255). Moreover, he highlights the interest of resources for research that does not exist for actors: '... we are explicitly or implicitly comparing the powers of *classes* or *types* of people' (2008: 251; emphasis in original). Despite his response to Peter Morriss and his approach of *atheoretical inductivism* (2008: 252), the reader is left in the dark regarding the criteria for the selection of the four proposed categories of resources.

Patrik Vesan and Paolo Graziano (2008)

The concept of resources also features in the literature on public–private partnerships. An example of this is the Working Paper by Patrik Vesan and Paolo Graziano on *Local partnership as a new mode of governance: A framework for analysis* (2008). The authors characterize these arrangements 'as a social co-ordination mechanism based on social dialogue, resource sharing and activity concentration...'. Basing themselves on Boerzel (1998), they consider such arrangements as 'a networked governance system, ie, a kind of social regulation where public and private actors depend on each other and are connected in a none hierarchical mode with the aim of sharing resources and coordinate interests and activities' (2008: 5). Among the resources exchanged and held in common, they mention 'time and dedication, financial resources for the co-funding of programmes and a partial delegation of some rights due to sharing of responsibilities for the use of the resources involved....' They continue: 'We will consider a partnership for local development as a form of a "political exchange" ... in which the actors involved invest some of their resources (material or immaterial) to obtain specific gains' (2008: 10). In this sense, the political authorities 'provide time resources, administrative and financial support, as well as a quota of their decisional power, to the partnership in exchange of "political gains", ie, acquisition or increase in political consensus' (2008: 11).

Alexandra Sauer (2008)

According to Alexandra Sauer in her article entitled 'Conflict pattern analysis: Preparing the ground for participation in policy implementation' (2008), the potential power of actors is their potential to exercise influence in a situation involving interactions. This power potential is based on the available resources and their intelligent use. She explains:

> Depending on the role and the main resources an actor possess (eg, working force, money, knowledge, capabilities, social capital and/or institutional support) four types of power potential are distinguished: (1) Definition power to shape a technical discourse. It depends on knowledge and on the credibility of this knowledge.... (2) Informal power to organise approval or rejection among other actors. It depends on the networking capabilities as well as the number and type of supportive actors or members (typical for associations). (3) Material power to directly influence actors and processes. It depends on material resources like budget, money, real estate and employees. (4) Normative power to define rules and norms that are respected by others. It depends on the legal and administrative legitimisation of an actor. The power potential of an actor can be estimated by assessing her formal and informal (execute) role and her available resources (eg, members of an association, political contacts, institutional framework, budget). (2008: 503)

Louis M. Imbeau (2009)

Seeking a more precise definition of the power of public policy actors, in his article entitled 'Testing the "veil of ignorance" hypothesis in constitutional choice: A "walk-talk" approach' (2009), Louis M. Imbeau explains that:

> In the context of public policy processes, the three most important power resources are: force or authority, wealth or things of value, and knowledge or information combined with rhetoric. Each power resource may be associated with a method and a main impact on incentive structures. Thus we identify three forms of social power: Political, economic and preceptoral.... (2009: 7)

According to Imbeau, political actors hold the resources force and authority. Given that power is distributed unequally,

> ...[s]ome individuals have more political power in the sense that they control the resources necessary to influence a larger number of people through the use of threat, coercion and heresthetic, thus maintaining or changing the distribution of political ... economic ... or preceptoral power – for example, by unilaterally imposing a theory or a belief as the truth thus making the defenders of this theory or belief more persuasive. (2009: 10)

Imbeau continues, confirming that:

> ...the same logic applies to the holders of economic power or perceptoral power. They can use the resources they control to maintain or modify the distribution of political, economic, or preceptoral powers. Wealth may be exchanged for a political appointment thus modifying the distribution of political power, or for a gold ring thus modifying the distribution of wealth, or for a university position thus modifying the distribution of knowledge. Knowledge may be used to persuade a politician to make a specific appointment thus modifying the distribution of political power. It may also be used to make one buy something that he would not buy otherwise thus modifying the distribution of economic power. (2009: 9)

The author identifies five resources – force, authority, wealth, things of value and knowledge – and stresses that an exchange of resources arises between actors.

Hugh Compston (2009)

Hugh Compston's article entitled 'Networks, resources, political strategy and climate policy' (2009), which is based on a research study of governmental strategies for strengthening public action to combat climate change, is perhaps the most rigorous, exhaustive and original contribution in this review of the literature. Compston starts from the theory of actor networks that suggests that these networks are constituted by the exchange of resources between the actors. Each actor wants something from another actor and is thus willing to exchange something they have in their possession for it. Quoting Roads (1985), a renowned expert in this theory, Compston confirms that 'policy making [consists] largely of a process of exchanges of resources using specific political strategies within understood "rules of the game"' (2009: 728). In this sense he confirms that a public policy is the result of interactions between a large number of actors, whereby each depends on other organizations to obtain the resources necessary to obtain their objectives. Exactly as in our policy analysis approach, he shows that the results of these exchanges are determined by the participants' resources and also by the institutional rules and the contexts in which these exchanges take place (2009: 729). This presupposes the existence of ownership rights to the exchangeable resources. Based on sociology and social psychology, Compston continues by confirming that power is conceptualized in terms of mutual dependence (Emerson, 1962). According to the latter, 'power resides implicitly in the other's dependency' (2009: 32). Each actor seeks or needs something that is controlled by other actors. The exchange of resources presupposes that the resources is transferrable: 'Consequently, we can define a resource in the context of policy network theory as being anything that (a) is controlled by a policy actor, (b) is desired by another policy actor and (c) can be transferred or exchanged in some relevant sense' (2009: 731).

Compston is insistent about the requirement of exchangeability for resources. Based on the actor holders, he considers the following resources as transferrable: law ('policy amendments') and 'access', with both being reserved to public actors; the following six resources can be in public or private hands: 'veto power', 'information', 'cooperation with implementation', 'recourse to the courts', 'political support' and 'patronage'; finally he attributes the resources 'private investment' and money ('fluid funds') to private actors.

Contrary to our approach, this list, which is considered exhaustive, differentiates between resources according to whether they belong to political-administrative actors and so-called private actors. Thus, Compston does not start from the idea, championed in this book, that each resource can be held by each of the actors involved in the analysed political game. A look at his comments would suggest that the resources identified by him correspond very closely to those presented in this book: 'policy amendments' and 'recourse to the courts' are more or less the same thing as Law and 'transferrable' because they consist in the possibility of a change '... in the choice of policy instrument(s) and/or settings in areas such as regulation, funding and taxation in the direction desired by the actor with whom the relevant resource exchange is taking place' (2009: 733). The resource 'access' corresponds to the Organization, 'veto power' and 'political support' strongly resemble Political Support, what Compston refers to as 'information' corresponds perfectly with the Information while 'private investment' corresponds to Property and 'fluid funds' to Money. Finally the resource referred to by Compston as 'patronage' bears a strong resemblance to Personnel.

Something else in this remarkable contribution that reinforces my approach is that the author arrives at concrete and convincing conclusions in the area of sectoral public policy (climate policies) through the application of the resources he develops. The conceptual effort consists in the rigorous application of the requirement of 'transferability' and the objectivabilty of resources. Finally, the logical attempt to develop an (exhaustive) typology appears to succeed and supports the similar attempt made in this book.

Heike Klüver (2011)

Heike Klüver proposes an interesting distinction between material resources and organizational structures in her article entitled 'Informational lobbying in the European Union: Explaining information supply to the European Commission' (2011). She uses resources as explanatory variables of the capacity of interest groups to influence European policies by marketing their information. She also bases her considerations on McCarthy and Zald (1977) and Knoke and Wood (1981), and defines material resources as:

> ...the equipment of interest groups with staff and money.
> Financial and personnel resources are a necessary condition

for every interest group to work towards goal attainment....
Interest groups need to acquire a high amount of material
resources in order to effectively lobby for their cause
and to supply the information required by the European
Commission.... The more material resources interest
groups possess, the higher the amount of policy-relevant
information they supply to the European Commission.
(2011: 4)

What is interesting about this contribution is that she does not consider
organizational structure as a resource, but as a different dimension
whose important characteristics in terms of an actor's power are
functional differentiation, professionalization and decentralization
(2011: 3).

Bruno Dente (2014)

In both conceptual terms and at the level of practical typology, the
analysis of public policy actors' resources presented by Bruno Dente
(2014) is probably the most similar to that presented in this book.
This is due to personal factors (intensive collaboration with the author
over a period of around 30 years), and also to the aim of his work,
which is both practical and focused on policy analysis, in particular
in the context of mandates carried out for the public sector. In order
to understand how and when actors are capable of intervening in the
process of policy-making, Dente starts from the concept of 'political
exchange' (2014: 35). Basing himself on Coleman (1964), he defines
this exchange as the capacity of actor A who is able to control outcome
X, which, in turn, is of interest to actor B, who, in turn, can influence
outcome Y, which is also of interest to actor A.

It is easy to understand how this concept is widely based
on the idea of power, considered as the ability to influence
other actors (actor B's behavior can only be explained as
a result of actor A's behavior) adding the consideration
that this is due to the actor A's capacity to generate rules
that actor B is interested in. These capacities are action
resources (or actors' resources) that can consist of the transfer
of any good that has a value for the receiver. One of the
main features of action resources is their replaceability:
the problem of not having a certain good in a sufficient

quantity can be solved by replacing it with something else.
(Dente, 2014: 35)

The typology proposed by Dente, which, unlike ours is not exhaustive, contains four categories of resources. In the introduction to his book he refuses to speak of the resource Force, even if it is often present in everyday interactions. The list he presents shows that resources sometimes incorporate certain actor qualities and do not make a clear distinction between actors and resources. The four resources defined are:

- 'Political resources', which are:

    ... the amount of consensus an actor is able to get. It can refer to the whole population or to specific social groups involved in the different public policies. It can be confirmed through elections or referendums, it can be modified through information and communication campaigns and often suffers from external events (a particularly ferocious murder alters the consensus to policies to combat crime). It can derive from countless factors: charisma of personal status of the policy actors, ideology of who grants it and who receives it, recognition of the fact that an actor has the intellectual capacities to tackle a policy problem .... (Dente, 2014: 36)

- 'Economic resources': 'the ability of an actor to mobilize money or any form of wealth in order to modify other actors' behaviour ... what counts is the importance of the wealth for whoever receives it.' Economic resources are worth as much as other resources that can be bought by them. Dente adds that from the perspective of the target group, other resources exist that are able to alter their behaviour. Consensus and the political resources available to the political-administrative actors are referred to explicitly.
- 'Legal resources': Dente defines these resources as:

    ... the advantages or disadvantages, attributed to particular subjects by legal regulations and in general legislative and administrative authorities' decisions. Examples of legal resources are: the fact that according to the law a certain duty is entrusted to a specific office (competence principal), the fact that a certain behavior is forbidden and violations are sanctioned; the fact that any individual has the possibility to challenge in front of a judge a public authority decision that violates his rights ; the fact that the sequence of the activities needed to reach a legally valid decision is strictly predetermined (existence of formal procedures). (2014: 39)

This definition strongly resembles our definition of the resource Law. The author stresses that law should be lived, and that it is the 'law in use' that describes the modalities of use that actors make of this resource that counts in decision processes. Actors may refrain from using Law because the costs associated with its application in terms of money, time and stress would exceed the benefits. 'This means public and private subjects often adopt illegal behavior simply because they know there are no counter-interested subjects that will object or might profit by using the law to modify or to sanction, this behavior' (Dente, 2014: 41). Dente concludes that law should be considered as a real resource that is accessible to all. Its importance consists precisely in the modalities of its use and its absence may be filled by political consensus, money or the resource knowledge (2014: 42).

- 'Cognitive resources': Again, the conceptualization presented by Bruno Dente for this resource, which is designated as Information in this book, is very close to mine. He stresses the increasing importance of this resource that manifests precisely in the increasing professional requirements regarding administrative personnel (Personnel), in the relative advantages that its availability provides to the key actors of public policies and in the dependence of the validity of a consensus between the actors (negotiated information). Finally, Dente presents a classification of this resource based on the type of information provided: its interpretation is based on either scientific information based on theoretical concepts and models or the information refers to substantive or procedural questions, whereby the latter are considered as 'strategic knowledge' (Dente, 2014: 45).

Comparison of findings

Overview

Table 3.1 summarizes the results of my analysis of the 19 contributions based on the dimensions used in my analysis. Only passages in the texts that correspond to the perspectives developed in this book are mentioned, hence the intention of this literature review is mainly to situate my ideas in the general scientific context and not to present the entire content of these texts. This means that even if there are considerable numbers of 'empty boxes' in the authors' columns, this does not mean that their work is weak in some regards, but simply that they consider other aspects of resources as important. In the majority of cases, what is involved here are actor qualities (last line), which, in my conceptualization, are not part of the objectivable and thus exchangeable 'public action resources'. Thus my reading of the literature is highly selective and focused on shared rather than diverging elements.

Discussion of findings

So many authors, so many conceptualizations, so many authors, so many typologies? In effect, the review of the literature, which becomes redundant in a way after around 20 texts, allows us to be eclectic without becoming heretical. This review enables us to maintain an essentially 'Crozierian' approach – or to quote Philippe Warin (2009), one of 'pragmatic constructivism', supported and reinforced by the following seven observations:

• The power of public policy actors can be conceived as their control, *hic et nunc*, over a finite group of public policy resources, the possession and use of which are regulated by institutional rules (10/19 statements).
• There is no universal typology of resources; even the typologies that include a finite number of resources vary hugely, and the quest for common elements makes little sense, as each typology depends on the specific research question that the 'conceptual framework' sets out to answer. The resources identified most frequently by the surveyed authors are (in decreasing order): Information (14/19), Law, Money and Property (each 13/19), Political Support (9/19), Consensus (7/19), Force and Organization (each 5/19) and Time (4/19). Moreover, the catalogue presented in this book is by far the most comprehensive found in the literature.
• On no account can I claim to have 'invented' the less common resources like Consensus (7/19), Time (4/19) and Organization (5/19). Apart from the fact that they are already tackled, in part, at least, in the 'classical' texts (see Lasswell and Kaplan, 1950; Dahl, 1961; Crozier and Friedberg, 1981), they also feature in the research of less well-known and more recent authors and authors with a stronger focus on empirical work and specific public policy fields.

Table 3.1: Recap of the literature review[a]

	Arnold J. Meltsner (1972)	Christopher Clapham (1978)	Didier Lapeyronnie (1988)	Jean-Patrice Lacam (1988)	Erik-Has Kiun (1996)	Michael Davern (2001)	Vincent Lemieux (2002)	Jens Newig (2005)	Peter J. Söderlund (2005)	Thierry Blin (2005)
Resources										
Force		X		X						X
Law			X	X			X		X	X
Personnel			X			X	X		X	X
Money			X	X			X	X		X
Property			X			X		X	X	X
Information	X			X		X	X		X	X
Organization							X			X
Consensus			X					X	X	
Time			X					X	X	
Political Support		X		X				X	X	
Number										
Finite number	X			X	X					X
Infinite number	?	X	X							
Exchangeability										
Exchangeable	X	X	X	X	X	X	X	?		X
Linked to the personal characteristics of the actors	?		X	X		X	X	X	X	X

	Paul Sabatier and Christopher Weible (2007)	Christopher Hood and Helen Margetts (2007)	Keith Dowding (2008)	Patrik Vesan and Paolo Graziano (2008)	Alexandra Sauer (2008)	Louis M. Imbeau (2009)	Hugh Compston (2009)	Heike Klüver (2011)	Bruno Dente (2014)	Total	Peter Knoepfel et al (2001, 2006 [2011])[b]
Resources											
Force	X					X				5	X
Law	X	X	X	X	X	X	X		X	13	X
Personnel		X			X		X	X	X	10	X
Money	X	X		X	x	X	X	X	X	13	X
Property		X			X	X	X	X	X	13	X
Information	X	X	X		X	X	X	X	X	14	X
Organization		X			X		X			5	X
Consensus	X	X		X					X	7	X
Time				X						4	X
Political Support	X		X	X			X		X	9	X
Number											
Finite number	X	X	X			X	X		X	10	X
Infinite number			X						X	3	
Exchangeability											
Exchangeable	X	X	X	X		X	X	X	X	14	X
Linked to the personal characteristics of the actors			X		X					9	

Notes: [a] 19 contributions, published between 1972 and 2014; the empty fields simply indicate that, in my view, the author or authors do not make a sufficiently explicit case. [b] See also Klok (1995), who used the same list in a publication we discussed in the frame of an international project ('Environmental Policies in Search of New Instruments', 1993/94, financed by the European Science Foundation).

- The value of a resource is always relative because it should be defined on the basis of the resource available to the other actors; this postulate is presented explicitly by at least half of the surveyed authors.
- The distinction between policy actors' resources and public action instruments is only rarely made; in the majority of the analysed texts, the authors scarcely differentiate, or do not do so explicitly, between action resources and public policy instruments.
- Although the review of the literature does not allow us to conclude that our catalogue is 'exhaustive', it confirms that no author presents a new category in terms of our definition. The majority of the 'resources' that do not feature in our catalogue, should not, in my opinion, be considered as resources as they are qualifiers or refer to the (subjective) capacities of the actors ('associated with the actors') and for this reason, they are not covered by our definition. The number of authors who consider these subjective qualifiers ('non-exchangeable') as resources, and erroneously in my view, is astonishingly high (9/19). This demonstrates a clear lack of consensus on the very concept of a public action resource.
- The approaches that are closest to mine are those of Dente (2014), Compston (2009), Hood and Margetts (2007) and Imbeau (2009). Those that differ most from it are by Söderlund (2005), Davern (2001) and Meltsner (1972). The question remains open as to whether these divergences or convergences arise from different disciplinary horizons, the use of the typologies for specific empirical fields, differences in the age of the authors or simply in their cultural contexts.

This survey of the literature was not carried out on a scientifically comprehensive basis; my model of the 10 public action resources was conceived using an inductive process that appears more productive to me than a deductive one, and I accept that this review of the literature is only useful to the extent that it confirmed the belief that the majority of attempts at the theorization of resources hardly provide more answers for practice. And practice is at the basis of the conceptualization presented here. It is an 'ex-post' conceptualization borne of the encounter between my preoccupations with both the research on policy actors' resources, on the one hand, and the (natural) physical, material and then immaterial resources of our environment, on the other, which still constitute the four types of human 'capital' according to The World Bank's terminology (2006, 2011, 2014), that is natural, manufactured, social and human resources.

Finally, it should be noted that what surprised me most about the results of the literature review is the low number of political science studies that have tackled the task of providing a typology of public action resources despite the fact that the use of the term 'resource' in relation to that of 'power' has become very common, since the 1980s at least, and, moreover, on both the level of everyday policy practice and the scientific literature.

Part II
New conceptual developments: Resource-based approach and analytical dimensions

Reminders

It is important to remember, first, that our conceptualization of the relationship between actors and resources starts with the idea that this relationship is strongly structured by the basic institutional rules of the political system – the Swiss political system in my case (for example, rule of law, human rights, executive federalism, principle of direct democracy). This structure is reflected in institutional rules governing possession (right to dispose of and thus mobilize a resource), behavioural institutional rules (permitted and prohibited use of a resource) and decisional institutional rules (time and space for mobilization based on the different stages of the public policy cycle). Neither the appropriation nor mobilization of these resources by the actors are chaotic processes; they are regulated like a Swiss timepiece, particularly during the implementation stage. Thus one can hardly refer to the mobilization of public action resources without referring to the rules that govern these processes. Hence the conclusion already drawn in the previous chapters to the effect that an actor who holds a relatively weak portfolio of resources can emerge victorious from an actors' game thanks to the intelligent activation of these rules that are sometimes enacted to protect such vulnerable actors.

Second, it should be recalled that the purpose of the mobilization of public policy resources is to influence the competent public actor(s) in relation to the decisions taken on each of the six products of the public policy cycle. Thus it is not primarily a question of influencing the social, economic or socio-cultural behaviour of a partner or adversary actor. Accordingly, in the area of company mergers, the mobilization of an actor's resources for the acquisition of a competitor company consists in the simple mobilization of these societal, economic and social resources[1] 'outside of public policies'. Given that the crucial product of the public policy on cartels is the approval or rejection of this cartel by the regulator (COMCO, the Competition Commission, in the case of Switzerland), the actor purchaser will mobilize specific public

77

action resources to 'convince' COMCO that, despite this purchase, it will not assume a dominant position in the market, a development that would contravene the aims of competition policy. Hence the mobilization of public action resources (and not societal resources) is strictly limited to attempts to influence public decisions that are in the process of production, that of the implementation of cartel policy through the eventual prohibition of a merger in the case in point. Moreover, this mobilization can be accompanied by support from eventual partners (third party losers like trade unions or local authorities fearing the loss of jobs if the merger does not materialize). However, as largely demonstrated later, in Chapter 10, on the resource Property, the fact that an actor has economic, social and or natural resources can consolidate its portfolio of public action resources considerably (transforming such resources into public action resources).

Third, let us recall that contrary to managerial conceptualizations of decision-making processes in the public sector, according to which these are merely internal phenomena within public administrations (Giauque and Emery, 2016: 5ff), our conception starts from the assumption that not only public actors but also (and above all) civil society actors (particularly target groups and beneficiaries) have public action resources that they regularly mobilize in the programming and implementation of public policies. This theory, which has been confirmed many times by empirical reality, constitutes a basic element of our approach and even structures the chapters of Part III of this book that are dedicated to mobilization and the exchange of each of the 10 resources based on these different actor groups.

Finally, a deliberate particularity of our approach is the avoidance of any theorization or modelling based on the development of algorithms (for example, if such an actor mobilizes the resource XY, the product will be Z). I firmly believe that such approaches lead to unrealistic prognoses and that they are counter-productive in that the objective is to demonstrate the variety of real situations, to arouse the interest of analysts, and to inspire new research on certain resource mobilizations and exchanges as presented here. As is the case in our basic textbook, I also reject attempts at the hierarchization of different resources, even though one of the analytical dimensions actually involves the substitution of missing resources with available ones. Chappelet and Emery (2009) provide a reasonable example of such a hierarchization for the aims of public management.

Aim

Part II adds some new conceptual developments to the approach based on my associates' studies on natural, manufactured, social and human resources (Chapter 4), and on the lessons learned from practical experience in the application of the conceptual elements presented in Part I in the studies by graduate and doctoral students over the last 10 years in Switzerland and abroad (in particular, in France, Ukraine and Spain[2]). It should be noted that Chapter 5 is conceived in part as a checklist, the purpose of which is to guide analysts and managers in their everyday work in relation to public action resources. At an initial glance, it resembles the checklist presented in Part IV, dedicated to the perspectives and advice on policy practice (in particular, the final section in Chapter 17 entitled 'Seven-point checklist for analysing the effects of the mobilization of public action resources on public decision-making'). This resemblance is merely apparent, however. The seven analytical dimensions presented in Chapter 5 are strictly limited to resources in themselves, while the checklist in the concluding chapter aims to be more comprehensive and synthetic.

Notes

[1]   As opposed to public action resources.
[2]   Where the author regularly gives courses.

4

Conceptual development of the resource-based approach

This chapter takes up the considerations initiated in the second part of Chapter 2. It describes the approach developed in the basic textbook while supplementing it with the help of a 'resource-based' approach in line with various studies on institutional resource regimes (IRR) carried out simultaneously by my associates and me (for an overview of the concept and methods, see, for example, de Buren, 2015; see also Knoepfel et al, 2001, 2003; Gerber et al, 2009). I begin by presenting the advantages of this approach for public policy analysis and then demonstrate its potential for the relevant analysis of questions relating to the governance of information-based public action resources.

Advantages of the resource-based approach for public policy analysis

According to traditional resource economics, a resource is defined as a group of basic interacting elements (stock) that produce flows of particular goods and services. For each good and/or service there is a group of interested actors that consider them as assets, which they set out to appropriate more or less permanently and exclusively through the acquisition of rights of use. In the case of a public action resource, the basic elements may be things (Property), armed persons (Force), competences/rights to produce or change (or instigate the changing of) public decisions (Law) or units of time such as minutes, hours and years (Time).

However, these basic interacting elements do not in themselves form the action resource or the power. The latter may be defined as the holding of a bundle of goods and/or services arising from the specific interaction between these basic elements. Depending on the established social mechanisms (conditions of the production of public action resources), these goods and/or services differ from each other and thus enable the actor-holders to distinguish themselves from other actors. This distinction concerns not only the level of the different groups of goods and services originating from different resources, but also that originating from one and the same resource. Money in the hands of a king is not the same as money in the hands of one of his subjects. In effect, given that the king has the monopoly on paper and ink, it can have a lower value in the hands of the king. Hence he can make these elements interact as often as he wishes; however, he runs the risk of making them lose their value (inflation) in the eyes of his subjects. A group of people who are authorized, obliged or disposed to use arms (stock of the resource Force) under the command of an actor from the target group ('private army') represents a good and/or service in the latter's portfolio that distinguishes it from political-administrative actors who may have access to the same groups of armed men, but are only authorized to use them as a last resort and in accordance with very restrictive rules.

Thus the goods and services of public action resources give the actors the capacity to distinguish themselves from others, and it is precisely this distinctive character of the goods and services that stimulates interest and provokes resource use rivalries. Even if the stock of the resource is abundant, there may be a scarcity of goods and services based on these stocks for one and the same public policy. It is the availability of these goods and services that constitutes the essential components of the actors' power.

To say that the resources (in limited number and varying quality) are constitutive of the actors' power is only correct if we incorporate the stocks and the goods and/or services produced by the stocks into the concept of resources. From the perspective of the regulation of the actors' power to act, this distinction may make sense because rules exist (in particular, possessive rules) that relate to the basic elements (definition of an armed man; the length of a minute; the colour of bank notes) and rules that concern the goods and services originating from the resource.

To put it more simply, I propose to refrain from applying this distinction in the empirical application of the proposed concept and to use the term 'resource' as a generic term that covers both the stock and the goods and/or services. I would like to stress, however, that the essence of an actor's power lies in the goods and/or services and not in the stock or the basic elements which, although an essential condition, are not necessarily sufficient for the true availability of the former.

Even if the usefulness of the analogy between natural resources and public action resources is not obvious at the level of this relatively abstract distinction between stocks and goods and services, its benefits come to fruition in the concrete analysis of each of the 10 categories of resources. The analogy would appear to be highly relevant in relation to the actor-users, the use rights and their regulation. In effect, any reference to different goods and services also covers different actor-users with an interest in the latter. This specific interest implies the existence of several uses by different actors that relate either to one and the same service provided by a resource (homogenous uses) or to different goods and services provided by one and the same resource (heterogeneous uses). This use is the result of the identical or different interest expressed by the actors in these services. And this interest is a function of the actors' objectives and strategies with regard to the content of the different products of a public policy.

Accordingly, a document (basic element of the resource Information) may provide its holders with the service 'of being informed' (as the first, exclusively), and this gives them a position of power over the non-holders. Based on this the holder will gain, for example, time over others, and this can strengthen the implementation of a public policy (in coalition with another actor that shares the same interest: homogenous uses), or the holders may use it to denigrate the other actors, for example, by challenging their interpretation of the same documented facts (heterogeneous uses). Thus the value that different actors attribute to the goods and services originating from a public action resource can vary on the basis of the nature of the interest in their use. This explains the selectivity in actors' acquisition strategies – varying degrees of exclusivity, speed – enabling, for example, exchanges for goods provided by other resources in their possession.

Whether homogenous or heterogeneous, all uses of such a good and/or service contribute to the emergence of situations of scarcity and rivalry, unless a true public good is involved (absence of subtractability, use of one good/service does not exclude the use of others and lack of possibilities for exclusion). This gives rise to the need, amply demonstrated in practice, for the application of (possession, behavioural and decisional) institutional rules. Together, these rules form veritable (general) 'institutional regimes', which lead to different 'local regulatory arrangements' (concrete, *in situ*) at the level of their implementation. According to my definition, such regimes and arrangements consist of groups of rules governing use rights that attribute the good and/or service in question to specific actors and describe their modalities of use in terms of the respect of other actors' use rights and thereby define the admissible uses in relation to space and time. The basis of these use rights can be found in civil law (physical or intellectual property rights) and/or in the provisions of public policies that impose limits on the owners or attribute use rights to non-owners.

This concept of institutional resource regimes (IRR) can be applied effectively and almost completely to public action resources. For reasons of nomenclature and variance among scientific communities, we simply use (and continue to use) different terminology that is based on the three categories of institutional rules already mentioned.[1] This analogy with natural and other resources draws our attention to the important role that civil and constitutional law can play in terms of actors' rights of use to the public action resources. It invites us to examine, at the level of each of the 10 resources, the legitimacy of activating these institutional rules constructed by these actors when they mobilize 'their' resources. As more and more institutional rules, which tended to be informal in the past, are codified today in the form of explicit legal norms, once again (see Part I) it makes sense to attribute a prominent role to (public and private) law in the management of public policy resources.

Finally, it should be noted that this alignment of 'public action resources' and 'institutional resource regimes' is a recent phenomenon. This process is merely starting: in introducing links between these two concepts for the first time, we remain some distance away from exploring the idea in detail.

Thus what about the risks relating to the bad exploitation of public action resources? It is already clear that each actor should take care to avoid uncontrolled rivalries. Rather than the simple disappearance of the stock, it is the devaluation of the resource that constitutes a major risk. Regarding Information, too much transparency – or too little at the right time – damages the credibility of the resource in its entirety. Property may be over- or under-valued in accounts, and this creates illusory impressions of wealth or poverty that also cast doubt on the actual state of the resource and distort the actors' strategies. The devaluation can arise through adverse attacks, for example, the use of Information as a weapon for undermining the credibility of an adversary's cognitive stock during an election campaign (such as the 2017 campaign on the Corporate Reform Act III in Switzerland), that is, if the behavioural institutional rules that frame the use of public action resources are essential (lawful or unlawful use of a resource, depending on the context; principles of proportionality, equality of treatment, for example, in the context of public procurement, rule of law).

In any event, time and patience are needed to systematically list the different types of use made of public action resources (and particularly the abusive uses, contested exclusive uses, or conversely, complementary uses). In this book, I simply attempt to establish this new research field between public policies and management.

Advantages of the resource-based approach for analysing the governance of complex public action resources (example: big data)

As confirmed in Chapter 3, some economic, social or environmental resources can transform into public action resources. Processes going in the opposite direction can also be observed. What we are witnessing today is, in effect, the transformation of public action resources into economic, social or environmental resources whose services are of interest not only to public policy actors, for which the later were initially conceived, but to an entire spectrum of civil society actor-users. This applies in particular to the resources Information and Organization. In effect, the impressive development that has taken place in the area of new information and communication technologies (NICT) and the simultaneous development of all kinds of social networks over the last two decades enabled the quasi-universalization of rights of use to computer data that were initially mainly collected for the management of specific public policies.

This process has particularly affected all kinds of public registries (land registry, commercial registry, registry of residents) and statistical databases in almost all areas of public policy activity (public health, environment, natural resources, transport, legislation and jurisprudence, economics and foreign trade). These databases are referred to as 'common pool resources' in the language of institutional economists (Ostrom, 1990). These resources are characterized by a use of their services which, in technical terms at least, can hardly be subtractable (use by one actor does not exclude use by others) or exclusive (difficulty, particularly technically, in excluding possible actor-users).[2] This non-exclusivity poses known problems with regard to the protection of data, their ownership and responsibility for their management – hence the need for the establishment of sometimes very sophisticated governance systems. It should be noted that this is equally applicable to historical data (archives) and 'live' data.

With a view to examining the governance of the *resource public documentary information* from the perspective of its durability, Mirta Olgiati Pelet demonstrates the usefulness and analytical scope of a resource-based approach. Taking the Swiss Federal Archives, the e-Helvetica[3] database, meteorology and climatology databases, Swiss federal statistics, soil monitoring, official cadastral surveying, civil status and value-added tax data, Pelet identifies three *main services*, that is, *addition, management and extraction*, for this public action resource. Figure 4.1, which is taken from her study (Olgiati Pelet, 2011) on archives, libraries and the Swiss federal administration, describes in detail the three groups of actor-users legitimized to use these services based on the use rights attributed to them. What is involved here is the strongly regulated right to submit data and thus add them to the stock of the resource in a controlled and systematic manner (depositor with right of addition to the resource), the right to store the data in accordance with strict rules enabling their traceability (management), and finally, the right to extract data attributed to end users with varying degrees of selectivity (extraction).

Figure 4.1: Actor groups of the resource information

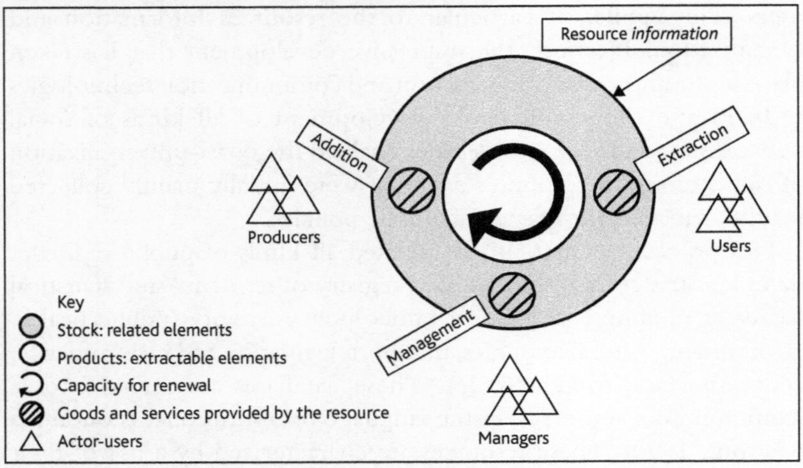

Source: Olgiati Pelet (2011: 79), translated from French original

Olgiati Pelet demonstrates the existence of rivalries between these user rights and user groups and analyses the regulations relating to them from the perspective of their extent (regulation possibly lacking and enabling the emergence of rivalries that could destroy the reproducibility of the resource) and their coherence (substantial and procedural coordination enabling the avoidance of contradictory regulations that can also make the resource's 'institutional regime' 'complex' rather than 'integrated'[4] due to the lack of 'tightness' of the regulation). Figure 4.2, which is taken from the same study, illustrates this basic concept.

Heterogeneous rivalries arising between the constitution of the resources (addition) and its exploitation (extraction) are considered as central use rivalries. This dichotomy originates in the basic rights defined by several articles in the constitution, for example, relating to the right to privacy (Federal Constitution of the Swiss Confederation,

Figure 4.2: Extent and coherence of regulations applicable to the resource information

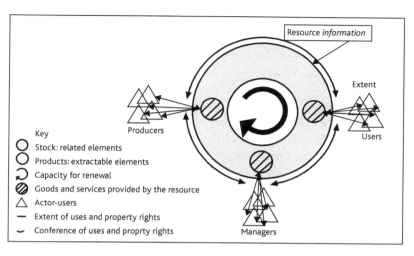

Source: Olgiati Pelet (2011: 99), translated from French original

Article 13) and freedom of expression and information (Article 16). In a democratic society, the legislation should find the point of equilibrium between the protection of the individual and access to information which, in the words of Joseph Zwicker, 'are ... at odds with each other – while being complementary at the same time' (2007, 166; author's translation).

The author explores this aspect of use rivalries in detail, which were already mentioned above and are closely associated to the IRR, stating that:

> ...other more significant heterogeneous rivalries can arise between the services of addition, extraction and management, which are characterized by needs specific to it on a temporal scale of a (very) long duration. Here is an example of rivalry to be managed between the services of addition and extraction: the implementation of a public policy sometimes necessitates the creation of internal files containing personal data (addition) which must be protect for the duration of their utilization (extraction). An example of rivalry between addition and management: the requirements relating to archiving (management) – for example concerning the choice of media – are often in conflict with the needs relating to the ongoing use of

information within an administrative body (addition). Finally, an example of rivalry between the service of management and extraction: the needs in terms of the use of the information (extraction) are often at odds with the respecting of the rights of the authors (management). (Zwicker, 2007: 90)

The resource-based approach enables Olgiati Pelet to confirm the existence of (admittedly minimal) differences between the degree of integration and sustainability of the institutional regimes of the eight data entities analysed and presented separately based on the extent and coherence of the relevant regulations[5] in Figure 4.3.

Pelet explains these differences based on the variations of the number of actors affected,[6] the standardization of the processes,[7] the regulatory powers of the managing actors,[8] the available means[9] and the actors games for retaining control of the information production process.

Figure 4.3: Summary of the gaps and incoherencies in the institutional regime of the resource information

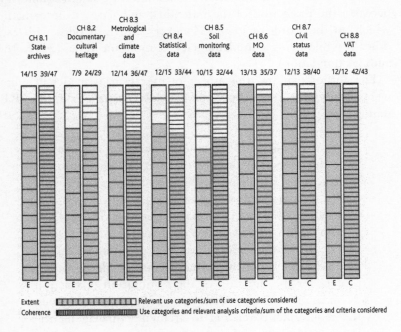

Source: Olgiati Pelet (2011: 257), translated from French original

She ultimately concludes that the applied resource-based approach:

> ...enabled both the systematic and global analysis of the nature of the challenges that characterize the use of the elements that compose the resource information in the early 21st century. Thanks to this, admittedly unusual, perspective, these elements are no longer considered as the assembly of a disjointed quantity of documents, information and individual data located at different points in their life cycle but, conversely, as components related to a basic resource that the public actors use every day in the context of their activities. (2011: 281)

Thus the resource-based process enabled her:

> ...to identify the complex network of problems in the form of a limited number of uncontrolled use rivalries, that is to identify precisely the gaps in terms of rules which, in the long term, risk jeopardizing the sustainability of the resource.... These – very limited – gaps are not the result of a poor evaluation of the needs in terms of rules but of the evolution of the resource in question. Based on the eight cases analyzed, we have shown that they concern in particular the identification of available information, its traceability, the selection of documents to be conserved, and, finally, their physical preservation with the aim of guaranteeing the long-term access to the information and, based on this, to knowledge. (2011: 281)

Given the absence of a consensus between the political-administrative actors, the target groups and/or beneficiary groups of the institutional policies in question, and also with other civil society actors, the resource-based approach as applied successfully in the case of the resource Information should have considerable analytical potential for studying the governance of other public action resources (Internet, Organization and Money) that are in the process of transformation from policy resources towards (societal) economic, social or environmental resources.

Notes

[1] Instead of the term 'institutional regimes' (see Gerber et al, 2009).

[2] Which characterizes them in the economic sense as 'public goods'; see Gerber (2009).

[3] Or publications by Swiss authors on topics relating to Switzerland.

[4] Complex: not sustainable; 'integrated': sustainable, according to Gerber et al (2009).

[5] The author analyses all of the – very complex – regulations contained in Swiss federal legislation (laws, decrees, directives) and codes (libraries, archives) for each of the eight analysed databases.

[6] 'The higher the number of actors involved, the greater the degree of integration of the regime' (Olgiati Pelet, 2011: 259).

[7] 'The more standardized the processes are for all of the actors involved, the more integrated the regime' (Olgiati Pelet, 2011: 260).

[8] 'The greater the regulatory power of the actors, the greater the chances are that the regime will be highly integrated' (Olgiati Pelet, 2011: 260).

[9] 'The greater the means of an actor to devote not only to the production and diffusion of the data but also to their management, the greater the chances that the regime that characterizes it has of being integrated' (Olgiati Pelet, 2011: 261).

5

The seven proposed analytical dimensions

Having considered the portfolio of resources at the disposal of the identified actors of a public policy and the 'resource-based' definition, it is time to move on to the actual in-depth analysis of these key resources that can be observed at work in the actor games. The criteria for the selection of the seven analytical dimensions proposed here are based on the aim of providing an empirical explanation of the essential aspects of the exchange of resources between the actors under consideration, in accordance with the approach applied here as the very essence of the power games at work in the implementation of public policies in particular. These aspects are the specific uses of the services in question provided by the different resources, the actors' rights of use, the modalities of production, acquisition and maintenance of these resources, their modalities of use or threatened use, and the substitutability and exchangeability of rights of use to the resources. Following a short section on the actors' strategic objectives, the proposed analysis demonstrates, in particular, the link between resources, actors and institutional rules already mentioned in Part I of this book. In this chapter this link is explored further from the perspective of the policy analyst and manager.

Strategic objectives of the actors

Let us recall here that the primary objective of resource mobilization is always to influence the decisions taken by political-administrative actors (in the context of public policy implementation: action plan and output). However, this objective is ultimately only attained if the target groups have actually changed their behaviour (in particular, changed modalities of use: Property) and the beneficiary groups have accepted the solution (degree of acceptance of the decision of the other two actors: Consensus). The ultimate aim of the mobilization of these resources will consist, therefore, in political-administrative decisions that apply to the behaviour of their addressees (target groups) and in the renunciation of various means of opposition (beneficiary groups).

In general, the strategic objectives that guide the mobilization of resources for the three actor groups, particularly on the level of implementation, are:

- Political-administrative actors: production of decisions that will result in real changes in behaviour instigated by target groups without encountering excessive opposition on the part of beneficiary groups.
- Target groups: to obtain decisions that are favourable to their interests (in particular, economic ones) without encountering overwhelming opposition on the part of beneficiary groups.
- Beneficiary groups: to obtain decisions favourable to the interests of the social groups affected by the existence of the problem that the policy proposes to resolve without provoking resistance that would have adverse impacts on the effective solutions.

The policy analyst and the manager are interested in empirically validating their hypotheses concerning the relative positioning of the actors in question, as in reality, variances from the maximalist strategies can be observed that are due to strategies that take either the long-term rather than the short-term perspective into account, the regional rather than the local one, or that can be explained simply by judgements in relation to costs and benefits that deviate from habitual practices. This unpredictability of the strategic objectives pursued by the 'adversary' actors of the triangle can be further boosted by the consideration of the interests of third party winners and/or losers (positively or negatively affected third parties). As already highlighted in Part I, both the target groups and the beneficiaries have an interest in concluding strategic coalitions – which are often crucial to the power relations within the policy triangle – with these groups, and in considering the latter's interests as imperatives when it comes to formulating their own strategic objectives.

Before moving on to comparative analysis of the resources at the disposal of the three actor groups, it makes sense to consider their objectives and motivations, which explain the intensity and modalities of their resource mobilization.

The (purposes of the) rights of use to resources

The goods and/or services provided by a resource can only be used by those who have the corresponding rights. Such rights are conferred by a possession rule in the form of ownership (in accordance with private law) and/or a specific provision of a public policy (the policy in question or another – institutional – policy relating to the management of the resource). It makes sense therefore to begin by identifying the specific use (goods and/or services) that the actor in question makes of the resource, that is, to respond to the question regarding the purpose to be fulfilled through its 'expenditure' or an offer of exchange to a third party actor. Behind all rational use of a resource lies the motivation to acquire a right of use to another service provided by the same resource (homogenous exchange) or a service provided by another resource held by one of the two partner actors (heterogeneous exchange). This motivation only exists under the condition that the actor that is willing to renounce their rights of use to one of the resources in their portfolio lacks something that prevents them from acting as they wish and intends to make up for this lack. In doing this, the actor always considers that they possess sufficient rights of use to this resource, even when they have 'relinquished' them in the process of a planned exchange. In effect, to be able to develop their strategy in the context of the implementation of the policy in question, they can expect a counter-service ('return') to which they attribute an at least identical if not greater value.

Accordingly, even if it means a loss of financial capacity in the future, the political-administrative actors involved in agricultural policy are willing to exchange rights of use to their Money ('subsidies') if farmers relinquish a good and service provided by their Property (right of use to agricultural land involving, for example, the spreading of volumes of fertilizers that are considered excessive and harmful to the soil). Thus, by signing a subsidy contract, the latter relinquish a previously exploited right of use to their Property. However, the farmers will only be willing to do this if they also have an interest in the financial service being provided, that is, if it is equivalent to their loss of profit (reduction in their right of use to their Property) and/or increases their stock of Consensus ('corporate image' enabling them to avoid disputes with the beneficiary actors of agro-environmental policy).

This example clearly shows that the exchange of the right to use resources is often a game involving multiple resources, particularly for the political-administrative actors. The target groups can become involved in exchanges of individual resources with the state if the political-administrative actors convince them that their loss of profits will be lower than the compensation they will receive (in the form of subsidies) or than other supplementary losses (penal procedures, fines). Such compensation may be boosted by gaining access to supplementary benefits in the form of the acquisition of new resources for their portfolios (for example, Consensus, Time, Property [future goods and/or services], Law [avoidance of legal procedures]). Thus, a detailed knowledge of the purpose of the use right and the role it plays in the actor's strategy and that of its 'adversary' is indispensible to the policy analyst and manager.

Public action resources: production and modalities of acquisition

The resource-based definition shows that the actors actually do produce 'entire' resources (without necessarily thinking about the specific services/goods they obtain from them) and that they acquire both resources and goods/or services of resources that they will then incorporate into their resource portfolio. The production of resources may be autonomous or heteronomous. As already indicated in Part I, political-administrative actors usually benefit from heteronomous production as they receive a large proportion of their resources from institutional policies (Money, Property, Time, Information, Political Support). In these cases, they receive 'budgets' from the centralized institutional policy actors of the public body in question.

It should be noted, nonetheless, that the political-administrative actors of sectoral policies are increasingly required to participate in the production of their own resources and even produce some of them themselves. This applies in particular to Money (levying of payments and charges earmarked for their own tasks), Information (production of their 'own' statistics on sectoral policies that may contradict, entirely or in part, the statistics produced by the general statistics services) and Political Support (so-called 'foreign affairs' policies in relation to substantive policies at the level of parliament or the executive). As opposed to this, other resources must be produced entirely by the specific political-administrative actors. This applies in particular to Consensus, Organization and Force. The specificity of these resources consists in their essential contributions to the secondary legitimization of these sectoral policies, which are based, in turn, on the quality of their services and their acceptance by the target groups and beneficiaries.

It is important for the policy analyst and manager to differentiate clearly between these two modalities of production. The 'home-grown' products frequently lead to 'sectoral' use rights that are of little interest to external actors. Hence they can suffer from a lack of Political Support. Moreover, the conditions of their production are volatile as, depending on its political positions, the body politic will also consider them as general taxes (which increase a country or canton's general tax burden) or as legitimate compensation for a specific service of the policy in question. It is obvious that the production of resources by the political–administrative actors is governed by very precise institutional rules (fiscal legislation and legislation specific to taxation, administrative charges) that are often the subject of lively political debate.

The production of resources at the disposal of political–administrative actors requires the sometimes considerable and even disproportionate availability of Personnel for both institutional and substantive policies. For this reason, a trend for attributing a high proportion of administrative costs to the target groups can be observed today. The most obvious example here is that of a traffic police force (for example, in Rotterdam) that must 'generate' revenue to cover the salary expenses of its officers by issuing fines.

With regard to social actors, the aforementioned distinction between taxes and payments operates on the level of the distinction between, for example, contributions or donations for a specific task and general contributions. It is still common today for both target group associations and associations that defend the interests of beneficiaries to juggle between contributions to specific activities (for example, revenue from commissions) and general expenses relating to their management (for example, costs of the general operation of secretariats).

For each of the resources, the modalities of production are regulated with varying degrees of intensity, particularly in the case of centrally managed resources (see 'institutional policies' in Part I, Chapter 1). In general, this also applies to the resources produced autonomously by the specific political–administrative actors, although the rules to be applied are often internal directives of the competent administrative bodies or informal roles created in the past. Hence the production of Consensus and Organization will arise through the careful and permanent maintenance of networks of contacts (regular meetings, discussion days, training seminars) and that of Time through schedules developed in close cooperation between the three groups. Similarly the production of Personnel is based on the regular conduct of further training, particularly in collaboration with university training centres. With regard to the production of Property, which is increasingly centralized (for example, in relation to information technology), this frequently necessitates recourse to public procurement that operates under close scrutiny on the part of competitors and specialist parliamentary committees (usually management committees) with a view to avoiding any kind of irregularity (corruption, cartel formation, excessive pricing).

As already mentioned, the fact of being a resource producer does not imply automatic access to more or less exclusive use rights. There is an entire series of institutional rules governing possession that allocate specific use rights to resources in public ownership, for example, in the form of the right to be informed about these resources. Accordingly, the objective law must be published in the official journal, planning permission decisions must be subject to public scrutiny and citizens even have the right of protection by the police in the case of public order problems (usually free of charge, Force).

Maintenance of resources

Given that actors' public action resources are, by definition, social constructs and not (only) 'things in themselves', they require constant care. As the lawyer Pierre Moor (1997) said, to retain its normativity, the law must be stated and restated; it has little chance of surviving if it is stored 'in a refrigerator'. A consensus reached at any given time can melt like the snow in spring if it is not constantly referred to by the actors that participated in its construction. Similarly, a piece of information loses its value without monitoring that facilitates its constant updating. This also applies to all kinds of infrastructure projects that require considerable maintenance investment, to Organization and, in particular, to Political Support that is likely to vanish in the absence of its redundant invocation by all actors of a public policy community.

In summary, all public action resources lose their value in the absence of maintenance activities consisting precisely in their (calibrated) redundant use. It is not possible to stockpile, accumulate and increase one's resources, like the 'treasure' of the kings of old or the *pater familias* of Roman times. It should also be noted that even solid gold coins have lost their economic value over the last two millennia and today, money is only worth as much as its holders would believe. This law, which applies to the financial world, is even more valid for the world of public policies in which the power and resources that constitute it can lose their value from one day to the next.

A concrete demonstration of this can be found in the (public and private) accounting rules applied to infrastructure resources – both public (HAM2[1] in Switzerland) and private (legislation on the taxation of company assets) – in the form of strict depreciation schemes that reflect precisely this loss of value by the assets involved. Similarly, we can apply this principle to all public action resources. Depending on the decision-making situations they find themselves in, the actors attribute different values to the goods and/or services provided by these resources. The availability of a well-trained army (Force) is only considered valuable in conditions of tension or war, and its value diminishes during long and sustained periods of peace (depending on political 'beliefs'). The provision of a time allowance of a few days will be of far less value at a time that is still far away from the agreed decision-making time, and its value will increase as the specified time approaches.

Modalities of resource use

The examples contained in Part III of this book present an impressive array of the modalities of resource mobilization through political-administrative processes from the formulation and implementation of public policies to their evaluation. The real world is more innovative than any conceivable scientific system. It should be noted, however, that among these wide-ranging examples there are two particularly common forms of mobilization: threat and renunciation. *The threat* of resorting to the use of a resource is very common and consists in the declaration of a consistent formal decision on the part of the political-administrative actors aimed at target groups in the event that they do not 'voluntarily' comply with the (more or less detailed) requirements of the legislation in force. Conversely, if the authority applies the legal provisions to the letter or too rigidly in the view of the target groups, they can also make threats through the unfavourable but legal use of their Property resources, for example, by moving to a different country or dismissing staff.

Finally, the beneficiary groups can also resort to making threats by announcing the mobilization of the Force at their disposal (for example, the occupation of building sites and organization of strikes targeting the products of companies that are considered non-compliant with the law) or Law (for example, by appealing decisions that they consider as being too 'lax' in relation to target groups). Such threats become even more credible if the actors that make them can rely on the support of allies from the third party winners or losers' camp (positively or negatively affected third parties). It should be noted that threats must be credible; credibility is often established through the activation of constitutional law principles or rights or rights arising from other public policies that are more favourable to the interests of one or other of the groups in question.

Renunciation may arise as an implicit or explicit indication of the acceptance of changes arising throughout the process of the production of administrative activities. These involve either changes to the provision initially subject to public enquiry by the authority, or a voluntary step by the target groups in the direction of the objectives of the policy in question. This kind of renunciation is also observed if the administration is satisfied with accepting the announcement of an imminent change on the part of a target group, and abandons its intention to proceed with a formal decision. Renunciations can also signal similar 'gratitude' on the part of beneficiary groups for the same changes in behaviour on the part of target groups. Moreover, the latter increasingly demand that the decision to renounce an administrative decision be appealed, just like the decision itself.[2]

Policy analysts and managers should observe the latter two forms of mobilization through non-mobilization. The simple fact of observing a case of non-mobilization does not necessarily indicate the absence of strong initial reticence on the part of the actors in question, and this obliges the analyst to research the cause of such a strategic transfer. Non-mobilization (renunciation of launching a referendum or submitting an appeal) can also be considered an indicator of the scarcity of the resource in question for the actor involved that would like to explore less costly solutions.

According to our statements about the rules of the game proposed in Part I of this book, all analyses of resource mobilization should take the (possession, behavioural and decisional) institutional rules into account that the mobilizing actor invokes to legitimize. The policy analyst and manager should always examine the conformity of resource mobilization acts with these general and special institutional rules. Based on this they can report the unlawful use of Money (corruption), Time (excessively tardy or precocious mobilization) and Information (recourse to confidential information or information subject to personal data protection). It should be remembered, finally, that all resource use takes the principle of the sustainability of these resources into account. Independently of the strategy pursued, any abusive use of one or other of the resources today risks leading to an incapacity to act in the future due to a lack of power (that is, resources).

Substitution and combination of resources within an actor's portfolio

In Part III of this book we will explore in detail some examples of the substitution of resources that may be missing from an actor's portfolio with other resources . It will emerge clearly that money is not necessarily the crux of the matter. In my view, in the case of political-administrative actors in particular, the lamenting of a lack of money and the less prominent lament of a lack of personnel are sometimes more indicative of a lack of creativity than of an absolute lack of resources. In reality, actors who lack resources know how to acquire them through exchanges with other actors in the policy triangle (that is, the target groups and/or beneficiary groups). The real administrative world also develops many strategies to overcome such (often temporal) lacks through their *substitution and/or combination* with other resources that tend to be available in abundance. The fact that the rules applied to public budgets today allow greater flexibility in using surpluses from some budget lines to compensate for losses in others is indicative of a relaxation of the rules governing the resource Money. One of the reasons for the advent of New Public Management was and remains that of making the use of the resources required by an administration more flexible for the production of the groups of outputs desired by political–administrative actors or the politicians who decide on public budgets.

The resources that remain relatively unknown among political-administrative actors, for example, Time, Property, Consensus and Organization, may be considered as possible sources of substitution for making public action more effective when so-called 'classical' resources are lacking. In effect, the existence of a solid consensus among the beneficiary and/or target groups can replace the production of extremely expensive expert knowledge or the appointment of additional personnel. The provision of more time for consideration (for example, a moratorium, authorized exceeding of all kinds of deadlines) through the extension of a deadline can have similar effects. Similarly, the use of scientific personnel available within the administration (generally more common today than in the past) can replace spending involving very large sums on new IT projects. And particular attention paid to the resource Political Support can contribute to the reduction of administrative, legal and political costs in situations blocked by external controversies at parliamentary or executive level.

My examples in Part III of this book also show that the *combination* of goods and/or services originating from different public resources can prove very effective in terms of bringing about changes in the behaviour of target groups (impact) or generating satisfaction among the beneficiary groups (outcomes). These observations are backed up by some cases encountered in practice, for example, the combining of Law and Information to explain the meaning of an administrative output by presenting it in the context of the public problem it is attempting to resolve, such as combining the installation of a speed reduction sign on the road with a mention of the words 'smog' or 'schoolchild'.

Other such examples include the combining of Law and Money (all subvention practices), Consensus and Property (making public or private premises available for the organization of meetings), Consensus and Political Support (involving the representatives of political parties in complex and controversial administrative procedures) and Information and Force (beneficiary groups: information campaigns explaining the reasons for the call to occupy a site).

The example of the public budget shows that strict rules sometimes exist in relation to such substitution processes. These institutional rules (which are usually decisional in nature) particularly concern the resources Force (to be used only as a 'last resort'), Law (no public intervention without a legal basis), Money (apart from budgetary rules, all of the rules regarding corruption, the public markets and accounting methods), Time (restrictive deadlines) and Organization (rules governing the obligations for the separation of the Confederation, cantons and communes). Again, the policy analyst and manager should observe the use of such substitutions and the institutional rules that allow them in detail.

Exchangeability and modalities of resource exchange

According to the concept proposed in this book, what distinguishes public policy actors' resources from their competencies and personal characteristics is the exchangeability of the resources arising from their objectivizable and transferrable nature. This exchangeability resides in the fact that each of the actors in a public policy community attributes a value to each of these resources that is specific to the actor in question as the possession of the resources increases their power. Hence, all actors can use them in the pursuit of their strategies, however they may differ. This value may also extend to third party winners and losers (positively and negatively affected third party groups).

What is involved here, however, is a relative value that is rarely shared, for example, by actors outside these communities. A specific piece of information is only of value to the actors that need it for the optimal pursuit of their interests. The resource Time (subjective) only has value for the actors that lack it and, moreover, in the context of the amount of time available to the other two actors in the triangle. Force has no value within a triangle of actors that has operated peacefully since the dawn of time, and Personnel is only of interest as a resource in actor constellations involving personnel with very similar qualifications (a similarity that may be explained by the fact that all of the personnel underwent identical training). The same applies to personnel with particular professional knowledge in relation, for example, to nuclear physics, which will represent a precious resource among communities of actors involved in nuclear power policy but will have no 'value' for a group concerned with social policies. The exchangeability of policy resources is limited, therefore, to communities of actors within the perimeter of specific and similar policies.

Again, the chapters in Part III will present an array of possible exchanges of resources between the three key public policy actor groups. As demonstrated in Chapter 4, it is quite easy to distinguish homogenous exchanges from heterogeneous ones. In the context of the resource-based approach, this distinction must also be relativized in that, in many cases, even homogenous exchanges concern different goods and/or services provided by identical resources.

For this reason, the very term 'exchange' presupposes by definition the existence of a differential, the sole objective and subjective criterion for generating an interest between two or more partners in engaging in an exchange. In the event that this differential does not exist – all of the actors have this good and/or service in equal and abundant quantities – an exchange does not make sense and no actor will be willing to 'pay the price' to obtain extra stock of the resource. Thus the existence of such a differential is the condition necessary for triggering a dynamic of exchange of resources between public policy actors. I even believe that without this exchange of resources, a public policy only exists on paper, in particular, during the implementation stages. The exchange of resources is quite simply a necessary condition for the existence of an effective public policy.

Such exchanges presuppose a *do ut des*[3] and the availability of use rights on both sides. The actor that does not possess any use rights cannot exchange the goods and services provided by resources. Such situations may arise if the resources are actual public goods or club goods to which the three groups hold similar use rights.

This last statement demonstrates the importance of the temporal sequence of the *do ut des*. Very often the *do* does not take place at the same time as the *des*. It is also possible that the *do*, always conditional on the *des*, is merely a simple promise of a future exchange (which risks never taking place) – hence the risks of uncertainty due to violations of the important rule of *pacta sunt servanda* ('agreements must be kept'), particularly in the frequent cases in which this 'future' unfolds after the political-administrative decision in question has been made. This distinction between 'before' and 'after' the decision merits more detailed consideration in the context of implementation processes. A promise of a *des* on the part of the target groups after the granting of planning permission is merely a promise of future behaviour consisting in the wish to construct a given project in accordance with the conditions of the planning permission. Even if the authorities do not verify the application of these administrative acts systematically, it is known that one or other of the conditions imposed on the owners will not be followed to the letter in many cases.

For this reason it is necessary to create a series of (possession, behavioural and decisional) institutional rules that enable the stabilization of the actors' expectations regarding such exchanges of resources over time. The *pacta sunt servanda* and good faith rules are probably the most important ones in this context.

Notes

[1] Harmonized Accounting Model for the cantons and municipalities of 2008/13: Swiss Public Sector Financial Reporting Advisory Committee (SRS-CSPCP), accepted by the Conference of the Cantonal Finance Directors in January 2008 and in January 2013 (amendments) (see www.srs-cspcp.ch/en).

[2] For Switzerland, in accordance with Article 25 of the Federal Act on Administrative Procedure; see Chapter 2.

[3] From the Latin, 'I give that you may give.'

Part III
The 10 public action resources

Logic behind the chapter presentations: possession, modalities of use and exchange

In terms of volume alone, this third part of the book is its *pièce de résistance*. Its aim is essentially illustrative in that it serves to apply the concept of public action resources presented and developed in the first two parts of this book with the help of a wide range of practical examples. The logic on which its presentation is based is simple: each chapter is dedicated to one of the 10 public action resources, which the text aims to illustrate by presenting their mobilization by each of the three main actors that feature in public policy analysis, that is, the political–administrative actors, the target groups and the beneficiaries.

The majority of the examples provided are taken from the Swiss context in the period 2012 to 2015; however, they are intended to be generic in that they could also come from other countries, in particular, European ones.[1] Despite trying to avoid it, the fact that my work tends to be focused on environmental policies and natural resources probably results in a bias in the selection of examples. For educational reasons, sources are not documented as they have been simplified with a view to highlighting the main characteristics. A large proportion of the examples come from practical studies carried out as part of our courses at the Swiss Graduate School of Public Administration (IDHEAP) and other universities, both in Switzerland and abroad, and this enabled me to cover a relatively broad field of substantive public policies. Furthermore, the reader will realise that the detailed structure of the following chapters sometimes forces me to supplement these wide-ranging examples from real life with some stylized and extrapolated ones. The structure also gives rise to some redundancies as observations of one particular social phenomenon served as an illustration for several resources and/or to illustrate the mobilization activities of two or even three actors. These overlaps clearly reflect the variety of the world of resource mobilization, particularly at the level of public policy implementation processes.

The relatively rigid basic structure necessitates processes of definition that are not always obvious but that prove productive due to their systematic limits. In effect, they should enable the discovery of counter-intuitive and almost inconceivable situations involving the use or exchange of public action resources.

The overlap between the examples provided in the individual chapters in this part is intentionally simpler than that between the seven analytical dimensions presented in Chapter 5 of the conceptual part of this book. These dimensions are revisited in the final chapter of Part IV, Chapter 17, in the form of a seven-point checklist for analysing the effects of the mobilization of public action resources on public decisions. The reason for this is that the examples are presented as illustrations and not as the results of systematic empirical analyses of the mobilization phenomena observed. Their aim is to stimulate the imagination of researchers and managers about what is possible and conceivable in terms of the mobilization of all kinds of public action resources in the early 21st century.

The main focus of the 10 chapters is on the three final sections that are devoted to resource mobilization by availability, mobilization by stage in the policy cycle (programming and implementation) and the actual exchange of resources; these sections are each structured on the basis of the three constitutive public policy actors. This sequence follows a simple phenomenological logic, starting at the level of resource portfolios (availability or non-availability), followed by the different modalities of mobilization (on the level of policy programming and implementation), and leading to the actual exchange of resources – or not.[2]

It is obvious that the reader is owed some bibliographical suggestions for each resource and, in particular, a precise definition of the resource in question. The definitions are based on our reference text (Knoepfel et al, 2006: 68ff [2011: 67ff], 2010: 61ff), and complemented by information that takes the conceptual evolution that took place in teaching practice over the last 10 years into account.

Chapter contents

Definition

In general, the definitions are based on those provided in our basic textbook.[3] However, as the concept has evolved considerably since this book was published, the 'Specifics' section incorporates further conclusions reached by the author over the last 10 years of work with the basic version of 2006. The level of detail of the definitions and specifications varies considerably, and reflects the requirements of the teaching of public policy analysis (and not those of the multiple disciplines to be considered).

Mobilization by availability

The starting point of these sections is both banal and simple: an actor can only mobilize resources if they have them (thanks to possession rules that provide access to the resources in question). However, the texts provided in these sections show that the availability of a resource doesn't always result in its mobilization. In effect, an actor can refrain from mobilizing a resource so as to ensure that another actor will refrain from using a resource in exchange, or they can use it for more important matters at the level of the policy product in question (or a subsequent product). When the resource in question is lacking, the actor may also substitute it with another resource.

These sections also include examples in which the mobilization of an available resource is rendered impossible by the presence of institutional rules prohibiting its use (behavioural rules) for a limited period of the public policy cycle in question (decisional rules).

Mobilization by stage

As already described, each product of the public policy cycle has a 'before' and 'after'. The line is most frequently drawn here between the programming and implementation stages. This distinction is also used to structure the 'mobilization by stage' sections. In effect, the content that is contested at the level of public policy programming (political-administrative programme, PAP, and the political-administrative arrangement, PAA) is usually more abstract, often less 'threatening' from the perspective of the different actors and, above all, likely to be redefined and re-debated at the level of concrete implementation (action plan and output). For this reason, the activities aimed at the mobilization of public action resources often differ based on these two stages. Moreover, they are of greater interest for actors and researchers because they are more varied during the implementation stage that often involves vital matters for both the target groups and the beneficiary groups. As the examples show, moreover, the mobilization of an actor's resource at the level of policy programming is often aimed at the modification of related legislative decisions with a view to developing a favourable position for specific actors.

Exchange

The fact that the development of a public policy's products closely resembles a negotiation process – at the level of both programming and implementation – enabled us to pinpoint the processes of resource exchange that these negotiations give rise to in the first textbook and in a number of applied studies carried out by our students and practitioners. These exchanges, which are all based on the *do ut des* ('giving-giving') model, can assume the form of a homogenous exchange (for example, Law for Law: 'I will refrain from submitting an appeal so that the authority shows itself willing to modify the content of an administrative decision during the enquiry period') or, more commonly, the form of a heterogeneous exchange (for example, Money for Law [corruption] or Time for Consensus etc).

This distinction will prove useful as it prompts the observer to focus particularly on sometimes surprising and unexpected heterogeneous exchanges, which strongly reflect the local and/or regional reality of national policy implementation.

In addition, the examples show the need for the existence of mutual interests between the actors participating in the exchange. The latter can only be discovered if the analysis specifies/indicates the strategic objective pursued by an actor and the actor's willingness to engage in an exchange. In empirical reality, this interest is often expressed by the fact that one or other actor is the initiator of a proposal for the exchange, or that the actor's availability to engage in the exchange is a response to a proposal made by a partner actor. These objectives may sometimes be different to those pursued by a particular public policy and concern the actor's position within another public policy context or in the policy area at local and regional level (electoral interests etc).

Recommended further reading

It has already been shown that the concept of public action resources as presented in this book has received relatively little attention in the Swiss and international literature (see Chapter 3). For this reason, in general the sections entitled 'Recommended further reading' don't just feature texts that explicitly deploy a resource concept that is similar to mine.

Most of our resources are covered by specialist disciplines which, even if they do not make an explicit link between these resources and public policy actors, focus in detail on important aspects of the management of these resources and, moreover, in the form of textbooks. Accordingly, in each chapter, I specify one or more textbooks currently used on courses in public administration. For example, Force is dealt with by textbooks for police science and criminology and security policy textbooks, Law is dealt with by public and/or administrative law textbooks, Personnel by textbooks on human resources management, Money by textbooks on public finance and economics, and Information by textbooks in several disciplines (archive studies, statistics, information technology). Similarly, textbooks on the sociology of organizations and/or management deal with Property (public finance and accounting, management of administrative and financial assets), and there is an increasingly abundant literature focusing on Political Support (classical political science).

To my knowledge, only Time and Consensus still lack their own, established university disciplines today, and they also lack individual institutional policies in the strict sense that are managed by centralized units within public administrations. However, we are fortunate to have two major textbooks that cover both the area of Swiss politics (Knoepfel et al, 2014) and Swiss public administration (Ladner et al, 2013), which we can refer to for recommended further reading.

It is important to remember that the objective of this book is not to present the content of these (Swiss and foreign) reference works, and the sole focus of interest is on these resources as policy actors' resources. As a general rule, the actor-based, resource-based or neo-institutional approaches in themselves do not form part of these reference works. For this reason, I only refer to these texts implicitly in the development of my arguments, and refer readers to Chapter 3, on the contextualization of the status of the literature.

In addition, I allowed myself to include 'home-grown products' in the reading recommendations involving studies carried out by collaborators at the Public Policies and Sustainability Research Unit at IDHEAP. These studies provide particularly detailed accounts of applications relating to the resources in question.

Reading guide

Based on the above-described sections, each of the 10 following chapters has a more or less identical structure with sections entitled: 'Mobilization by availability', 'Mobilization by stage' and 'Exchange'. In addition, these sections also contain the same sub-sections: 'Political-administrative actors', 'Target groups' and 'Beneficiary groups'. This enables readers to consider the usefulness of the systematic declension of each of the 10 resources.

This approach has one disadvantage, however; it runs the risk that the reader will confuse the sub-sections relating to one resource for those relating to another. To avoid this pitfall, readers are advised to clearly identify the sections, which are easy to consult on a selective basis, within the context of the resource to which they wish to refer.

Notes

[1] For this reason, I decided not to change them for the English edition, which is aimed at an international academic audience.

[2] This logic is close to that of the presentation of possession institutions (constitutive of the extent of the resource portfolio), behavioural institutions (modalities of mobilization, in particular, based on the distinction between programming and implementation) and decisional institutions (modalities of mobilization, in particular, the exchange of resources).

[3] For this chapter, the texts are taken from the 2010 version, *Analyse des politiques suisse de l'environnement*; the examples have been modified in some cases as they were too 'environmental'.

6

Force

Definition

… constraint through force is easy to understand. In effect, the closure of plants considered as illegal by the authorities (for example, the closure of a plant that emits hazardous pollutants through police control), physical control and violence on the part of the law enforcement agencies in response to the opposition of target groups or beneficiaries (for example, occupation of lands intended for the construction of a controversial road) are all examples of the use of force which can be dissociated conceptually from the other resources, even if they are legitimated by the law and generally dependent on human resources.

Public policy actors do not often avail of this resource. First, entire policy sectors do not have access to specialized police forces that can act in this way (for example, specialized police brigades allocated as a priority to a particular area are rare) and, second, the solution involved here is deployed as a last resort. Nonetheless the capacity of public actors to physically constrain an individual or target group of a policy with a view to modifying a behaviour should not be neglected. To this end, the threat of recourse to force can be a determining factor in the policy implementation process.

To avoid being arbitrary, the use of force by a public authority must always be proportional to the intended objective and be based on a legislative provision. When target groups or beneficiaries use violence by deploying mostly illegal means (for example, "ecoterrorist" actions such as the blockage of a property-related resource available to another actor, for example, a nuclear waste convoy), they are seeking a resource that enables them to express claims that are perceived as legitimate but not legally recognized.

The use of force is a very delicate matter and generally requires Political support. In the absence of such support, it runs the risk of prompting the loss of the resource

Consensus for a long period of time. Moreover, in certain situations the recourse to Force should be highly publicized to be effective. In the area of road safety, for example, it would appear to be impossible to physically control those who contravene the rules of the road at all times and in all places. On the other hand, the deployment of the police and intensification of controls during holiday weekends, during which very high numbers of fatalities generally arise, has a real impact if the measures are accompanied by extensive media coverage targeting the drivers involved and the population as a whole. (Knoepfel et al, 2010: 70-1)

Specifics

Although highly visible, particularly in the context of the implementation of controversial policies, Force presented some problems in relation to identification in the past, to which the following specifications respond.

In view of recent developments, it is necessary to consider various new forms of Force, particularly the psychological forms (nudging) and those associated with cybercrime (electronic wars), which are both becoming more widespread and can cause considerable material and non-material damage. These two forms are deployed by both political-administrative actors and civil society actors today.

The use of all forms of Force is far more common, however, at civil society level. Accordingly, this is a resource of social or economic action deployed by individuals or social groups with the aim of obtaining, as a 'counter-service', all kinds of objects (things, money, information etc) or of eliminating those considered as serious enemies (attacks all dealt with in the Swiss Penal Code). The forms the exercise of Force can assume at the level of public policies or civil society are identical in principle. When it comes to its use as a public action resource, the aim is to put one of the two other groups of actors involved in a specific public policy under physical or psychological pressure by presenting them with the *fait accompli*, that is, denying them all freedom of choice and obliging them to act in accordance with the will of the actor behind the action involving Force and against their own will. The civil society actors (target groups and beneficiaries) have access to the resource Force in that their existence and legal status enjoy constitutional protection ('right to physical integrity'). Nevertheless, this possession rule guaranteeing access to the resource is subject to a large number of behavioural rules (formal rules and, above all, informal and customary rules). The situation of public actors is similar, in principle, because the authority holds the monopoly on legitimate force and the use it makes of it is obviously subject to highly restrictive and stringent regulations.

The use of Force generally has a beginning and an end. It is limited, targeted and traceable. The 'forces' on both sides (attack and defence) usually wear each other out. The capacity of 'instruments' to exercise force (for example, the human body, guns and various other kinds of arms) diminishes, and armistices, round tables, solemn acts involving the conclusion of peace agreements or the successful imposition of their will by one actor (often the political–administrative actor) ensue.

The aim of the use of Force by the political–administrative actors is generally to defend the public order and, more specifically, the safety of citizens. The main concern is the maintenance of the objective law, which encompasses both an effective implementation act (if necessary, against the opposition of actors that make justifiable use of Force) and the protection of the right of all those to physical and psychological personal integrity. Apart from military and national defence policies, the main examples of the use of Force in this context include the tasks of the traditional police, which have the justified objective of preventing the use of force by criminals, the indictment of crimes that have been committed and the implementation of sanctions stipulated in the Penal Code (for example, theft, attack on the integrity of the person).

Because the use of Force, in societies under the rule of law, is also considered abnormal in the context of the relations between public agencies and civil society actors, the ordinary penal legislation contains a large number of institutional behavioural rules regarding its mobilization. The uses explicitly mentioned and sanctioned (for members of the target group, beneficiaries or third party groups) under Title Fifteen of the Swiss Criminal Code, 'Offences against Official Powers', include: violence and threats against public authorities and public officials carrying out an official act (Article 285), prevention of an official act (Article 287), removal of seized property (Article 289), the famous 'breaking of seals', that is, removal or destruction of an official mark (Article 290) and, in particular, 'contempt of official orders' (Article 292).[1] Also included are the publication of secret official proceedings (Article 293), the breach of an activity prohibition order or a contact prohibition and exclusion order (Article 294) and failure to comply with probation assistance or instructions (Article 295). What all of these offences have in common is the fact that they concern an illegal act of defence against political–administrative actors who legitimately apply the resource Force in the context of their policy implementation activities.

Such a use of Force on the part of target groups and beneficiaries constitutes the expression of their clear desire to avoid the application of the objective law to a given local and concrete situation. They consider a violent attack (or threat of such an attack) against the public actors involved in the implementation of a policy as a legitimate means of opposing the state and defending (public or private) projects or interests that are considered legitimate and protected under the constitution by an institutional rule of possession (legitimate defence, Swiss Criminal Code, Article 122, nos 5 and 6). The 'weapons' used here include the physical blocking of access by public inspectors, monitors etc to a private enterprise, the destruction of items of proof relating to accounting practices, and the physical occupation of a site for the construction of a plant or installation, for which planning permission has been obtained but which is nonetheless considered 'unacceptable' by the beneficiaries of protective public policies (for example, environment, labour, public health). In these two cases, the actors who make use of Force frequently refer to constitutional or 'universal' (*jus*) rights that are considered as prevailing over the law governing the public policy in question (within the political-administrative programme: *lex*).

Force is probably one of the resources whose use is often threatened. This observation is linked to that of cases in which the threat is not carried out, which are also very common. The two cases are indicative of the fact that a situation of general mistrust (absence of Consensus) can be overcome through the anticipation by both parties of the damage that might be caused by the voluntary and prolonged use of Force. This observation, in particular, prompts me to draw the attention of policy analysts to the 'latent presence' of the use of Force in public policies, which is more extensive than initially assumed.

Another aspect concerns the relationship between the target groups and Force. For example, situations can often be observed in which, prior to decisions being made about legislation or the advent of a local policy implementation act, the target groups threaten the 'departure' of their company, a development that would have negative impacts on the public finances (tax revenue) and labour market. If such a departure actually takes place, should we consider it as the expression of the use of Force? Similarly, should the stopping of investments in a sector or country be seen as a lawful or unlawful use of Force by investors?

In the past I would have answered these questions in the affirmative. The corresponding analyses prompted the considerable extension of the concept of Force at the expense of the resource Property. This no longer appears justified today. Even if the consequences of a hostile use of Property in reality can prove more serious than that of Force as it is presented here, for example, the blocking of investments or dismantling of an important site of economic activity, in my view, our old definition of Force, which also included such activities, is too extensive and imprecise. This clarification once again highlights the importance of the resource Property in the portfolio of public action resources held by target groups. This was probably underestimated in our basic textbook.

A final aspect of Force concerns the increasingly costly mechanisms that exist for the protection of other action resources, such as Information and Property, against acts of theft or destruction by other 'partner' actors who thereby establish a favourable portfolio compared to the actors that have been subject to such an attack. Such breaches, which are common at the level of economic activity in civil society (outside the realm of public policies), can be justified by specific institutional rules (fight against 'terrorism', use of stolen data by fiscal policy actors, pursuit of 'state interests') or can be unlawful (abuse of police power of political-administrative actors, theft of data by target groups or beneficiary groups – cybercrime). This explains the increase in the mechanisms for securing all kinds of data as a preventive use of Force that feature increasingly in the portfolios of public policy actors.

Force: Mobilization by availability

Force/availability: Political-administrative actors

Apart from the very restrictive requirement of an explicit legal basis (Law: powers of intervention and substantive objectives clearly defined at the level of the objective law), the use of Force presupposes the availability of armed persons who are accustomed to and capable of making use of violence in a proportional manner in accordance with a formal oath. Such policing interventions can assume very different forms, for example, arresting of a person, confirmation of an offence through subsequent arrest, the physical closure of a company whose directors repeatedly violate labour or environmental law, the demolition of a building constructed without planning permission or authorization for residential use, breaking up of an illegal demonstration through the use of water jets or tear gas, slaughter of an animal or physical evacuation of people illegally occupying a building or site, data capture on the internet. Legally speaking, what is also involved here are material acts by the state[2] (which include 'nudging', in my view).

In view of this diversity and often technical specificity and also the rigorous requirements of jurisprudence in relation to the proportionality of such interventions, it is obvious that the availability of Force is extremely limited and, as a result, that political-administrative actors may find themselves in many concrete situations in which they are unable to avail of it (behavioural rules). For this reason, in practice, all kinds of alternative solutions are adopted, the majority of which are challenged on political grounds, for example, privatization of the police through the engagement of private security companies (that have not sworn an oath), assumption of police functions by the umbrella associations of target groups (solutions involving so-called 'corporatist' governance), acceptance of unsanctioned offences corresponding to the acceptance of public policy implementation deficits, recourse to particularly severe sanctions as a means of dissuading actors committing potential offences.

Other solutions, which are often considered more promising because they are more proportional, consist in the selection of less strict intervention instruments to replace Force through the mobilization of other resources available to the political-administrative actors, such as Information (for example, information campaigns), Personnel (strengthening of communication requirements among administrative personnel) and Organization (an increase in the density of preventive monitoring networks with a view to reducing offences against the implementation of specific policies – community policing).

Force/availability: Target groups

Even if it is not very common in Switzerland or other European countries, policy implementation can be accompanied by acts of violence resulting in fatalities or considerable material damage. This is not exclusive to battles between political-administrative actors and policy beneficiaries (see below), and can also involve acts of opposition on the part of target groups. Examples here include the famous owner of an agricultural or artisanal operation who uses his military gun or dog to face down representatives of the public authority responsible for inspecting his land or, in a more subtle way, financial companies that are involved in mafia circles. Today, companies can also be observed resorting to computer-related crime, for example, for the purpose of laundering money. Anecdotes presented by newspapers and specialist publications bear witness to the 'creativity' deployed in the use of this mode of violence against fiscal officials and the financial police by economic actors. It should be noted that it is very difficult to sanction such 'innovative' uses of Force based on the penal legislation, as its provisions take effect too late in many cases.

Force/availability: Beneficiary groups

The use of Force by beneficiary groups in the implementation processes of all kinds of infrastructure policies, for example, the occupation of strategic sites for the construction of military practice locations (Rothenturm, canton of Schwyz, Neuchlen-Anschwil, canton of St Gallen), nuclear power plants and nuclear waste disposal sites (Wolfenschiessen, canton of Nidwalden), new road and railway sections (railways: rail 2000 programme in the canton of Solothurn, Mattstätten) and trial sites for research on genetically modified organisms is generally better known as it is widely publicized in the media. Such opposition activities, which are sporadic in duration, are often accompanied by the successful or unsuccessful use of Law (provided that the actors have a formal right of appeal against the granting of planning permission or an operating licence). In addition, and unlike the target groups, the opponents make considerable use of Information (information campaigns attacking the promoters and/or public authorities responsible for decisions authorizing such measures) and, if necessary, they will also avail of Organization (common today in the form of recourse to social networks).

Force: Mobilization by stage

Force/stage: Political-administrative actors

I must admit that I am not aware of cases in Switzerland or Europe in which political-administrative actors physically destroy influential people or groups capable of effectively opposing a legislative proposal or the localized implementation of a public policy. And if such examples existed in reality, the actions carried out by the public authorities would be subject to strict confidence, rumours or suspicions that would be unlikely to be discovered and substantiated by a policy analyst. In any case, debates of such cases by historians and other intellectuals only take place when the confidentiality requirement is lifted (after 40 years).

Nonetheless, in the context of policy implementation, the considerable satisfaction experienced by executives (particularly at a local level) when opponents are physically absent during the consideration of controversial projects should be noted. Based on my experience, this absence may be provoked deliberately through the scheduling of the crucial meeting at a time or on a day that is at least 'uncustomary' and when it is unlikely that the adversary will be available (for example, the scheduling of a public inquiry during school holidays or at the same time as another meeting that the 'enemy' is obliged to attend). Other similar situations may be engineered at implementation level if the authority actively participates in campaigns to discredit people with the aim of weakening their position in the administrative procedure (nudging, subjection to psychological pressure).

Force/stage: Target groups

In Western Europe, at least, cases in which the actors targeted by a future legislative act avail of Force to oblige the legislator to change their opinion are rare. The creation of *faits accomplis* using, for example, the physical destruction of their own companies or wooded areas (forest fires) or the triggering of collective fraudulent bankruptcies rarely form part of an anticipated defence strategy on the part of target groups that feel threatened by a future legislative act. The adoption of individual strategies by the members of a target group in response to the threat of the implementation of a public policy that is considered hostile, as referred to above, could be more plausible. It should nonetheless be recalled that the creation of *faits accomplis* tends to be a strategy adopted more by target groups that avail of the resource Property (for example, withdrawal of funds by banks threatened with imminent regulation, blocking of investments). It is also possible to imagine the use of 'nudging' by this group to target an unpopular competitor or the representatives of beneficiary groups.

Force /stage: Beneficiary groups

Unlike the strategies of target groups, those of beneficiary groups frequently include the use of Force and, moreover, in both the programming and implementation stages of public policies. Hence strategies involving the occupation of sites and staging of demonstrations prohibited by the authorities are part of the arsenal for defending environmental or public health interests and are deployed precisely before the opening of debates on a new law (for example, on nuclear power) in the chambers of the federal parliament, cantonal parliamentary sessions or communal assemblies, even if these decisions merely have the character of a political–administrative programme at this stage and not of individual and concrete, local implementation acts.

Force: Exchange

Force/exchange: Political-administrative actors

As far as possible, the political-administrative actors respond to the use of the Force mobilized by civil society actors (target groups, beneficiary groups and third parties) with force, but in a way that is proportionate and compliant with the strict rules governing its use. This applies both to so-called 'normal' situations and urgent ones. This exchange of resources cannot, however, be considered entirely 'homogenous'. The authority is obliged by these rules (for example, on proportionality) to follow procedures that are sometimes rather slow and strict, subject to limitations, and also that render it incapable of providing an immediate and 'efficient' response. These limitations should be considered as the price to be paid for the principle of the rule of law that subjects all political-administrative actors who avail of the resource Force to strict rules that sometimes render them 'impotent' in reality when faced with the violence perpetrated by civil society actors. It should be recalled that these limitations are nothing more than the assets of these civil society actors who were formerly exposed to the tyranny of the royal sovereign (*habeas corpus* of 1679).

For the same reason, the political-administrative actors threatened by the use of Force on the part of civil society actors tend to react by resorting to the use of other less violent resources, for example, Law (for example, granting of a right of appeal to minorities that feel suppressed by the democratic majority; modifications at the level of material law enabling the affected civil society actors to obtain 'more just' treatment), Money (strengthening of the welfare state for the benefit of disadvantaged groups, as implemented by the first Prussian legislative acts benefiting 'the poor') and Information (explanation of legislative content or implementation acts involving possible stumbling blocks to the disadvantage of [certain] target groups). The use of these instruments based on alternative resources will obviously depend on a previous 'armistice' by which the civil society actors undertake to renounce the use of violence (for an agreed period at least). Similar arrangements may lie behind the renunciation by political-administrative actors of the use of their own Force (homogenous exchange) in reaction to the unlawful acts committed by such civil society actors (for example, the conclusion of a rental agreement with the occupants of rental properties belonging to a local authority, an amnesty).

Force /exchange: Target groups

The recourse to the different modalities of use of Force by the target groups described in this chapter arises not only in cases in which they feel threatened by legislative or implementation acts, but also in anticipation of or in reaction to the use of this resource on the part of a public authority. In such cases, the target groups will consider this recourse a legitimate defence (Swiss Criminal Code, Article 122) or as being necessary to protect the real interests of the state (situations involving a *coup d'état*). In such situations, the homogenous exchange of Force is initiated (formally, at least) by the target groups who may themselves refrain from its use under the condition that the political-administrative actors also refrain from the use of the resource and propose more favourable decisions. What arises here, therefore, is a heterogeneous exchange of resources between public actors and target groups that can materialize at the level of the (re-)establishment of a relationship of trust (exchange of Force for Consensus), armistice contracts accompanied by clauses providing for an amnesty, moratorium or simple non-application of a specific legislative act to contested cases.

Force /exchange: Beneficiary groups

It is easy to speak here of a homogenous exchange of Force in all situations involving violent clashes during public demonstrations between the authorities and public policy beneficiaries who see themselves, with justification, as deprived of such benefits by new legislative or implementation acts that they consider a direct cause of (new) social, economic or ecological hardship. For the political-administrative actors (who may or may not be identified by eventual target groups who themselves feel threatened by the riots) to make use of their Force, such manifestations must be likely to cause damage or fatalities and thus be at the root of serious public order problems. This is precisely the reason why such demonstrations are 'forbidden' or 'not authorized'. In addition, in such situations involving the opposition of street violence and police violence, the exchange of Force is not entirely homogenous as, again, the police are obliged to observe stricter rules than the demonstrators.

In the majority of cases, the opponents will be willing to abandon their violent activities if the authority proposes changes to the incriminating legislation or implementation acts in exchange. No government can remain unscathed by street violence in the long term, and experience shows that there will always be negotiations that ultimately lead to concessions being made by the public authority. Apart from Law, the resources mobilized by the political-administrative actors to calm the situation on the streets and re-establish social stability vary considerably (see above).

Recommended further reading

Textbooks and specialist literature

Cusson, M. (ed) (2008) *Traité de sécurité intérieure*, Lausanne: PPUR.

Cusson, M. (2010) *L'art de la sécurité. Les enseignements de l'histoire et de la criminology*, Québec: Editions Hurtubise.

Flückiger, A. (2018) 'Gouverner par des coups de pouce (*nudges*). Instrumentaliser nos biais cognitifs au lieu de légiférer', *Les Cahiers de Droit*, 59(1): 199-227.

Imbeau, L.M. and Couture, J. (2010) 'Pouvoir et politiques publiques', in S. Paquin, L. Bernier and G. Lachapelle (eds) *L'analyse des politiques publiques*, Montréal: Presses de l'Université de Montréal, pp 32–72.

Travis, J., Chaiken, J. and Kaminski, R. (1999) *Use of force by the police*, Washington, DC: National Institute of Justice.

'In-house' applications

Condo Sales, V. (2017) 'Conflits dans la mise en œuvre de la politique de grands projets miniers et la stagnation de ceux-ci. Etude de cas autour de trois grands projets miniers au Pérou', Thèse, Lausanne: IDHEAP-UNIL.

Knoepfel, P., Müller-Yersin, H. and Pestalozzi, M. (2004) *Grundlagen zu den Verhandlungsempfehlungen UVEK: Fachbericht*, Bundesamt für Umwelt, Wald und Landschaft (BUWAL), Schriftenreihe Umwelt, 365.

Knoepfel, P., Eberle, A., Joerchel Anhorn, B., Meyrat, M. and Sager, F. (1999) 'Cas de Neuchlen-Anschwilen. Conflit autour de l'extension de la place d'armes de Neuchlen-Anschwilen dans le canton de Saint-Galle', in P. Knoepfel et al (eds) *Militär und Umwelt im politischen Alltag: Vier Fallstudien für die Ausbildung/Militaire et environnement: La politique au quotidien: Quatre études de cas pour l'enseignement*, Bern: EPA, pp 33-168.

Weidner, H. (1995) 'Innovative Konfliktregelung in der Umweltpolitik durch Mediation: Anregungen aus dem Ausland für die Bundesrepublik Deutschland', in P. Knoepfel (ed) *Lösung von Umweltkonflikten durch Verhandlung – Beispiele aus dem In- und Ausland*, Basel and Frankfurt am Main: Helbing & Lichtenhahn, pp 105-25.

Zuppinger, U. and Knoepfel, P. (1998) 'Swiss Border incident: A case study of the Ciba-Geigy special waste incineration plant in Basel, Switzerland', in B. Dente, P. Fareri and J. Ligteringen (eds) *The waste and the backyard: The creation of waste facilities: Success stories in six European countries*, Dordrecht: Kluwer Academic Publishers, pp 117-60.

Notes

[1] Article 292: 'Any person who fails to comply with an official order that has been issued to him by a competent authority or public official under the threat of the criminal penalty for non-compliance in terms of this Article is liable to a fine.'

[2] According to Article 25a of the Swiss Federal Act on Administrative Procedure of 1968, in many cases these acts are not preceded by a formal decision in the sense of Article 6 of the same Act. The legal protection of affected people remains limited, nonetheless, to actors who obviously refer 'to their rights or their obligations'.

7

Law

Definition[1]

> It [the law] is the ultimate source of legitimation of all public action. The different actors are allocated legal resources by all of the general rules of constitutional, civil and public law and by the rules specific to a given sectoral policy. By way of illustration, we can refer here to the right of appeal of NGOs, the rights guaranteed under private law contracts and property rights, the permanent legal basis enabling a public authority to impose speed limits and driving bans (for example, to reduce smog levels in Berlin), the rule defining standing or locus standi for the formulation of opposition in the context of submission to a public enquiry. As a resource, the law consists in the capacity of an actor to act by means of legal norms and provisions.... It is common ... for an actor to be unable to mobilize the resource law due to an institutional rule prohibiting this (for example, impossibility of appealing a decision further when all other means of appeal have been exhausted). (Knoepfel et al, 2010: 61-2)

Specifics

Let us recall the identification of the four functions of the law (as specified at the end of Chapter 3): it cannot be stressed enough that only the mobilization of the law (the fourth function) is used to define the resource Law. This function describes the law 'as an important resource of the public action whose main service that can be mobilized by an actor is the *right to be able to impose a behaviour that complies with the objective law on another actor* based on their authority (political-administrative actor, including the courts).' To be able to mobilize this service the actor must have a right of use (opposable subjective right) that is conferred on them by a rule that features in the objective law. For the public actors, this right consists in an explicit norm of competency. It should be noted that the nature of the mobilization can be highly varied and range from a simple substantiation to misappropriation, circumvention or innovation (Schweizer, 2015: 80ff).

Legal rules are obviously also decisive for the recourse to all other public action resources. Even if everyone can invoke/activate the (objective) law as a framework at any time in the public policy cycle, the right to mobilize it as a true public action resource is reserved for the holders of the corresponding rights (for example, rights of appeal against a norm or decision or a specific material administrative act).

This specification obliges us to not consider every statement by an actor referring to the law as the mobilization of the resource Law. Only situations in which a (legislative, governmental or judicial) political-administrative actor makes use of their competence to modify the objective law (programming stage) or takes (or deliberately refrains from taking) a decision (administrative act or order of a court – implementation stage) are considered as the mobilization of this resource. With regard to civil society actors (target groups, beneficiaries), the use of Law is equivalent to submitting (or not submitting) an appeal (threat or actual act) against a political-administrative programme (rare in Switzerland)[2] or against an administrative or judicial decision.[3]

Law: Mobilization by availability

Law/availability: Political-administrative actors

If a cantonal administration with responsibility for the environment encounters a pollutant for which an emission limit value is not specified in the Ordinance on Air Pollution Control in the context of an environmental notice issued during a planning permission procedure, it lacks a legal basis for the regulation of this pollutant, however dangerous it may be. In this case the Ordinance gives it the right to create an *ad hoc* norm based, in this instance, on the resource Information (obligation to consult the latest scientific research enabling the determination of a threshold value).[4] Or, as another example, in the process of developing a proposal to establish a communal regulation on begging, the municipality of the city of Lausanne becomes aware that it does not have the right to simply prohibit begging on its territories (lack of provisions in the cantonal legislation). With a view to overcoming this obstacle, the police administration with responsibility for the development of such a regulation draws on another legal source based, in this instance, on its competency in relation to spatial planning (creation of zones in which begging is prohibited). If a political or judicial, cantonal or federal instance confirmed that this new regulation also lacks a legal basis, the commune would find itself in the position of being incapable of acting on this issue by means of public policy, which it nevertheless considers the only possible effective approach.

In practice, a large number of strategies exist for circumventing the lack of legal bases not only by referring to a different legal text (as the saying goes, 'a legal basis can always be found if needed'), but also by replacing this missing resource with another resource that is available and accessible to the political–administrative actors, for example, Consensus: the planning authority provides planning permission for a site outside the zone 'approved' by the neighbours, the municipality and the canton that is illegal in terms of the requirements of the Federal Spatial Planning Act,[5] but is not legally challenged by any of the three partners. In this case there would be no declaration of an 'overriding public interest in protection'. This can arise, in particular, in relation to the protection of the landscape, for example, wind farm projects in areas in which the second condition (absence of overriding public interest in the form of a national interest in the production of renewable energy) did not yet exist.[6]

Contrary to the strict rules of Swiss executive federalism, the federal political administrative actors (federal departments = ministries) sometimes have a right of appeal against cantonal decisions in relation to policy implementation. Such a provision exists, for example, in the area of spatial planning and asylum policy. So as not to lose Consensus among cantonal authorities or organizations that defend the interests of beneficiary groups, the federal authorities frequently refrain from exercising their right of appeal and only become involved in the case of cantonal decisions that have attracted a lot of media attention. Accordingly, they will only intervene in asylum matters when required to do so by public opinion, under particular pressure from target groups (in this case, neighbours of residences for asylum-seekers and overnight shelters for foreigners), or in the explicit case of foreigners being sent back to their country of origin or to their place of first registration (in accordance with the Schengen regime). Another example of intervention by the federal authorities in the area of spatial planning arose against the cantonal approval of a communal land-use plan that was clearly in contravention to the federal legislation that had been strengthened in 2015, and prohibits all zoning of lands for development if the commune cannot demonstrate an urgent need for it and propose the simultaneous de-zoning of other development land.

On several occasions the Swiss National Council (lower house of parliament), which has recently been dominated by a centre-right majority following the elections of 2015, refused to introduce the

Federal Council's (government) proposals for legislation that had previously been considered necessary by simply deeming the legislation in question 'useless' or a matter of cantonal competency. This has arisen in particular in the areas of environmental policy (for example, a federal ban on littering, a ban on the distribution of plastic bags in shops and failure to consider proposals relating to the 'green economy') and social policy.

Such 'non-decisions' are even more common at policy implementation level. During the initial activities for the implementation of federal legislation on environmental protection (in the mid-1980s), several cantons refused to pass orders for the clean-up of polluting installations that clearly exceeded the newly imposed emission limit values as the factories in question played an important role in the local economic fabric. Also worthy of mention in this context are the (sometimes unique) local bistros that were protected from sanctions for the violation of public health rules due to the strong opposition of their customers – who are, in theory, the beneficiaries of food-related public health policy.

Law/availability: Target groups

By way of example of a target group, let us take the Swiss Farmer's Union (SFU) and its initiation of a referendum against the revision of the Federal Act on Agriculture. The proposed revision involved changes to the direct payments regime (replacement of payment based on livestock numbers with an area-based payment), and the SFU set about obtaining Political Support for the retention of the old system. The same organization also declared its intention to refrain from exercising this right to initiate a referendum if the parliament would modify the law contrary to the wishes of the Federal Council and parliamentary commission (concessions by the holders of the theoretical parliamentary majority through its non-exploitation by its holders).

The mobilization of the resource Law by target groups is very common at policy implementation level. However, it should be noted that its use in Switzerland is far from being as widespread as in other countries, for example, Germany and France, which have a much longer tradition in this regard than Switzerland: the mandatory right of appeal of administrative law was only introduced at cantonal level in 1968 and the establishment of a Federal Court of Administrative Law came very late in 2007. It should also be noted that, even if it is successful, the submission of such appeals – which are more common than those made by policy beneficiaries and limited to cases specially provided for by the law – can only result in the weakening of policy implementation acts and not in their reinforcement. This situation – which is also recurrent at the European Court of Justice (see, for example, Scharpf, 2009) – clearly demonstrates the costs associated with the rule of law (Scharpf, 1970) and its system of liberal legal protection on the level of the effectiveness and, above all, efficiency of public policies.

Another much debated example concerns the appeals submitted by participants in public tendering procedures that generally give rise to long delays for the project owners (concrete cases: the blocking of the building site for the Gotthard railway tunnel for several months following the submission of an appeal by a company whose tender for the technical railway installations in the tunnel was rejected; multiple blocking of small construction projects at the level of public projects carried out by communes). Cases involving such appeals on the part of a tenderer in response to administrative decisions that are considered as favouring another company and would theoretically have the potential to reinforce the implementation of public policies are becoming increasingly common (self-monitoring of its own 'black sheep' by the sector).

In the event of the rejection of an appeal, the appellant can nonetheless try to establish a direct arrangement with a beneficiary. For example, if a neighbour wishing to oppose the construction of a house that will block their view of a lake submits their letter of objection a week after the deadline for the submission of objections, they relinquish their right of intervention and planning permission will be granted against their will. The only means of action that remains is that of an eventual private law agreement with the neighbour based on which the neighbour 'repurchases' their view (Money) and the new neighbour agrees to build a less intrusive house from the perspective of the neighbour.

Law/availability: Beneficiary groups

Swiss law does not grant a right of appeal under general administrative law for all public policy beneficiary groups (see above). Like German law, it starts from the principle that an *actio popularis* (*action populaire* in French, *Popularbeschwerde* in German) is not admissible, as such a right would violate the principle according to which the representation of the 'public interest' is the sole responsibility of the administration. To obtain this right, both in the past and today, organizations that protect the interests of beneficiaries must knock on the door of every substantive policy that can grant them this right of appeal in the form of a specific legal clause. As already mentioned in the first two chapters of this book, the volume of such appeals in Switzerland is quite remarkable compared to abroad. Beneficiaries have acquired this right in relation to, *inter alia*, environmental law, labour protection law and consumer protection law (including telecommunications).

A study by Flückiger et al (2000), compiled in the context of the popular vote of 2008, the objective of which was to eliminate this right of appeal in relation to environmental protection policies, demonstrated, among other things, that such appeals had a success rate of around 70 per cent, thereby demonstrating the necessity of this instrument in the authors' view.

As a final example, on 3 December 2004 the Swiss Federal Supreme Court accepted the appeal made by an environmental protection organization (Association Transports et Environnement, ATE) against a neighbourhood plan involving the construction of a new football stadium at the former Hardturm football stadium in Zurich, and confirmed that the project was not compliant with Swiss environmental law. The decision of the Federal Supreme Court obliged the Zurich authorities to modify the plan despite the fact that it had been approved and supported by a majority of the communal council (legislature) and communal executive (Law versus Political support).

Law: Mobilization by stage

Law/stage: Political-administrative actors

The example I present here involves the threat made by the Swiss Association of Property Owners (Association des Propriétaires Fonciers, APF) to launch referenda against the introduction of taxation on the increase in the value of land arising from the inclusion of a site in a development zone as proposed in the federal chambers' draft revision of the Federal Act on Spatial Planning, which was finally accepted in a popular vote on 3 March 2013. The Association wanted the chambers to transform this binding norm into a norm to be delegated to the cantons, as was the case under the spatial planning regime defined in the old Federal Act on Spatial Planning (Article 5). In doing this, it used its right of initiative (mobilization of the resource Political Support) in exchange for the resource Law as held by the federal parliament in the sense of the competency to produce law.

Another example involves the threat by political–administrative actors to avail of their resource Law (legislative competency) if target groups do not succeed in resolving a public problem in 'their' social arena themselves and, moreover, in agreement with the beneficiary groups. Everyday political life in Switzerland is teeming with examples of calls for self-regulation solutions (referred to as 'subsidiarity of public intervention'), particularly in the area of banking policy (for example, 'gentlemen's agreements' between bankers regarding money laundering before the passing of restrictive legislation in this area; unfair competition policy: 'commission' for the monitoring of advertising; health policy: self-regulation of health insurers; agricultural policy: labelling of agricultural products; labour market policy: extension of general obligation of collective work contracts by the federal or cantonal government). It should be noted that such proposals often originate from target groups represented by economic sector associations with the aim of avoiding the passing of restrictive legislation in the future.

A similar phenomenon consists in the threat by the 'Confederation' to legislate in an area that is reserved in principle for intercantonal solutions. For example, in the area of education policy (primary and secondary schools), an area of cantonal competence par excellence, the Swiss Federal Constitution contains provision for a power of harmonization at federal level if the cantons do not succeed in agreeing their education plans by *concordat*, that is, an intercantonal agreement to be concluded and approved on the level of each individual canton. The area of foreign language teaching (which [national] languages should be taught from which class?) is an example currently [in 2016] under discussion.

For a discussion of the use (or non-use) of Law by political-administrative actors at implementation level, please refer to the previous section.

Law/stage: Target groups

Many cases exist in which the target groups themselves launch popular initiatives or referendums or, more commonly, agreements with political partners (political parties, specific associations) in return for sometimes significant financial undertakings. Cases involving real collective changes in behaviour with a view to avoiding the consequences of the eventual acceptance of a popular initiative also exist. For example, a popular initiative of the left concerning the taxation of legacies required the cantonal authorities to have the right to tax successions that took place prior to the popular vote on the initiative in question (from 1 January 2011). If this initiative had been passed by the Swiss population and cantons, successions taking place before the vote would also have been taxed (retroactive effect). Fearing such a development, many Swiss landowners transferred their assets to their children in December 2011. In the event, the initiative was rejected by the Swiss people and cantons on 11 June 2015.

Conservative, populist and nationalist parties and circles (which increasingly see themselves as the target groups of asylum policy because this policy obliges them to accept foreigners) succeeded in having a constitutional provision stipulating the mandatory expulsion of all foreigners who receive a prison sentence for a serious crime put to the vote. Following the acceptance of this initiative, the winners demanded (unsuccessfully) a broader interpretation of the term 'serious crime' in the legislation for the application of this constitutional norm. They claimed that in cases of doubt the restrictive interpretation of this term would be contrary to the previous decision of the people and cantons.[7]

For a discussion of the use of Law by target groups during the policy implementation stage, please refer to the previous section.

Law/stage: Beneficiary groups

As is the case for the target groups, the use of popular initiatives and the right to request a referendum as a means of producing or rejecting objective law based on the securing of Political Support is a tool that is frequently used by groups representing the interests of public policy beneficiaries. An attempt to withdraw the right of appeal of these associations in relation to the implementation of environmental policies in 2008 was rejected by the Swiss population thanks to the strong mobilization of opposition to the proposal by the groups in question. Since then, the organizations have continued to make use of their right of appeal and, moreover, with success. The areas favoured for the use of such popular rights by the organizations that protect the interests of policy beneficiaries are numerous and various. In recent years, they included the areas of political asylum, pensions, public health (health insurance), energy, agriculture and foodstuffs. It should be noted that in many cases the promoters of such initiatives are not political parties but the actual representatives of beneficiary groups (see Chapter 1).

During the implementation stage, these groups sometimes find themselves faced with the following alternatives: launch a referendum (against a decision of the communal legislature, main resource: Political Support) or take the legal route (resource Law). However, one does not necessarily exclude the other, and the risks of failure differ in nature even if the objective remains the same. Accordingly, a movement opposing a neighbourhood plan that is contested due to environmental impacts that are deemed excessive can launch a communal popular referendum (with the risk that the plan will be accepted) or approach an association (with a national reach) that has a right of appeal with a view to attacking the plan legally for a claimed violation of federal environmental law (with the chance that the cantonal or federal administrative court will accept the plan against the will of the majority of the communal legislature).

With a view to minimizing the risk involved in an appeal for the beneficiary groups, the federal and cantonal political-administrative actors increasingly advise that these groups be included in planning etc processes at as early a stage as possible. The recommendations made by the Federal Department of the Environment, Transport, Energy and Communication (DETEC) in 2004, which cover the majority of the Confederation's infrastructure policy and thus the policies most prone to attracting such opposition movements, are an obvious example of this attempt to find negotiated solutions to environmental conflicts with a view to avoiding long drawn-out legal proceedings.

Law: Exchange

Law/exchange: Political-administrative actors

The case of waste processing provides a good illustration of this point. Despite the fact that a communal waste regulation provides a right of appeal to property owners who are liable for the payment of a flat-rate tax for the collection and processing of household waste, the municipal council responsible for the environment division tries to convince an important property owner to withdraw their appeal and, moreover, despite the forfeiture of the strict control by the authorities of the latter's obligations in relation to the sorting of waste.

An example of heterogeneous exchange is the granting of planning permission to a tourism promoter for the construction of a chairlift on a site outside a zoned area in exchange for a payment of CHF 10,000 to the commune or municipal council with responsibility for the sub-section in question (Money: corruption).

Law/exchange: Target groups

Similar heterogeneous exchanges with, in this case, the property owner as the initiator of the exchange are exemplified by the following case: the owner whose plot is located within the area subject to a neighbourhood plan renounces the option to assert their right of appeal against the plan in exchange for a promise on the part of the communal building service to respect their interests in a (subsequent) procedure for the granting of permission to construct a building contained in the plan that disturbs the property owner. This 'right' to priority treatment will enable the latter to assert their desire to protect their unrestricted view of a lake.

As another example, a company refrains from launching an appeal against a decision condemning it to pay a fine for an infraction against labour protection law in exchange for the state refraining from pursuing it for an offence in relation to environmental protection.

Or, a building company pays a considerable sum to the cantonal work inspector (Money) in exchange for his or her agreement not to assert his or her right (and obligation) to inspect its building sites (in particular, regarding measures relating to work safety, environmental protection and/or the salaries paid to foreign workers).

Or, a wine producer refrains from exercising their right of appeal against a cantonal decision to grant AOC status to a wine cooperation in its commune if the latter includes its vineyard within the boundaries of the AOC (Property of the winemakers within the AOC area).

Law/exchange: Beneficiary groups

An example of heterogeneous exchange arises when an environmental protection group, as claimant, feels aggrieved about the planned construction of buildings in its vicinity under a neighbourhood plan but refrains from submitting an appeal because the promoters of the plan offer to pay a considerable sum for the management of a biotope or to simply contribute financially to the organization's basic operating costs.

Another example involves the case whereby an environmental protection organization refrains from making use of its right of appeal against a project for the raising of a dam water level under the condition that the promoter (target group) undertakes to manage new biotopes in the mountain and turbine water retention basis in the valley (Cleuson-Dixence hydroelectric dam in Valais).

Recommended further reading

Textbooks and specialist literature

Commaille, J., Dumoulin, L. and Cécile, R. (2010) *La juridication du politique*, LGDJ – coll. 'droit et société'.

Dente, B. (2009) 'The law as a policy resource: Some scattered thoughts', in S. Nahrath and F. Varone (eds) *Rediscovering public law and public administration in comparative policy analysis: A tribute to Peter Knoepfel,* Lausanne: PPUR, pp 3–44.

Flückiger A. (2013) 'Les instruments de soft law en droit public', in A. Ladner, J.-L. Chappelet, Y. Emery, P. Knoepfel, L. Mader, N. Soguel and F. Varone (eds) *Manuel d'administration publique suisse,* Lausanne: PPUR, pp 299–313.

Flückiger, A., Morand, C.-A. and Tanquerelle, T. (2000) 'Evaluation du droit de recours des organisations de protection de l'environnement', *Cahier de l'environnement. Droit,* 314, Bern: Office fédéral de l'environnement, des forêts et du paysage.

Kaluszynski, M. (2006) 'La judiciarisation de la société et du politique', *Colloque RIAD, Association internationale de l'assurance de protection juridique,* Paris, 21–22 September.

Lienhard, A. and Kettiger, D. (2016) *The judiciary between management and the rule of law,* Bern: Stämpfli Verlag.

Moor, P. (1997) 'Dire le droit', *Revue européenne de sciences sociales,* XXXV(105), Genève and Paris: Droz, pp 33–55.

Moor, P. (2010) *Dynamique du système juridique – Une théorie générale du droit,* Genève: Schulthess.

Moor, P. (2016) *Perméabilités du système juridique. Essais sur le droit de l'État de droit,* Québec: Presse de l'université de Laval.

Moor, P. with Poltier, E. (2011) *Droit administratif. Vol II: Les actes administratifs et leur contrôle,* 3rd edn, Bern: Stämpfli.

Moor, P. with Bellanger, F. and Tanquerel, F. (2016) *Droit administratif. Vol III: L'organisation des activités administratives. Les biens de l'Etat,* 2nd edn, Bern: Stämpfli.

Moor, P. with Flückiger, A. and Martenet, V. (2012) *Droit administratif. Vol I: Les fondements généraux,* 3rd edn, Bern: Stämpfli.

Morand, C.-A. (1991b) 'Les nouveaux instruments d'action de l'Etat et le droit', in C.-A. Morand (ed) *Les instruments d'action de l'Etat,* Basel: Helbing & Lichtenhahn, pp 237–56.

'In-house' applications

Dupuis, J. and Knoepfel, P. (2015) *The politics of contaminated sites management – Regime change and actors' mode of participation in the environmental management of the Bonfol chemical waste landfill in Switzerland,* Berlin and New York: Springer International.

Girad, N. and Knoepfel, P. (1997) *Cleuson-Dixence: Tout est bien qui finit bien?*, Etude de cas de l'IDHEAP, no 8, Chavannes-près-Renens: IDHEAP.

Knoepfel, P. and Descloux, M. (1988) *Valeurs limites d'immissions: Choix politiques ou déterminations scientifiques?*, Cahier de l'IDHEAP 48, Chavannes-près-Renens: IDHEAP.

Savary, J. (2008) *Poltiques publiques et mobilité urbaine, analyse de processus conflictuels dans quatre villes suisses*, Zürich and Chur: Rüegger.

Schweizer, R. (2015) *Stratégies d'activation du droit dans les politiques environnementales – Cas autour des bis valaisans*, Zürich and Chur: Somedia, Rüegger.

Notes

[1] See also Part I (Chapter 2, on the role of the law).

[2] Essentially in contravention of cantonal legislation or (indirectly) a federal ordinance (public law appeal to the federal court).

[3] In the past I erroneously provided a broader definition of such uses by admitting that all actors that invoke the (objective) law make use of the resource Law. This claim has been excluded from the new specifications on this resource (see Chapter 2).

[4] Article 4 of the Ordinance on Air Pollution of 16 December 1985 (RS 814.318.142.1).

[5] Loi fédérale 22 juin 1979 sur l'aménagement du territoire (Federal Act of 22 June 1979 on Spatial Planning), RS 700.

[6] Prior to a decision of the Federal Supreme Court of 2012 and, in particular, prior to the decision of the federal chambers of May 2016 explicitly acknowledging such an interest equivalent to that of the protection of the landscape.

[7] Vote of 28 February 2016 on the initiative concerning the application of the initiative of 2012: yes 41.1%, no 58.9%; see www.admin.ch/ch/f/pore/va/20160228/index.html

8

Personnel

Definition

> The strategies developed and actions carried out by public policy actors require increasingly qualified personnel. When an administration or NGO does not have sufficient personnel (for example, biologists for the compilation of biotope inventories, lawyers for compiling a notice of opposition), the problem may be alleviated through the purchase of specific skills from outside the organization, in particular through the commissioning of private consultancies, a measure that corresponds in a way to the purchase of human and cognitive resources. This trend for 'outsourcing' can affect the modalities of implementation of public policies through a growing dependency of the political–administrative authorities on the expertise of private actors. (Knoepfel et al, 2010: 62)

Specifics

Today, every large organization, whether public or private, has a human resources policy. This policy reflects the importance accorded to this resource. From the 1970s there was a trend for the centralization of human resources management involving the establishment of entities at the level of the administrative staff and centralized services with the transverse function of providing support to the operational entities. However, since the late 1990s, the opposite trend for the new de-centralization or integration of human resources management in the management of operational processes can be observed. This makes it possible, in particular, to overcome recurring tensions between centralized service policies, which are perceived as being too schematic, and the often very human resources requirements of the operational entities.

Even in the 'decentralized model', in both the public and private sectors, human resource management policies pursue the objective of equality of treatment of personnel in terms of working conditions and salaries, the adequate supply of qualified personnel for operational units, a specific positioning of the organization in question on the labour market, and the promotion of a shared corporate spirit (often expressed in the form of a company slogan, behavioural codes for personnel and 'personnel policy strategies'). In addition, with the advent of a certain 'economization' of the public sector, human resources policies are today considered as a means of increasing the efficiency and effectiveness of administrative production, as was the case for a very long time in the private sector.

The acquisition and use of the resource Personnel is strongly regulated (as is the case for Money) both under public law (for political-administrative actors) and the law of private obligations (contracts of work). These are sometimes supplemented by very detailed rules in the collective agreements negotiated between (public and/or private) employers and the relevant trade unions. In both cases (institutional policies of public labour law and substantive policies for the protection of workers), the beneficiaries benefit from a relatively strong position compared to other public policies. Their associative rights are strengthened moreover by the right to strike (Force), which public sector workers in Switzerland also enjoy since the new Federal Act on the Personnel of the Confederation of 24 March 2000.

The acquisition and use of human resources are based on a set of institutional rules, mainly originating from private law, which are combined in the contract of work. As is the case for the personnel of the Swiss Confederation, the old distinction between public and private contracts is in the process of disappearing today in many European countries (see the aforementioned Federal Act on the Personnel of the Confederation). This applies not only to the nature of contracts (contract of limited or unlimited duration), but also to the modalities of wage setting: in the case of management, salaries in the private sector are generally higher than in the public sector), the obligations associated with obedience and individual exercise of the function in question, and the obligations relating to professional confidentiality, strikes and sanctions. The rules regarding dismissal and redundancy have been made more flexible in the new (federal and cantonal) legislation compared to the classical era of the public service in force until the late 20th century: the regime remains in place but is more restrictive for the public sector than the private sector. Accordingly, the modern status of state employees ('post-public service') is more similar to that of a private sector employee than in the old period of 'Weberian bureaucracy' referred to as the 'public service' or *functionnariat* (Emery and Giauque, 2005, pp 200–201). Similar changes can also be observed at the level of policy personnel employed by public policy target groups and beneficiaries.

Considerable changes have arisen at the level of the individual professional profiles required for appointments. These no longer tend to involve general requirements like loyalty to the common cause ('public interest', the defence of individual interests in the case of target and beneficiary groups), but specific capacities like personal availability, operational/professional confidentiality, professional requirements (the end of the domination of the jurists and economists and a shift towards more specialized professions in a multi- or interdisciplinary context), and leadership (management skills and capacities in group work contexts). Socio-professional criteria (promotion of women's equality), socio-political criteria (inclusion of political representatives close to target and/or beneficiary groups, in particular, in recruitment policy) and the need for multilingualism are added to these requirements in the public sector. A trend involving the increasing recruitment of former public service managers in the private sector can be observed. Such appointments are sometimes explicitly prohibited for periods specified in the legislation on public personnel with a view to avoiding potential conflicts of interest. It should be noted that many of these changes arose with the introduction of new public management in the Swiss federal administration and, particularly, at the level of the cantons. Criticism has been expressed at the decline in the reach of the rule of law, the economization and individualization of the public service ('satisfying the client while upsetting the citizen', as David Giauque puts it in Emery and Giauque, 2011), the excessive focus on performance evaluation, and the use of market-type incentives.

One of the main concerns of human resources policies involves the long-term exploitation of the resource Personnel and its capacity for regeneration. This concern is expressed in the form of training activities aimed at guaranteeing the quality of services at the level of the public policies involved, but also at maintaining the employability of staff in the medium and long term through participative performance evaluations, regular interviews between senior staff and their employees, and the more detailed definition of job descriptions for all employees. In addition, it is possible to observe the emergence of a particular focus on the arrival and/or departure of employees that enables the maintenance of the 'memory' of the organization involved (Information). As is the case with other resources, sustainable use of the resource Personnel requires the protection of basic elements (people) against abuse: in this instance, all kinds of stress caused by the intensification of (public policy) tasks and squeeze on time (Time) and, more broadly, all kinds of professional maladies (for example, 'burn-out').

Such situations involving demotivation and stress, which are increasingly common according to surveys, are particularly prevalent at middle management level in all organizations, both state and private. The state's human resources departments need or are obliged to protect personnel against the demands of politicians and/or those responsible for sectoral policies. This applies in particular to periods of staff shortages imposed by governments or parliaments. Every employer, whether public or private, with an economic and social responsibility knows that such over-exploitation of personnel leads to losses in productivity in the medium term that are difficult to recoup in retrospect.

Despite the aforementioned activities aimed at counteracting the loss of employability, internal resource exchanges (homogenous: Personnel for Personnel) appear to have declined in recent times due to hyperspecialization. As mentioned in relation to outsourcing, multiple heterogeneous exchanges continue to arise (Personnel for Money and Personnel for Consensus: recruitment of representatives of target groups and/or beneficiary groups by the state; Personnel for Time: engagement of employees with short-term contracts for high-pressure periods; and again, Personnel for Organization: administrative reorganization enabling the reduction of the number of people employed).

Personnel: Mobilization by availability

Personnel /availability: Political-administrative actors

This is illustrated using the cases presented below, which are taken from real-life situations.

The Swiss Federal Office for Civil Protection made 300 of its employees available to the organizers of a winter sports event in the Bernese Alps (Lauberhorn to Wengen ski race) free of charge as the organization of this event is in the national interest.

The Swiss Federal Office of Public Health made some of its employees available to the Conference of Cantonal Directors of Public Health (whose secretariat is located at the Maison des cantons in Bern) for the conduct of an anti-AIDS campaign at local and regional levels in compliance with federal AIDS prevention policy.

The Swiss army made a few hundred soldiers and part of its air force available to the Davos Forum (free of charge) to guarantee the security of participants in this event that is considered to boost Switzerland's image and international relations.

The Federal Police deemed itself to be inadequately staffed to be able to ensure the effective combating of organized crime, specifically, money laundering, if it was not allocated around 20 new collaborators. For this reason the Federal Office of Police requested an increase in its personnel and the request was accompanied by a press release aimed specifically at the victims and above all, the target group of this security policy (banking operations targeted by the action against money laundering etc to gain their support against the 'black sheep').

The companies of the Basel chemicals industry financed a chair in biotechnology at the University of Basel and also made around 10 researchers available to enable the fulfilment of their mission in the area of basic and applied research, the aim of which is one of the objectives of the new university policy, the objective of which is to boost the Swiss market. The exact content of the contract between the university and the companies is a secret.

The State Secretariat for Migration threatened the federal parliament with a demand for a huge increase in its staff if the latter decided to reduce the duration of a standard asylum procedure to two weeks, as it did not believe that the proposition was feasible with the personnel available at the time.

A regional job centre refused to accept responsibility for the placement of people with disabilities, claiming that its already overworked staff had neither the qualitative nor quantitative capacities to fulfil this new task that the cantonal government wanted to impose on it in accordance with the new federal legislation relating to invalidity insurance. This legislation stipulates the reintegration of people with disabilities into the primary and/or secondary labour market as the main axis of state activity in this area.

Insufficient personnel is one of the most common arguments used by the public sector to reject attempts to allocate new tasks to existing services (no new tasks without an increase in personnel) in the context of new legislative requirements (Law and Political Support).

A large number of administrative services developed outsourcing strategies to circumvent the famous hiring freeze imposed by the parliaments on all levels of the public service in Switzerland. These strategies consist in enlisting the services of personnel from the external labour market to fulfil tasks for which there are no internal (and/or sufficiently qualified) personnel available within the authorities. As a result, according to the periodic reports produced by the management committees of the two parliamentary chambers, there are hundreds –

even thousands – of people who work directly for the federal, cantonal and communal administrations in Switzerland but who are public sector employees in the strict sense.

Personnel /availability: Target groups

The Swiss Bankers Association issued a statement saying that all legislative provisions that would oblige the banks to require their foreign customers to provide a statement to the effect that the money they deposit is tax-compliant would transform its employers to fiscal police, a role for which they are not trained. Moreover, this measure would require an increase in personnel which, in turn, would cause a rise in the cost of banking services. Accordingly, the Association fought the planned reinforcement of money laundering legislation by the federal legislature.

In the early years of environmental policy in Switzerland (1970s), the Federal Office for the Protection of Water Bodies (now the Federal Office for the Environment) felt it was obliged to recruit experts in science (particularly chemistry) from the chemicals industry that was among the Swiss private sector's biggest polluters at the time. The environmental organizations and their supports feared that these appointees would lack independence as a result.

Based on its so-called 'dual' concept, Switzerland's professional training policy is strongly reliant on the support of companies and obliges apprentices to enter into an apprenticeship agreement to be able to attend courses in the professional training colleges (which are public or organized by the private sector – resource Law). Only those who have completed mandatory courses and an apprenticeship with a company can obtain a Federal Vocational Education and Training Diploma. This model ensures that the business community has a significant influence on professional training (Personnel). The public sector services at cantonal and federal level, which are also obliged to provide apprenticeships, are also involved in the system as employees. Once again, this is a case where a state service forms part of the target group.

In many cantons, the agricultural officials in charge of monitoring agricultural operations in receipt of direct payments are themselves farmers who often act as part-time 'public officials'. Thus a large proportion of the personnel involved in the implementation of agricultural policies belong to the 'agricultural community' itself. The existence of such 'professional bodies' that exercise both public functions and a private profession which is subject to public monitoring (for example, energy policy, professional training policy [see above], food policy and, formerly, civil aviation policies) can also be observed in other public policy contexts. It should also be noted that the old 'appeals commissions' that existed before the different chambers of the current Federal Administrative Court were incorporated into the federal administration (in 2007) were often composed of 'people from the profession' selected by professional associations.

Increasing numbers of public policies require companies to designate individuals for specific tasks that require specialized professional training (particularly in the case of large companies: safety, waste, accounting, energy). It is not uncommon for the associations representing these target groups to oppose draft legislation containing such provisions with the argument that this highly qualified personnel is not available on the labour market or that such appointments would have negative impacts on production costs.

Personnel /availability: Beneficiary groups

Today, as in the past, the staff of the services in charge of the environment are often members of environmental protection organizations which, according to the Swiss legislature, are supposed to represent the interests of the environment. Hence the heads of sections, divisions and services, and even the staff of the Federal Office for the Environment itself, are recruited from the professionals who work for the environmental associations. Moreover, it is not unusual for an organization to make personnel available to others in the form of temporary secondments.

Despite their association-based structures and sometimes large numbers of members, some organizations, for the protection of the specific interests of public policy beneficiaries, suffer from a lack of professional personnel (for example, associations that represent and protect the interests of consumers, the environment, employees, patients, television audiences, auditors). As a result, these organizations are increasingly unable to obtain a comprehensive overview of the different public policy products (in particular, outputs) that are likely to have a negative effect on the interests of the groups they represent. Different strategies aimed at overcoming these deficits can be adopted: the delegation of particular tasks to the secretariat of a regional section specializing in one or other of these areas, the establishment of working groups for specific issues, inter-organizational cooperation (for example, the sharing of observation and intervention areas between different environmental protection organizations) or the simple abandonment of monitoring activities in less important areas.

Another way of overcoming the lack of professional personnel in these associations consists in organizing joint fundraising campaigns, requesting subsidies from the state either for specific projects (often successful) or to cover structural expenses (a strategy that is declining in popularity as such requests are frequently rejected). As public interest organizations (not-for-profit), these organizations are normally exempted from taxation, collect contributions from their members, and sometimes engage in semi-commercial activities with the aim of covering their operating costs and thus engaging the personnel they require.

Personnel: Mobilization by stage

Personnel /stages: Political-administrative actors

During legislative procedures, the personnel policy actors frequently accuse the administration of being incapable of creating the ordinances necessary for the correct monitoring of policy implementation (at cantonal level). This argument is used to challenge a new law in its entirety or at least prompt its partial modification so that it does not give rise to administrative costs that are seen as excessive.

At the level of implementation activities, (institutional) personnel policies frequently clash with rules that limit the flexible engagement of supplementary personnel in anticipation of temporary or permanent increases in the volume of cases to be processed. Numerous examples of such situations exist, such as the influx of asylum-seekers, submission of tax declarations in the summer, increase in the number of applications for planning permission submitted prior to the entry into force of legislation restricting secondary residences or the guaranteeing of safety by the policy during major events. In general, the solutions adopted consist either in the exceptional payment of overtime for existing personnel or the employment of supplementary personnel based on temporary private law contracts. Once the extraordinary situation has passed, this strategy makes it possible to reduce the number of personnel to its initial number. However, problems arise here in relation to the training of temporary personnel and their placement in the labour market at the end of their contracts. For certain sensitive functions (for example, the police, fire brigade, tax service collaborators), questions regarding the reliability of the temporary employees may also arise.

The lack of personnel is often felt when it comes to monitoring (changes in) the behaviour of target groups. This lack of monitoring is often criticized by representatives of the beneficiary groups. This phenomenon is especially prominent in Switzerland due to the small size of the cantonal administrations with responsibility for policy implementation.

Personnel /stages: Target groups

Nowadays certain target groups organized in the form of associations for the representation of their political interests (for example, the economiesuisse organization that represents the interests of the Swiss business community) tend to employ their own 'policy personnel'.[1] They may be employed on a permanent or temporary basis, for example, to operate the secretariat, to collect signatures for the purpose of launching a popular initiative or referendum, or for the operation of referendum campaigns on controversial topics. It is not uncommon for these people to be recruited among former federal and cantonal officials. Such appointments are often made with particular public events in mind (popular votes, processing of a specific issue in the federal chambers), and are thus intended to be limited in duration. Once the campaign or 'fight' is over, the number of such policy personnel employed declines. This phenomenon can be observed during both the policy programming and implementation stages.

Personnel /stages: Beneficiary groups

Similar fluctuations in personnel can also be observed at the level of organizations that claim to defend the interests of the beneficiaries of certain aforementioned public policies. In effect, the committees for popular initiatives or referendums are usually dissolved on the completion of the corresponding votes and the temporary employment of lawyers is concentrated on the stage involving the initial implementation of contested legislation (for example, the Federal Act on the Limitation of Secondary Residences adopted in 2015). In these cases, questions arise regarding the conditions of employment of those involved as they are often appointed in accordance with private law under temporary contracts of work.

Personnel: Exchange

Personnel /exchange: Political-administrative actors

Apart from the exchange of personnel between sectoral public policies, which arises in the federal, cantonal and communal administration by means of internal selection processes for vacancies and is becoming increasingly difficult due to the greater specialization of professional profiles, a large number of situations exist involving the exchange of human resources between the state, the private sector and non-profit social organizations (beneficiary groups). Such – homogenous – exchanges are more common today in both the public and private sectors as professional profiles have become increasingly specialized, and individuals with specialist qualifications are known to each other as they have followed similar or identical (postgraduate) training. However, such practices sometimes encounter difficulties due to salary policies or in relation to professional confidentiality, for example.

With regard to senior officials in particular, political-administrative actors continue to appoint 'political' personnel who tend to be close to business circles that are usually represented by the centre-right political parties or conversely, circles active in protecting public policy beneficiaries represented by NGOs, which protect specific interests and/or centre-left parties. Moreover, in addition to fulfilling leadership tasks within the administration, the appointment of these people should ensure Political Support that is deemed necessary for the promotion of the policy in question (heterogeneous exchange). Sometimes such appointments also serve in procuring Consensus in terms of the trust of the communities involved in a sectoral policy. It is easy to imagine a strategy that combines the simultaneous acquisition of the two resources through the appointment, for example, of the old chief economist of the Swiss Federation of Trade Unions (Union syndicale suisse) as director of the State Secretariat for Economic Affairs (SECO), which both promotes the participation of a key actor in labour market policy (Consensus) and that of the left-wing political parties for future federal policy in the area of the labour market (Political Support).

Personnel/exchange: Target groups

Depending on their strategic objectives, target groups can be interested in such homogenous exchanges (*pantouflage*, practice by which high-level civil servants obtain work in the private sector in France) operating in both directions. On the one hand, the interest may consist in 'placing' one of 'their own' at the decision-making centre of a policy that these strategic groups consider as crucial to their activities and, on the other hand, the same groups will appoint former political representatives (commonly, federal councillors, councillors of state or former presidents of major Swiss cities), who generally have large political and social networks, to their leadership or administrative councils. This strategy enables them to increase their political influence in negotiations with political-administrative decision-makers.

These examples clearly illustrate the heterogeneous nature of the exchange. In effect, the transfer primarily serves to fill a leadership post and increase the political influence of business circles (Political Support) with a view to fulfilling a second, more political objective, that is, to increase the visibility of a particular candidate during a selection process and making them stand out from several candidates with professional qualities that are deemed 'equivalent' (Personnel). Such exchanges are often criticized by the public and thus governed by specific preventive mechanisms (for example, mandatory waiting times before being allowed to take up such appointments, professional confidentiality, withdrawal of pension benefits).

Personnel/exchange: Beneficiary groups

Similar symmetrical exchanges of personnel can also be observed between political-administrative actors and organizations for the protection of specific interests (see above).

Such exchanges also serve in stabilizing or increasing the portfolios of Consensus and Political Support at the disposal of the organizations representing the interests of specific public policies and, as in the case of the target groups, in both directions, either through the placement of 'one of their own' within the administration or through the nomination of a former elected representative as a president, member of the administrative council or director of the organization's secretariat. Given that the salaries paid by NGOs are significantly lower than those paid by the public sector and business associations, the problem of salary scales is probably more acute in this case than in corresponding appointments to positions in the federal administration.

Recommended further reading

Textbooks and specialist literature

Bellanger, F. and Roy, C. (2013) 'Evolution du cadre légal et réglementaire de la fonction publique suisse', in A. Ladner, J.-L. Chappelet, Y. Emery, P. Knoepfel, L. Mader, N. Soguel and F. Varone (eds) *Manuel d'administration publique suisse*, Lausanne: PPUR, pp 461-79.

Berman, E.M., Bowman, J.S., West, J.P. and van Wart, M.R. (2015) *Human resource management in public service: Paradoxes, processes and problems*, Los Angeles, CA: Sage.

Emery, Y. (2013) 'Nouvelles politiques et processus de gestion publique des ressources humaines', in A. Ladner, J.-L. Chappelet, Y. Emery, P. Knoepfel, L. Mader, N. Soguel and F. Varone (eds) *Manuel d'administration publique suisse*, Lausanne: PPUR, pp 481–500.

Emery, Y. and Giauque, D. (2005) *Paradoxes de la gestion publique*, Paris: L'Harmattan.

Emery, Y. and Giauque, D. (2011) *Motivations et valeurs des agents publics à l'épreuve des réformes*, Laval: Les Presses de l'Université Laval.

Emery, Y. and Gonin, F. (2009) *Gérer les ressources humaines*, Lausanne: PPUR.

Fredericksen, E.D., Witt, S.L., Patton, W.D. and Lovrich, N. (2016) *Human resource management: The public service perspective*, New York: Routledge.

Giauque, D. (2009) 'L'administration publique fédérale suisse en comparaison internationale: à la recherche d'une tradition administrative', in A. Ladner, J.-L. Chappelet, Y. Emery, P. Knoepfel, L. Mader, N. Soguel and F. Varone (eds) *Manuel d'administration publique suisse*, Lausanne: PPUR, pp 31–46.

Giauque, D. (2013) 'Motivation et identités des agents publics suisses', in A. Ladner, J.-L. Chappelet, Y. Emery, P. Knoepfel, L. Mader, N. Soguel and F. Varone (eds) *Manuel d'administration publique suisse*, Lausanne: PPUR, pp 523–40.

Hendry, C. and Pettigrew, A. (1990) 'Human resource management: an agenda for the 1990s', *The International Journal of Human Resource Management*, 1(1): 17–43.

Koller, C. (2009) 'Profil du personnel de la function publique', in A. Ladner, J.-L. Chappelet, Y. Emery, P. Knoepfel, L. Mader, N. Soguel and F. Varone (eds) *Manuel d'administration publique suisse*, Lausanne: PPUR, pp 501–22.

Padioleau, J.-G. (1999) 'L'action publique post-moderne: Le gouvernement politique des risques', *Politiques et management public*, 17(4): 85–127.

Patton, D.W., Witt, S.L., Lovrich, N. and Fredericksen, P. (2016) *Human resource management: The public service perspective*, New York: Routledge.

Varone, F. (2013) 'Administration fédérale', in A. Ladner, J.-L. Chappelet, Y. Emery, P. Knoepfel, L. Mader, N. Soguel and F. Varone (eds) *Manuel d'administration publique suisse*, Lausanne: PPUR, pp 103–18.

'In-house' applications

Bréthaud, C. and Nahrath, S. (2011) 'Entre imbrication, instrumentalisation et infusion', *Annales valaisannes*, 2010-2011: 69-89.

Note

[1] This expression is used to designate target group managers dedicated to the follow-up of public policies.

9

Money

Definition

This resource is indispensable to public policy actors in that it enables them to procure many other resources (for example, the promoters of a shopping centre exchange the resources money for law by financing the improvement of access to the site by public transport, pedestrians and cyclists in exchange for the granting of planning permission). This resource draws its importance from the fact that it is very easy to exchange, particularly as many actors enjoy a certain level of budgetary autonomy. This is precisely the reason why the annual and rigid budgetary process of public administrations is the subject of criticism by analysts who support the trend of new public management. They suggest that multi-annual budgets be replaced by service contracts which would enable the more flexible management of this resource. (Knoepfel et al, 2010: 62-3)

Specifics

The saying that 'money has no smell' (*pecunia non olet*) can give us the wrong idea, that is, that money should be seen as a 'super resource' and dominant in the hierarchy of all public action resources. In my view, this is not the case at all. First, it is important to differentiate this resource from the resource Property (administrative and financial assets) held in public or private hands. The constitutive values of administrative assets (which render an actor 'rich' or 'poor') are usually unsaleable and cannot therefore be converted into money. The value of financial assets, although convertible into money, is not always 'available' as it is associated with objects with varying degrees of saleability. Thus it is advisable not to consider financial assets as forming part of the resource Money in all cases.

Furthermore, the use of this resource, which is universally available in civil society, is far more limited and regulated than other public action resources in the public policy sphere (for example, measures to prevent corruption, misappropriation of funds and other abuses by the authorities, public procurement, the strict regulation of the use of subsidies). In this sense, as a public action resource, Money does indeed have a traceable 'smell' that is consciously regulated by multiple possession, behavioural and decisional institutional rules and, moreover, by substantive public policies (such as anti-money laundering policy and monetary policy). It is important to remember, finally, that no actor can 'buy everything': the exchange of public action resources for Money is strongly restricted by public and private regulations, and is also frequently associated with 'bad smells'.

Money: Mobilization by availability

Money /availability: Political-administrative actors

The story is told that one evening in summer 1983, Federal Councillor André Chevallaz arrived at a meeting being held at the Hôtel de la Croix Blanche in Vugelles-La-Motte in the canton of Vaud with a small suitcase containing several thousand Swiss francs to be distributed to the 'poor' citizens of the commune to compensate them for the disturbance caused by the noise generated by the Swiss army. The latter had an open-air shooting range in the upper ranges of the village. The shells from the canons used at the range flew over the village before landing in the valley below it. This use of Money by a former public representative to compensate for the disturbance suffered by the local population clearly belongs to a bygone mode of action. The Federal Finance Administration has since developed a public spending policy that includes a large number of rules governing the use of this resource.[1] These rules mean that all spending by the state (whether related to a specific purpose or 'free') is subject to a strict regime and, moreover, at federal, cantonal and communal levels.

This applies not only to subsidies but also to public acquisitions that must be carried out in compliance with the federal and cantonal legislation imposing strict procedures for public tender procedures. The latter apply to political-administrative actors in the broadest sense of the term (including public foundations). The Swiss Federal Audit Office and the Control Committees (*commissions de gestion*) of the National Council and Council of States monitor the federal departments and offices' compliance with these strict rules which, as demonstrated by the activities of these bodies, are often circumvented using familiar and not so familiar strategies (for example, division of the total sum of an order into several purchases that do not exceed the threshold for a mandatory tender procedure, highlighting the unique qualities of a supplier with whom the service has been working for years, fictitious billing for IT consultancy services).

Another case that has triggered a fierce public debate, something that is relatively rare in Switzerland, is the misappropriation of public money for private, associative or political purposes (such as payment of private holiday travel by the state or rental prices that do not correspond to market prices for buildings belonging to the state).

However, the non-use of Money is a far more common subject of political debate today than its possible misuse. The focus here is on the multiple economic restrictions adopted in the federal, cantonal and communal annual budgets for many years now. The cautiousness (and sometimes the cold political calculations[2]) of the public paymasters was often considered as the explanation for the excessively restrictive (conservative) budgets: an under-estimation of revenues often results in gains at year end, and such cases are a source of general rejoicing for the parliaments and responsible ministers. However, they prompt critical reactions on the part of the collaborators of the administrations involved and, in general, the parliamentary left. These criticisms are due, in part, to the fact that ending the year with unused budgetary items increases the risk of 'punishment' for the following financial year (additional cuts of the sectoral budget). It is a well-known fact that to avoid such situations, the administrations at all levels in Switzerland are more inclined to spend money in November and December than in January ('December fever').

In the case of a lack of Money, political-administrative actors can avail of savings programmes (see below) with or without the (qualitative and/or quantitative) reduction of services, find ways to increase their revenue (direct taxation of physical or moral entities, indirect taxes like VAT, taxes and fees that are normally associated with particular services of specific sectoral policies), resort to borrowing, generate more revenue from financial assets, or reduce the cost of borrowing (restructuring of debt).

When referring here to the lack of Money, I use a generic term, which does not include the taxes and fees that form the revenue generated by specific public policies. In effect, a public policy can introduce, increase etc this revenue that it collects from the specific target groups or beneficiaries in exchange for their services (for example, fees for planning permission, procedures for the entry of toxic substances, waste processing in accordance with 'the polluter pays' principle, local high-resolution meteorological forecasts, vehicle registration documents for car owners). Such revenues are regularly earmarked and not available for purposes other than the production of the services involved.[3]

Political-administrative actors tend to respond to a lack of Money by proposing quantitative or qualitative reductions to the services they provide. Such measures are implemented at the level of the federal administration, which carries out more or less systematic reviews of all of the public policies implemented with a view to reducing their number or, more commonly, to negotiate a retrenchment (*renoncement* in French and *Verzichtsplanung* in German) of tasks and missions. Similarly, the main products of each public policy are examined with a view to dispensing with some of them.

Similar operations are carried out in the cantonal administrations responsible for policy implementation involving the examination of strategies for the rationalization of procedures for the production of outputs (for example, the simplification of planning permission procedures, the use of standard expressions), and the elimination of the mandatory authorization of various activities that generate excessive administrative costs and whose benefits are marginal. It is obvious that such operations for increasing the efficiency of production can have negative impacts on the effectiveness of the federal policies involved. Experience shows that such measures tend to have a particularly negative impact on activities for the monitoring of target groups (such as inspections and police reports).

Money/availability: Target groups

Nowadays the large organization of economic target groups tends to have specific budgets dedicated to their political actions. This also applies to major companies in the financial and industrial sectors in Switzerland, irrespective of the 'labels' they use to designate the corresponding budgetary allocations (often 'cultural' or 'social' activities, for example). This money is reserved for the funding of policy personnel, lobbying, the funding of campaigns for popular votes and again, the support of political parties. It is a well-known fact that, depending on the issue involved, the cost incurred in defending the interests of target groups at political level are considerable, and frequently exceed the budgets available to the beneficiaries of the contested policies.

The object of influence changes according to the positioning of the contested product in the public policy cycle. It should be noted that such interventions among policy decision-makers are also considered as necessary in the case of important outputs (for example, provision of a permit or licence for the construction, raising etc of a hydroelectric dam) and public policy evaluations. In such cases the target groups use their political budgets to fund legal fees, scientific reports or simply – and happily less commonly in Switzerland – attempts to corrupt decision-making officials with a view to obtaining favourable outcomes in relation to tendering procedures, planning applications, import quotas or the authorization of the placing of chemical products on the market.

The latter example demonstrates, moreover, that relatively strict rules exist in relation to the use of money as a resource available to target groups involved in public policy processes. These rules no longer simply concern classical and private corruption, but also financial transparency in general, the financing of political parties and the payment of lobbying representatives.

If, despite all of the individual and collective efforts, the target groups' 'war chests' are empty and they see themselves forced to reduce their investment in their political activities, like every other actor they will seek allies (mobilization of Organization) at the level of the political-administrative actors involved in policy programming (Political Support from centre-right political parties), or they will try to block output production processes at policy implementation level that they consider as having a negative impact on their development (for example, environmental policies, spatial planning, building regulations). Their success at this level depends on their capacity to mobilize the resources Law (appeal) or Information (for example, withholding of the information necessary for the production of outputs, such as data on their energy consumption, their taxable assets, the chemical composition of their products). This capacity mainly involves Property (right in rem in respect of land, production plants; actual capacity to maintain confidentiality; right of intellectual property).

Money /availability: Beneficiary groups

The organizations for the protection of the interests of public policy beneficiaries devote a considerably larger proportion of their funds than the target groups to 'political' work, even if the sums involved could only be defined as modest in absolute terms. The Money they use comes mainly from membership contributions, sometimes the sale of services associated with the sectors in question (for example, general subscriptions, car insurance sold by the environmental transport organization Association Transports et Environnement), subsidies (for concrete projects or, less frequently, for the operation of the organization's basic structure) and donations. This money cannot be used in an entirely arbitrary way. These associations, which are subject to internal and sometimes external financial auditing, must keep meticulous records of their spending. Indeed, it can be confirmed that the rules of transparency governing these beneficiary groups are probably stricter than those governing the political work of target groups.

Volunteers carry out a considerable proportion of the political work of these organizations. The organizations can also save on expenses, in particular in relation to legal procedures, by engaging expert volunteers (for example, lawyers and biologists) at preferential rates.

As already stated, Money is the Achilles heel of groups representing public policy beneficiaries, and can even lead to their disappearance when sustainable funding is lacking. Hence the groups tend to mobilize their capacity for organization (Organization) that enables them, among other things, to establish coalitions among themselves or with political-administrative actors or political parties. They also mobilize Consensus in the form of the withdrawal of their members from platforms, commissions etc, thereby visibly indicating their distrust of the two other groups of the policy triangle and undermining the credibility or legitimacy of certain public policy products (in particular, the action plans and outputs).

A phenomenon that can frequently be observed in relation to policy implementation is the preventive filing of opposition during inquiry procedures for major projects which, in many cases, do not require major financial investment but enable the beneficiary groups to delay any imminent public action (gain of Time).

Money: Mobilization by stage

Money/stages: Political-administrative actors

It makes sense for all policies that plan to change the behaviour of target groups with the help of financial incentives (subsidies, tax deductions, taxation of non-compliant behaviour) to differentiate between the use of Money for policy programming and implementation. Twenty-eight of the Swiss Confederation's 51 tasks as defined in the Federal Council's steering programme for public policies of 2012[4] involved transfer payments to public bodies (cantons, communes) and private ones. According to the Federal Council, on the basis of around 350 constitutional and legal provisions, 60 per cent of federal spending in 2010 (CHF 35 billion) was allocated to subsidies (43 per cent for social welfare, 15 per cent for education and research, 15 per cent to transport and 10 per cent to food and agriculture).[5] The sum relating to general costs and the modalities of payment of these transfers will always be the object of political battles in the context of the policy budgeting procedure, and target groups and/or beneficiary groups will mobilize all kinds of resources during these battles to obtain the desired federal contributions.

The Federal Council, cantonal governments and political parties have the growing tendency to invest (public and private) money in popular vote campaigns with a view to covering the sometimes enormous advertising, logistical and other costs associated with them. This spending is justified by the state actors in the strict sense as information campaign costs (which are more or less compatible with the principle of neutrality of the state) and not as partisan propaganda, a term reserved for the activities of the political parties and umbrella organizations representing the target and beneficiary groups.

Similarly, the political–administrative actors invest considerable sums in 'informing' and making the political groups, target groups and beneficiaries and eventual third party winners and losers (positively and negatively affected third parties) comply with major projects that form part of public policy outputs. Accordingly, funding will be allocated for the compilation, printing and distribution of documents that explain the operation, public interest etc of new high-voltage power lines, projects for increasing the capacity of, for example, dams, motorway projects and football stadiums, which will be the object of communal votes (district plans), planning permission or licensing procedures that are likely to be rejected at the ballot box or contested through administrative law appeals.

Moreover, the Confederation and, above all, the cantons make provision in their legislation on subsidies for the conclusion of service mandates, contracts or agreements between the bodies providing the subsidies and the organizations that receive funding for the production of public services. These 'contractual' arrangements regularly contain a more or less implicit definition of the problem that the public policy aims to resolve. They indicate, moreover, the target groups whose behaviour should be changed through the services (outputs) to be produced directly or indirectly by the contracting public bodies, the services themselves and, moreover, the periods of time allocated for the production of these outputs and the evaluation clauses (evaluative statements) relating to the policy outputs, impacts and, less commonly, the outcomes.

To overcome the inconveniences associated with the principle of annuality of the (federal and cantonal) budgets, the political-administrative actors of the Confederation increasingly avail of multi-annual financial frameworks, which are valid, for example, for a four-year period. This instrument has all of the characteristics of an action plan, in particular, the spatial and temporal prioritization of the phasing of implementation processes and the predictability of public action in time and space (for example, by means of waiting lists).

Money /stage: Target groups

The above-described use of Money contained in the political budgets of the target groups obviously arises before the parliamentary chambers decide on the corresponding issues. At implementation level, the target groups often find themselves in the position of promoting contested projects and support the communal authority by covering the cost of renting premises or commissioning reports that justify a project, for example. It should be noted that, in any case, they cover the cost of developing projects.

By definition, the target groups are those that must change their behaviour and bear the costs of this change that can affect their economic and social assets and, accordingly, their stock of the resource Property. They will have attempted to reduce these costs during the programming stage with greater (for example, farmers) or lesser (for example, companies responsible for air pollution) degrees of success, in particular, through attempts to influence the choice of action instruments deployed by the policy in question (avoidance of regulatory modalities of intervention in favour of incentive-based or persuasive instruments).

For the incentive-based policies, the moment of truth arrives at the implementation stage when the target groups must demonstrate the effectiveness of the instrument by formulating real requests for subsidies, the quantity and quality of which correspond to their earlier promises. 'Too few' requests equates to a failure in the implementation of the policy in question, which may be due to the over- or under-estimation of the incentivizing effect of the measures taken. In the latter case, changes in the behaviour of the target groups progress so 'easily' and/or correspond so perfectly to the strategies that have been selected (for example, cyclical replacement of haulage fleets if new trucks are all fitted with a catalytic converter, replacement of civil aviation fleets) that public money ends up being 'poured down the drain' ('free-rider' effects).

Money/stage: Beneficiary groups

Within the limits of the possible, the groups representing the interests of beneficiaries also invest their money prior to the decision-making of federal, cantonal and communal parliamentary bodies. It is interesting to note that these NGOs often take the precaution of reserving some of their money for eventual legal proceedings and/or eventual expenses arising from the monitoring of the – in their view, negative – consequences of the implementation of the policy projects in question.

According to our definition, public policy beneficiary groups are not generally the 'beneficiaries' of subsidies or groups 'targeted' by subsidy payments, which tend to be aimed at the target groups. However, public services aimed at policy beneficiaries can be observed in the area of social policy. In this instance, the aim is to induce beneficiaries to actively avail of services rather than avoiding them.[6] According to our definition, the public policy proposes to positively alter their poor (social, environmental, economic) living conditions that are rightly considered as posing a real public problem (altruistic or egoistic motives: protection against criminality). The work of their organizations essentially consists, therefore, in monitoring the behaviour of the authorities responsible for these policies; they must promote the services among their members and propose indicators capable of describing the different aspects of the latter's 'quality of life'. Thus their field of action involves the monitoring of policy implementation (production of outputs) and producing evaluative statements during public policy programming.

When applied to social policies, the statement made in the previous paragraph shows that, based on a probably general trend for the 'accountability' of the beneficiaries of social services, the addressees of the outputs of these policies include employers (obligation to pay contributions, obligation to create jobs), all employees (obligation to pay contributions) and also socially vulnerable people (such as those who are unemployed, who have a disability and those dependent on social welfare). Thus the latter must also change their behaviour as social welfare payments are conditional and increasingly subject to explicit counter-services, for example, exemptions, attendance at courses, participation in other active measures defined in the labour market policies. The often implicit *raison d'être* of this assumption of responsibility by the public policy sometimes consists in the fact that these policies propose to resolve the collective problem which is, among other things, precisely that of the assumption of responsibility by the family members of these people, and this is considered socially unacceptable. According to our conceptualization (see Chapter 1), family members are not positively affected third parties but actual secondary beneficiaries whose situation must be improved according to an often inexplicit objective of the political-administrative programmes (for example, the often very onerous support of very elderly parents by their children who are themselves of retirement age). Hence the failure to avail of these social services is not a 'success' ('state makes savings'), but clearly a failure of these social policies.

Money: Exchange

Money /exchange: Political-administrative actors

Many public policies exist that involve transfers of money (subsidies, tax exemptions) aimed at obtaining money from the same (target) group, usually in the form of a tax. Such homogenous exchanges arise, for example, in the tax exemption regimes for very wealthy foreigners living in Switzerland. The Swiss state refrains in part from levying taxes considered excessive by these people with the aim of obtaining at least a guaranteed sum of taxation from them. Similarly, temporary tax exemptions for companies newly established in a given canton are justified by the fact that this instrument will enable the creation of jobs in the future and the generation of extra tax revenue as a result. Based on this concept, the company will pay tax in the long run, and based on this expected outcome, the state accords it a 'subsidy' in the form of tax exemption in its initial state.

The incentive-based intervention mode can also be motivated and more often by a concept of heterogeneous resource exchange in that the subsidy destroys the opposition of the target groups that threaten to avail of Property (for example, moving abroad, open declaration of non-compliance with implementation outputs and opting to pay a fine). The political-administrative actors also use their Money to obtain a series of other resources that are available among the target groups and beneficiaries, for example, Consensus (payment of subsidies for NGOs with a view to making them comply with a sectoral policy process), Information (purchasing of expert reports through commissions to compile them), Personnel (temporary appointment of additional collaborators) and Political Support ('purchasing' of parliamentarians in the case of a fragile majority).

Money /exchange: Target groups

The initiative for the above-described fiscal arrangements can also originate from the taxpayers themselves who declare their intention to move to particular canton if the state agrees to refrain from collecting a defined proportion of their taxes. It is a well-known fact that companies make good use of the intercantonal competition today. Accordingly, all cantons aim to create a 'favourable fiscal climate' and sometimes become involved in veritable battles for the hosting of these companies (tax competition). Another exchange constellation involving Money is that demonstrated above and involving target groups that invest large sums in a popular vote concerning legislation that will guarantee them fiscal privileges or, in the case of agriculture, subsidies. The sums invested in the popular vote appear to depend on the level of the subsidies or fiscal privileges involved.

Multiple monetary transactions also exist that are initiated by target groups and are also considered as more or less legitimate. They form part of the array of (part-time) 'consultancy mandates' offered to members of the federal chambers, cantonal parliaments or communal executives. Another less controversial area – because it is universally rejected – is that of corruption involving the provision of an entire range of counter-services in the form of resources as varied as Time (extension of a remediation deadline), Consensus (invitation of decision-makers and beneficiaries to serious excursions or Berlusconi-style 'parties'), Law (provision of 'purchased' driving licences) and Information (provision of access of a confidential file containing data relating to the competition). Other less controversial heterogeneous exchanges are those that arise in the rental of public premises for private events (for example, courses or social events organized by the UBS bank in university buildings, celebration of the 'birthday' of a major NGO in the federal parliament building). It should be noted that such activities are less common as they are considered as 'desecrating' the symbolic locations of political life (just as Jesus drove the traders and bankers out of the temple).

Money /exchange: Beneficiary groups

As the organizations that protect the interests of public policy beneficiaries generally lack money, they are unlikely to be able to participate much in the financial games surrounding public policies. Nonetheless, it is possible to conceive two constellations involving such organizations that involve, first, an attempt to obtain structural or project-related subsidies through acts of corruption aimed at political-administrative actors (dubious NGOs, as were once encountered in Eastern European and in developing countries) and second, the sale of labels created by the same questionable organizations to public bodies (public marketing) or companies that do not entirely fulfil the conditions required by the label. It is also possible to imagine the adoption of such 'commercial' practices by an NGO if the service is 'sold' at a much higher price than the cost of its production for the simple reason that this service has a high symbolic value for the buyer.

However, given that the money is not readily available in the resource portfolio of the beneficiary groups, they rarely initiate exchanges involving this resource. Apart from the above-described homogenous exchange (corruption in exchange for subsidies, sale of false labels), NGOs can sometimes be seen to use Money with a view to boosting their Property stocks, for example, by acquiring plots of land that are of strategic interest to them. This ownership may also enable them to access the resource Law (right of appeal as a neighbour) in the context of spatial planning. A recent example of such a strategy involved the leasing of a site by Greenpeace close to the Bonfol hazardous waste landfill (canton of Jura) with a view to obtaining a right of appeal against the cantonal decision on a clean-up plan for the contaminated site; the NGO felt that the cantonal decision was too advantageous to the former operators of the landfill site, a Basel-based chemical concern. Another example involves land leasing in the US that results, in practice, in the privatization of the governance of the lands involved, that is, the 'purchasing' of access to a less restrictive landscape protection regime than that applicable to normal lands.

Despite legal and, above all, moral objections from one party or another, it is also possible to observe cases that involve the purchase of the withdrawal of an appeal submitted by an organization for the protection of beneficiary interests. Accordingly, the compensation agreed in negotiations aimed at enabling the avoidance of appeal proceedings can take the form of payments for the financing of compensatory measures that remain rather vague and difficult to verify. In such cases involving the exchange of Law and Money, the (undeclared) interest of the beneficiaries lies more in the revenue attained in this way than in the actual realization of the compensatory measure.

Also worthy of mention here are strategies for the heterogeneous exchange of resources between target groups and beneficiary groups, which consist, for example, in the purchase of (small) blocks of shares by NGOs with a view to obtaining a right of participation in the shareholder meetings of major companies (exchange of Money for Law/Force and or Property). Such strategies generally yield little success.

Recommended further reading

Textbooks and specialist literature

Athias, L. (2013) 'La contractualisation de services publics: Une analyse économique', in A. Ladner, J.-L. Chappelet, Y. Emery, P. Knoepfel, L. Mader, N. Soguel and F. Varone (eds) *Manuel d'administration publique suisse*, Lausanne: PPUR, pp 679-98.

Bergmann, A. (2009) *Public sector financial management*, Harlow: Pearson Education.

Bonoli, G. and Bertozzi F. (eds) (2008) *Les nouveaux défis de l'Etat social = Neue Herausforderungen für den Sozialstaat. Contributions à l'action publique*, Lausanne and Berne: PPUR, Haupt.

Dafflon, B. (1994) *La gestion financière des collectivités publiques locales*, Paris: Economica.

FDK-CDF, Conférence des directeurs cantonaux des finances (2008) *Manuel – Modèle comptable harmonisé pour les cantons et les communes – MCH2*, Bern: CDF.

Kirchgässner, G. (2013) 'Economie politique de la dette et des déficits publics', in A. Ladner, J.-L. Chappelet, Y. Emery, P. Knoepfel, L. Mader, N. Soguel and F. Varone (eds) *Manuel d'administration publique suisse*, Lausanne: PPUR, pp 587-602.

Schönenberger, A. (2013) 'Finances publiques en Suisse', in A. Ladner, J.-L. Chappelet, Y. Emery, P. Knoepfel, L. Mader, N. Soguel and F. Varone (eds) *Manuel d'administration publique suisse*, Lausanne: PPUR, pp 567-86.

Soguel, N. (ed) (2011) *Des politiques au chevet de la conjoncture/Die Politiken als Retterinnen der Konjunktur*, Lausanne: PPUR.

UN (United Nations) (2004) *United Nations handbook on practical anti-corruption measures for prosecutors and investigators*, Vienna, September.

Warin, P. (2010) 'Les politiques publiques face à la non-demande sociale', in O. Borraz and V. Giraudon, *Politiques publiques 2. Changer la société*, Paris: Presses de Sciences Po, pp 287-312.

'In-house' applications

Dupuis, J. and Knoepfel, P. (2015) *The politics of contaminated sites management – Regime change and actors' mode of participation in the environmental management of the Bonfol chemical waste landfill in Switzerland*, Berlin and New York: Springer International.

Gerber, D. (2012) 'The difficulty of integrating land trusts in land use planning', *Landscape & Urban Planning*, 104(2): 289-98.

Gerber, D. and Rissman, A.R. (2012) 'Land-conservation strategies: The dynamic relationship between acquisition and land use planning', *Environment and Planning A*, 44: 1836-55.

Joerchel, B. (1999) 'Vugelles-La-Mothe/VD: Echos de tirs dans le vallon', in P. Knoepfel, A. Eberle, B. Joerchel Anhorn, M. Meyrat and F. Sager, *Militär und Umwelt im politischen Alltag, Vier Fallstudien für die Ausbildung/Militaire et environnement: La politique au quotidien. Quatre études de cas pour l'enseignement*, Sur mandat de l'Office fédéral du personnel, Bern: OCFIM, pp 168-324.

Knoepfel, P. and Zimmermann, W. (1986) 'Oekologisierung von Landwirtschaft', *Schweizerische Landwirtschaftliche Forschung/Recherche agronome en Suisse*, 25(2): 195-212.

Notes

[1] In particular, the requirement of a precise legal basis, the correspondence of an item of expenditure to a clear budget line, accounting rules for annual operational, investment, budgeting etc expenses.

[2] In particular, centre-right federal ministers of finance.

[3] In the particular case of regulatory taxes (for example, taxes on volatile organic compounds, VOC), products that damage the ozone layer, CO_2 levy – climate), the tax revenues are redistributed to the population (through a reduction in health insurance premiums normally paid to each insured person in December). Note that Swiss health insurance companies are supposed to be 'neutral'.

[4] According to my own calculations cited in *Revision of the indicator system for the Federal Council and Parliament* by Sabrina Baumgartner and André de Montmollin, published by the Swiss Federal Chancellery (FCh) and the Federal Statistical Office (FSO) (2012), p 32.

[5] According to the Federal Council's management report of 8 August 2016 (see www. bk.admin.ch/dokumentation/publikationen/00290/00929/index.html?lang=fr).

[6] Problem of the failure to avail of social services; see Warin (2010).

10

Property

Definition

This resource includes all of the material assets (for example, buildings, meeting rooms, equipment, lands, IT equipment, etc) at the disposal of different actors that own or hold rights of use for the implementation of their different activities. These assets are not only indispensable to the implementation of the regular activities of these actors, they also play a central role in the communication functions of the latter with their social, political and economic environment. The assets controlled by public actors are highly diverse and range from motorways, rivers and forests to various old buildings (historical heritage) and more recent ones (administrative and cultural centres, schools, prisons etc).

All environmental policies [the public actors of all public policies] are endowed with varying quantities of public assets.... While the public ownership of a number of strategic infrastructures has long been considered an essential condition for the implementation of public policies, in particular those relating to spatial planning (transport, telecommunications, energy, schools, the military etc), the current processes involving liberalization and privatization of certain infrastructure (airports, telecommunications, urban networks) challenge the capacity of the state to mobilize infrastructure resources. Thus a new question arises in relation to maintaining the capacity of public actors to attain their objectives in a context in which the proportion of these infrastructure resources (for public use) held by private actors is on the increase.

Two main functions may be associated with this resource.... The first ... involves the capacity of public policy actors to directly manage a service or to impose restrictions more directly, for example in cases in which a public body is the owner or manager of such a good. It is easier to restrict public access to an ecologically sensitive area if it is owned by the state than if it is in private hands. The state can use the lever of purchasing lands to place an area under protection or for granting surface rights to enable construction (of houses) to locations that are most suited to such purposes in terms of spatial planning. Hence it is easier for the state to act in such contexts than if it must impose restrictions on private owners. For example, entire sections of the lakeshores in Switzerland are not accessible to the public, despite the fact that this contravenes the principle enshrined in federal law (Spatial Planning Act).

The second function involves the capacity for communication (in the broadest sense of the term) that this infrastructure provides the actors of the political-administrative system. The administrative assets include a vast collection of the equipment necessary to govern and, in the language of public policy, to produce implementation acts on the interface between the state and civil society. It is true that the characteristics of this equipment depend largely on the use made of them by the actors that manage the organizational and cognitive resources. Hence, administrative buildings represent a production space that enables the establishment of a multitude of communication processes between the individual members of the administrative organization in question, on the one hand, and between the latter and the target groups and/ or end beneficiaries, on the other. Thus a vast array of administrative equipment supports communication in the modern administration, be it in the form of paper, software or other IT equipment. It should be noted that this resource is undergoing a partial process of "dematerialization" today following the spread of "new communication technologies" (cyberadministration). Finally, it should also be noted that the capacity to mobilize the resource property is equally important for private actors, whether beneficiaries or target groups. (Knoepfel et al, 2010: 65-7)

Specifics

Let us recall that the analysis of this resource – and indeed the others – cannot be limited to the political-administrative actors, and that a large part of its regulation is based on private law. While the attribution of rights of use to the resources Money, Personnel and in a way, Information, is regulated by the law of obligations, that relating to the real right (right in rem) is governed by civil law (for Switzerland: Civil Code, Article 655ff: movable and immovable property) known as property. In principle, this property law is the same for public and private property. Moreover, it enjoys constitutional protection and, according to the Swiss Federal Constitution, any major limitation of the rights of use to the goods and properties covered must be compensated in full (Federal Constitution, Article 26; see also Chapter 1, this volume).

The exchange of property rights operates through the transfer of titles recorded in the land registry (immovable property) or through the transfer of possession (movable property). Such exchanges are accompanied by formal contracts of sale. This is equally applicable to the transfer of limited property rights (limited real rights such as easements or mortgages) in relation to immovable property which, to be valid, must also be included in the land registry.

It is important to note that, strictly speaking, public policy actors are not landowners or the owners of movable property. The owner is the public body that employs them. It and it alone has legal status; in the case of Switzerland, the public bodies in question are the Confederation, the cantons, the communes and other public law corporations. The federal and cantonal legislature can, however, create legal entities (for example, public establishments, public law corporations, limited companies) that have their own legal state and can, accordingly, be listed as entirely separate public owners in the land registry. All public actors involved in public policies that wish to formally mobilize the resource Property by means of property transactions or the purchase of movable property (such as computers, office materials, equipment) must approach the institutional policy actors responsible for holding and applying the immovable and movable property rights of the public body in question (at federal level, the Federal Office for Buildings and Logistics of the Federal Department of Finance; similar attributions often exist at cantonal level).

The same restrictions exist for private actors and, in particular, policy target groups that, depending on the applicable internal rules, must refer to their responsible intermediary (committee) or supreme bodies (for example, general assemblies, foundation boards). A directorate representing a member of an individual target group in policy implementation processes is not usually authorized to make unilateral decisions on property-related operations involving, for example, an exchange of lands with the state.

When we refer to the property resources of public policy actors, we are not simply referring to property operations that arise in the few policies that deploy them as action instruments (for example, structural improvement, spatial planning, infrastructure policies, such as the construction or modification of road and rail networks, the renaturation of rivers and streams). The mobilization of Property is a far more widespread phenomenon and also covers the modalities of political use that the owners make of their movable and immovable properties.

The economics of natural resources teaches us that an actor-owner holds rights of access and use to all of the goods and/or services provided by the resources (often land or water) in their possession. This fact is also important for public policy analysis. In effect, the owner exercises their rights of concrete use to their property, machines and other equipment on a daily basis. This exploitation corresponds to a behaviour that may or may not be compatible with eventual public policies. It is precisely by differentiating between uses that are favourable and unfavourable to the public interest that public policies propose to limit the freedom of choice of the owners of property resources and, moreover, at the level of both the (social) target groups and political-administrative actors – in this sense, a change in the behaviour of the target groups triggered by a public policy and considered necessary to alleviate the suffering of the policy beneficiaries in prohibiting the exercise of rights of use that are not compatible with the policy's objectives. Lawyers regularly refer to public law restrictions on ownership.

This observation applies not only to traditional policies relating to space, such as spatial planning policies, infrastructure or agricultural policies; it also applies to social policies (housing sector: limitation of land ownership; child labour sector: limitation of owners in relation to the exploitation of these property resources through child labour; social welfare sector: limitation of profits from the exploitation of property resources through the obligation to pay contributions). The same applies to incentive-based policies that aim to channel the exploitation of the target groups' property resources in a particular direction by imposing financial sanctions on modalities of exploitation that are considered negative.

It is possible to observe the emergence of a very particular resource service in this context, probably due to the quasi-universal presence of property issues in the context of public policies and the fact that property is a resource whose importance is bolstered by the very strong constitutional guarantee granted to it in Switzerland (Federal Constitution, Article 26). The service in question is *abstract* (in contrast to the aforementioned concrete service), and may be considered a *political service of the resource Property* which, in accordance with the terminology used in this book, is nothing more than the public action resource referred to here, strictly speaking, as Property, and features regularly in the resource portfolio of actor-owners (in particular, the target groups). To put it into everyday language, the owner of this resource is 'rich' and thus considered a powerful actor in the formulation and implementation of public policies. Or, to adopt the terms used in Chapter 4, the economic, social and/or environmental resources at this actor's disposal are transformed into a public action resource.

Hence there is an interaction between the two uses of Property, that is, its concrete use (lawful or unlawful modalities of exploitation of the rights of use to a resource) and abstract use (exploitation of a use right that gives the holder significant influence in the context of public policies). In effect, the abstract use rights give the owner generally acknowledged political influence in the context of public decisions dealing specifically with the concrete use of these property-related resources. Therefore it is unsurprising that, at the policy implementation level in particular, property-owning target groups enjoy a procedurally guaranteed or informal right of participation that far exceeds that of the beneficiaries (often referred to by the lawyers as 'third parties'). Hence, whether or not they live in the commune in which they hold property, owners are contacted by registered letter with requests to comment on changes in land-use plans while the beneficiaries are often only informed through the medium of an official gazette (access to which can vary considerably). It should be recalled that, before the entry into force of the Federal Act of 22 June 1979 on Spatial Planning (Article 4), such participation on the part of beneficiaries was not explicitly provided for, and that, in many cantons, the procedure for the creation of communal land-use plans resembled a quasi-contractual and bilateral process that was conducted in the form of a negotiation between the authority and property owners.

It comes as no surprise to learn that the same distinction between the concrete and abstract (political) use of property can be observed in the activities of political–administrative actors. In effect, the latter avail of this distinction in two senses through a strategic use of their assets. They suggest to their communes and/or cantons that they should acquire plots of land referred to as 'strategic', and plan the construction of their infrastructure projects there to avoid the mobilization of the resource Property by private owners, and in this way avail of the concrete use rights conferred on them through the acquired resources. By means of such operations local authorities sometimes attempt to oppose (as owners and not only as authorities) policy implementation acts that originate 'elsewhere', that is, public policies other than their own that come from the Confederation or canton and that are perceived as a threat to their own policies.

When we refer to the mobilization of the resource Property in this book, we always consider this *distinction between concrete and abstract uses*, which is sometimes difficult to make in the context of political reality (in particular, at communal level), as one supports the other and vice versa. Although this book is dedicated to the political use of property, this ambiguous relationship between the two uses is crucial. It should be noted that beneficiary groups can also acquire Property, even if this is unusual. By way of example, we can refer here to the environmental protection organizations (for example, Pro Natura, the second biggest landowner in Switzerland) that have been purchasing extensive natural lands since the 1980s with a view to protect them against degradation or to the end beneficiaries of housing policy (cooperative movements that advocate the role of both owner and tenant).

Finally, I would like to indicate that it makes sense to distinguish, in principle and for the three groups of actors, *'administrative' property from 'financial' property*. This distinction is particularly important for the political–administrative actors, as their administrative property (assets, moveable and immovable property) is a vital condition for the exercise of their public activity. For this reason, the property in question is allocated to public tasks and may not be sold or mortgaged without a formal act of abandonment (for example, the sale of the Swiss Federal Palace, national roads, but also the abandonment of surface rights, rights of public way for a country road or a communal building). It is generally considered that the state owner needs this property to provide political–administrative actors with premises, office material, communication tools and so on. The construction, modification, amortization and purchase of this property is the responsibility of an institutional policy (relating to Property) of the public law body that 'attributes' rights of use to different services, directorates etc.

As opposed to this, financial property is composed of non-allocated assets and liability and remains freely available to different public paymasters within the limits of the institutional rules concerning, for example, indebtedness, accounting methods,[1] treasury modalities and daily payments to be made. In our conception, this financial property resides in part in the resource Money. This applies equally to the two other groups of public policy actors; the interest here concerns their 'administrative' property that is necessary to the management of public policy interventions.

Property: Mobilization by availability

Property/availability: Political-administrative actors

The uses that a public policy's political-administrative actors make of the Property at their disposal tend to be relatively exclusive (appropriation: 'our' meeting room, 'our' logo, 'our' telephone numbers, 'our' software), not very communal (two different public policies rarely make use of the same premises), not very economic (offices and meeting rooms are often empty but heated and cleaned) but nonetheless respectful of the property (no use for private meetings or telephones). Moreover, these uses are increasingly more ecological in nature (the RUMBA resource management and systematic environmental management programmes at federal level target the separation of different kinds of waste, energy saving and so on) and often highly regulated (big offices for the bosses, small offices for the subordinate employees, even in cases where the subordinate employees have far more interaction with the public than the bosses).

The premises, websites and signage used by a public policy make an important contribution to its image and identity, and the infrastructure resources involved are located at the interface between the state and the public (particularly at the level of cantonal policy implementation). For this reason, the political-administrative actors also maintain the aesthetics, architecture and so on of their resource property to create a welcoming atmosphere (Consensus) in their interaction with the public (for example, cafeterias, modern art, landscaping, architecture). There is an increasing focus today on ensuring access to public administration using e-administration tools that enable target groups and beneficiaries to rapidly access different policy products (such as reports and outputs), for example, by means of electronic request forms and through the availability of geocoded data etc. Drinks events with parliamentarians (Political Support), annual press conferences (even if there is nothing new to report) and the particularly accommodating reception of the media (sometimes well monitored) are also considered part of the indispensible communication tools.

It is possible to observe an increasing 'dematerialization' of (administrative) Property resources in that public bodies are focusing on arrangements for the rental of buildings constructed by themselves and often based on the formula of 'public–private partnerships';

for example, the city of Neuchâtel recently became the tenant of a private property company that owns the football stadium, of which the commune is a shareholder.

The availability of Property provides the political-administrative actors with access to choices regarding the concrete uses they make of the resource, in particular, withdrawals by means of a transfer of financial property to the administrative property and reassignment to uses with a public interest. This enables them to implement public policy projects without being dependent on property operations that would have to be agreed on with the private property owners ('active property policy of the communes and canton').

But what do political-administrative actors who lack Property do? The example of the establishment of the canton of Jura in 1978 is a typical illustration of this problem for all cantonal public policies involving the implementation of federal policies. The day after the federal vote of 24 September that year, the new public body had to rent apartments, in particular in the commune of Delémont, to accommodate its first officials and, moreover, without being certain that it would be able to find and fund these apartments. The road traffic policy actors had to produce vehicle number plates, which were important symbols of the existence of the new canton and an integral component of the new 'Republic's' Property. It was also necessary to produce new flags and other emblematic signs attesting to the existence of the new canton.

The risk of a lack of Property renders a political decision necessary that cannot be made without access to Money. Public administration cannot function without administrative buildings, vehicles (for the police), digital information networks and signage. A lack of Property may also be caused by the profligate use or waste of space (excessively large offices and corridors), excessive maintenance costs (heating of administrative buildings during holidays) and the rental of excessively restrictive premises (lack of flexibility in the rules governing the use of conference rooms, for example, prohibition of multiple use; see 'exclusive use' in this chapter and in Chapter 4).

In the case of under-exploitation of Property, the responsible institutional policy actors will attempt to identify the causes. Based on recent experience, this process is carried out through changes at the level of accounting rules (HAM2 rules, see note 1 in this chapter). It is a well-known fact that due to the payments for buildings and, above all, materials and equipment from the operating budgets rather than investment budgets, the value of these items is one symbolic Swiss franc (fully amortized when purchased). All analytical accounting must take into account the true costs of producing public services that include the real (market) value of the administrative property and the costs associated with its maintenance and depreciation. Even if this activation of property poses problems (lack of comparable market prices), experts in public accounting agree that just a short time ago the budgets of public bodies hugely under-estimated the value of this property, and that this under-estimation constituted one of the reasons for the waste that resulted in property 'shortages' in the public sector. Its moderate activation was able to fill these gaps by obliging substantive policy actors to be more economical in their use of the properties in question.[2] The political disadvantages of such operations include the need for politicians to reduce taxes (because 'we are richer than we thought') and/or – in diametric opposition to this but arising from the same causes – the demand for increases in spending.

Property /availability: Target groups

The use of the administrative property[3] (for example, headquarter buildings, IT) for public communication and political ends appears even more marked on the part of organizations representing public policy target groups. Far from being the simple workplaces of the (political) personnel of these associations, their premises have become locations that attract journalists as well as their members. Drinks parties, exhibitions, debates, networking, training courses for lobbyists, concerts and so on are all organized there. All of this is done in the interests of maintaining the organization's image, and in this way contributes to gaining Consensus (credibility), even if such events can actually have the opposite effect (undermining credibility).

Based on what I have said about the relationship between concrete and political uses, it is obvious that the availability of the considerable (administrative) productive property of a group of companies as a target group enables them to take decisions about concrete uses of the resource (investments, extensions, closures) that will have positive or negative economic, social and/or environmental consequences for the objectives of an entire series of public policies. Hence, the scope of their property strengthens the credibility of their possible threats to refuse to change their behaviour. This demonstrates the importance of this resource as both a social (economic, social and environmental) and political basis of power.

It is difficult to identify a lack of Property among target groups. In effect, economic actors today do not necessarily attempt to become the owners of the plots, buildings or equipment they use for their production activities. The purchase of vast lands as reserves for eventual expansion is an approach that has been consigned to the past. Long-term contracts (of varying degrees of exclusivity) are preferred along with the assurance of rights of use through a financial stake in the 'new' owners, that is, real estate foundations, real estate companies and real estate funds. Compared to that of the real estate sector, which has become an entirely separate sector of the economy, the proportion of the productive sector of society's Property accounted for by land assets has declined considerably.

Despite the large number of new investment 'vehicles' on these markets, which has resulted in a high degree of opacity in relation to the real responsibility for the actual use made of land resources,[4] it would probably be incorrect to speak of a decline in the importance of Property as a resource for target groups today. Hence what we are witnessing is the transformation but not the disappearance of this resource. It is my belief that the former owners retain their control of both the concrete and political uses of the resource.

Property /availability: Beneficiary groups

As a general rule, beneficiary groups are not well endowed with Property. Nevertheless, with the increasing power of social networks, the creation and updating of a website has become an important objective of organizations representing the interests of beneficiary groups. This component of their 'business capital' enables them to maintain the resource Organization, which is important for their capacity to intervene in public policies. A website is considered even more important for them than the acquisition and operation of (expensive) premises. The virtual presence enables them to reduce the cost of maintaining physical premises without relinquishing their power of intervention. There is also a trend for them to sell expensive 'administrative' buildings in urban centres and to rent less costly buildings in suburban communes whose postal address is becoming less important as a symbolic component of their property.

If these groups had held enormous quantities of the resource Property (in the sense of the definition presented above), it would probably not have been necessary to create a public policy that protects their interests. They themselves could have decided on the use of their own funds, and this would probably not have run counter to their own interests. These groups can actually acquire property so as to attain a similar position to owners involved in public policy implementation procedures (see the example of Pro Natura previously mentioned, on p 168). A typical case is the already cited example (see Chapter 7: Law) of the leasing of a plot of land by Greenpeace located near the old Bonfol chemical landfill with the sole of aim of gaining the right of appeal against the cantonal decision relating to the remediation of the site. According to Greenpeace, the decision did not fulfil all of the requirements of the environmental legislation. The appeal was accepted by the Administrative Court of Jura in 2008.

Property: Mobilization by stage

Property /stage: Political-administrative actors

As the aforementioned examples show, the political-administrative actors primarily mobilize their Property on the level of public policy implementation. To my knowledge, major transformations of administrative property into financial property involving attempts at exploiting the resource in the form of the sale of lands, buildings or equipment have only arisen at federal level in connection with military policies. In effect, the Confederation remains the biggest landowner in Switzerland, and holds a vast portfolio of properties that were formerly used in the conduct of military policy, for example, barracks, airports, bunkers and also vehicles and other mobile equipment. The auction of objects that are considered 'saleable' (in contrast with those considered unsaleable) are common today. A similar situation can be observed in relation to railway policies whereby a distinction is made between properties that are needed to operate railways and lands that are of no direct use for the activities of the Swiss Federal Railways (SBB). The latter are placed on the property market and sold at the maximum price to cover the deficit in the SBB pension fund and other expenses.

At policy implementation level, the political mobilization of Property through assets belonging to the communes and cantons, or the Confederation (national roads), is quite customary in connection with spatial planning policies (purchase or strategic use of plots before or after the formulation of land use plans), infrastructure policies (network of secondary communal roads, railway networks, drinking water and wastewater networks in communal or intercommunal ownership, whose holders often exclude the non-owner communes intentionally so as to force them to pay sometimes exorbitant contributions for their use), education policies (construction of school buildings in public utility zones sometimes located outside development zones and thus at a low and advantageous price for the communes), economic development policies (reestablishment of surface right in an industrial zone to attract new companies), housing policies (reestablishment of surface rights to the builders of low-cost housing) and communal fiscal policy (generation of revenue through the sale of lands acquired at agricultural prices and rezoned as development land and sold to investors, based on the 'money-making machines' model).

In our terminology, all of these cases involve the exchange of Property for Money and result in an increase in the Property held by the investors, who are often the target groups of the public policy in question. If necessary, the latter can mobilize this same resource against the political-administrative actors of the policy in question, particularly in the case of the lapse of the right of surface. Accordingly, the public bodies that sell off their property risk losing political power (Property). Cantonal regional and economic policies often contribute to this exchange through tax exemptions (see the renunciation of Money, as described above).

Property /stages: Target groups

An interesting case of the mobilization of Property on the part of target groups in advance of a legislative decision at the policy programming stage arose in association with the popular vote of 2012 on the constitutional article concerning the ban on the construction of secondary residences. In effect, the members of the target groups opted to exploit their concrete rights of use in all kinds of different ways with the sole aim of proving an intention to build on the land they owned in the areas threatened with a ban on secondary residences under the new legislation. According to the legal requirements, this intention should have existed (demonstrably) prior to the date on which the new federal act entered into force.

Another example involves similar steps taken by landowners prior to the vote of March 2013 on the revision of the Spatial Planning Act that contained a provision for obliging communes to declassify some of their development zones that were considered as excessively large. The owners submitted applications for planning permission and deposited building materials on their plots to 'prove' their imminent intention to build on them and the existence of investments made prior to the entry into force of the revised legislation. As was the case before the entry into force of the emergency federal decree on emergency spatial planning measures in 1972, these measures were clearly not aimed at changing the mind of the legislature at the last minute, but at establishing an advantageous position when it came to the mobilization of Law by invoking the material expropriation of the lands through an act of refusal of planning permission or, if necessary, the right of residence for the hastily constructed building.

It should be noted, finally, that almost all changes in the behaviour of target groups prompted by an administrative or judicial decision (public policy output) involves an infringement on their assets; their response will consist in the mobilization of their Property, either in the form of the correct follow-up or a violation of the content of the decision. Thus what is involved here is a heterogeneous exchange of the resources Law (political-administrative authority) and Property (target group).

Property / stages: Beneficiary groups

Beneficiary groups can only be concretely observed availing of Property (as explained, a rare phenomenon) at the level of public policy implementation. Such action must obviously take place prior to the administrative decision considered as potentially harmful, its aim being to obtain a priority procedural position in the process of the production of the decision.

An example here is the already mentioned continuation of a policy involving the purchase of natural lands (or rights of surface etc to such lands) by the Swiss nature conservation organization Pro Natura (formerly known as the Swiss League for the Protection of Nature) following the approval of the Federal Act on the Protection of Nature and Cultural Heritage of 1966, the emergency federal decrees on emergency spatial planning measures of 1972, 1974 and 1976, and the entry into force of the Spatial Planning Act of 1979 with the main aim of saving characteristic natural landscapes. This strategy demonstrates a certain distrust of public policies on the part of the organization as, unlike landed property, they could be altered more easily and thus weaken the obligations imposed on the landowners by democratic means (communal land use plan). In this instance, Property was considered more reliable than the resources Law and Political Support (see below), which the organizations in question had at their disposal when the decisions on these different legislative acts were made by the parliamentary chambers. The protection of the properties through the possession of the corresponding titles appeared more effective to the organizations than the (often communal) decisions relating to the communal land use plans that are sometimes unpredictable and reflect the changing power relations.

Property: Exchange

Property/exchange: Political-administrative actors

The exchange of Property with target groups initiated by political-administrative actors can be homogenous (exchange of lands as part of a land reorganization process; see above) but is more often heterogeneous in nature (for example, property in exchange for Money: sale of temporally limited right of surface, sale of disused assets, properties or movable items from the administrative assets). Such exchanges regularly affect the concrete use rights of the target groups (buyers) in that these uses must be compatible with the objectives of the public policies in question, for example, housing, nature and landscape conservation, economic development (see above).

It is increasingly common for organizations that protect the interests of target groups or beneficiaries to organize their events in public spaces (squares, roads) or public buildings (such as the Federal Palace, Cantonal Chamber, meeting room in the Swiss National Bank building in Bern). The exceptional refusal of such uses (which are usually authorized for payment) on the part of the political-administrative actors involves the mobilization of their Property and Consensus in the sense that the state actors challenge the credibility of the groups requesting to use the corresponding resource.

Property/exchange: Target groups

Conversely, the target groups try to gain the trust of political-administrative actors by making their premises or equipment available to them for the meetings in which the former are involved and possibly in the majority. The political-administrative actors are well aware of the risks associated with such 'non-neutral' meeting locations and, to avoid the excessively obvious exploitation of Consensus on the part of the target groups that issue such invitations, only accept them with caution and under the condition that the topics to be discussed are clearly defined. This situation arises in particular in connection with discussions about projects that are subject to disputes at the level of cantonal or communal policy implementation.

Another case arises when the target groups propose to refrain voluntarily from making a concrete use of their property that could prompt a deterioration in the situation of the beneficiary group. This often enables them to avoid a legislative or administrative decision that they consider more restrictive than a simple 'gentlemen's agreement'.

These cases involving the proposal of self-regulation (see above) are known as strategies that are likely to prompt the political-administrative actors to refrain from mobilizing their resource Law. They are equally common at the levels of policy programming and implementation. Such – heterogeneous – exchanges of resources enable the political-administrative actors to gain Time and Personnel.

Property/exchange: Beneficiary groups

With the exception of the cases referred to below, the organizations for the protection of the interests of beneficiaries have limited portfolios of Property, and the initiative for such exchanges, whether homogenous or heterogeneous, is unlikely to come from these groups.

If appropriate, the acquisition of strategic moveable or immovable goods (see above) with the objective of gaining a right of appeal may lead to a heterogeneous exchange of resources in that the organization in question ultimately refrains from mobilizing its right of appeal if the authority alters the content of a decision that has not been challenged in principle by public opinion (complete renunciation of the exploitation of Political Support).

Recommended further reading

Textbooks and specialist literature

FDK-CDF, Conférence des directeurs cantonaux des finances (2008) *Manuel – Modèle comptable harmonisé pour les cantons et les communes – MCH2*, Bern: CDF.

Hugues, F., Hirczak, M. and Senil, N. (2006) 'Territoire et patrimoine: La co-construction d'une dynamique et de ses ressources', *Revue d'économie régionale & urbaine*, 5: 683-700.

Lajarge, R., Pecquert, B., Landel, P.-A. and Lardon, S. (2012) *Ressources territoriales: Gouvernance et politiques publiques* (https://halshs.archives-ouvertes.fr/halshs-00700760).

Lambelet, S. and Pflieger, G. (2016) 'Les ressources du pouvoir urbain', *Métropoles*, 18 (http://metropoles.revues.org/5329).

Sager, F. (2013) 'Structures politico-administratives de la politique des transports', in A. Ladner, J.-L. Chappelet, Y. Emery, P. Knoepfel, L. Mader, N. Soguel and F. Varone (eds) *Manuel d'administration publique suisse*, Lausanne: PPUR, pp 811-34.

Soguel, N. (2013) 'Présentation des états financiers publics', in A. Ladner, J.-L. Chappelet, Y. Emery, P. Knoepfel, L. Mader, N. Soguel and F. Varone (eds) *Manuel d'administration publique suisse*, Lausanne: PPUR, pp 623-44.

'In-house' applications

Dupuis, J. and Knoepfel, P. (2015) *The politics of contaminated sites management – Regime change and actors' mode of participation in the environmental management of the Bonfol chemical waste landfill in Switzerland*, Berlin and New York: Springer International.

Gerber, J.-D. (2006) *Structures de gestion des rivalités d'usage du paysage – Une analyse comparée de trois cas alpins*, Zürich and Chur: Rüegger.

Gerber, J.-D. (2016) 'The managerial turn and municipal land-use planning in Switzerland – Evidence from practice', *Planning Theory & Practice*, 17(2): 192-209.

Knoepfel, P. (2006) 'Der Staat als Eigentümer', in J.-L. Chappelet (ed) *Contributions à l'action publique = Beiträge zum öffentlichen Handeln*, Lausanne and Berne: PPUR.

Knoepfel, P., Kissling-Näf, I. and Varone, F. (2003) *Institutionelle Regime natürlicher Ressourcen in Aktion/Régimes institutionnels de ressources naturelles en action*, Basel and Genf: Helbing & Lichtenhahn.

Knoepfel, P., Csikos, P., Gerber, J.-D. and Nahrath, S. (2012) 'Transformation der Rolle des Staates und der Grundeigentümer', *PVS Politische Vierteljahresschrift*, 53(3): 414-43.

Knoepfel, P., Nahrath, S., Csikos, P. and Gerber, J.-D. (2009) *Les stratégies politiques et foncières des grands propriétaires fonciers en action: Etudes de cas*, Cahier de l'IDHEAP 247, Chavannes-près-Renens: IDHEAP.

Knoepfel, P., Kissling-Näf, I. and Varone, F. (eds) with Bisang, K., Mauch, C., Nahrath, S., Reynard, E. and Thorens, A. (2001) *Institutionelle Regime für natürliche Ressourcen: Boden, Wasser und Wald im Vergleich – Régimes institutionnels de ressources naturelles: Analyse comparée du sol, de l'eau et de la forêt*, Basel: Helbing & Lichtenhahn.

Nahrath, S. (2003) 'La mise en place du régime institutionnel de l'aménagement du territoire en Suisse entre 1960 et 1990', Thèse présentée à l'IDHEAP.

Nahrath, S., Pflieger, G. and Varone, F. (2011) 'Institutional network regimes: A new framework to better grasp the key role of infostructure', *Network Industry Quarterly*, 13(1): 23-6.

Nahrath, S., Knoepfel, P., Csikos, P. and Gerber, J.-D. (2009) *Les stratégies politiques et foncières des grands propriétaires fonciers au niveau national: Etude comparée*, Cahier de l'IDHEAP 246, Chavannes-près-Renens: IDHEAP.

Notes

[1] In Switzerland, in accordance with the 'Harmonized Accounting Model for the Cantons and Municipalities HAM2' of 2008/201; see the website of the Swiss Public Sector Financial Reporting Advisory Committee (SRS-CSPCP), Principles approved by the Conference of Cantonal Directors of Finance in January 2008 and January 2013 (amendments) (http://www.srs-cspcp.ch/).

[2] This activation does not constitute an invitation to transform the administrative property into financial property that would enable the sale or exploitation through the rental of these properties. It consists, in particular, in the demonstration of possible substitutions for a lack of Money through the mobilization of Property. Nor is this an invitation to politicians to over-activate this Property to enrich the commune and thus reduce taxes. According to its statement of October 2016, the city of Zurich reported that its wealth could have increased by several billion Swiss francs thanks to a simple modification of the accounting rules imposed by the canton of Zurich.

[3] Necessary for production and not for its funding ('financial property').

[4] 'Securitization', 'fragmentation', rising power of intermediary actors, extension of the decision-making chain, 'anonymization' of ownership and dilution of responsibilities (see Nahrath et al, 2009).

11

Information

Definition

This comprises the knowledge acquired in relation to historical or current technical, social, economic and political data about public problems to be resolved. Although they constitute an essential condition for the development and conduct of effective public policies, relevant knowledge, insight and information are scarce commodities. This is particularly true of contemporary policies which require increasingly sophisticated scientific expertise. In this respect, the successful functioning of public policies generally requires an equivalent level of knowledge of the problem among the actors involved.

The production and processing of statistical data is often assigned to a specialized state service, for example the Swiss Federal Statistical Office. It is also possible for the public actors responsible for a particular policy to organize their own data management (for example, the statistics produced by the individual federal offices in Switzerland) and for private associations to establish their own data monitoring body in parallel to that operated by the state (for example, second opinions, inspections and qualitative testing of water bodies by fishing associations and environmental NGOs, the reports compiled by the national spatial planning and environmental platform ASPAN for the cantons and communes in the context of the implementation of the Spatial Planning Act).

In the case of environmental policies, it is not uncommon for the target groups to have more cognitive resources at their disposal than the administration, for example in the area of hazardous substances (chemicals) and major risks (nuclear threats, banking etc). In these cases, the cooperation between political–administrative actors and target groups can be very close, with the latter contributing to the development of legislative instruments intended to regulate their own future behaviour, a phenomenon that points to the major challenge regarding the independence of public actors. (Knoepfel et al, 2010: 63)

Specifics

Information is in the process of becoming a veritable 'common pool good' from which the exclusion of use rights is increasingly difficult, first, on account of the enactment of all kinds of legislation regarding administrative transparency and second, due to the fact that all attempts to protect information against cybercrime (see 'Force: security systems' in Chapter 6) come up against encounter theft or diffusion techniques that are becoming increasingly sophisticated and difficult to combat effectively. Although the use rights involving addition (right to submit data) and management (right to organize data based on specific criteria enabling their traceability) (see Chapter 4, according to Olgiati Pelet, 2011) still withstand such criminal activities today, sampling activities already appear to be particularly under threat.

One of the consequences of this situation is a return to the oral exchange of information, both within the public sector and between it and the target groups and beneficiaries, for example, through the exchange of information in restaurants, on golf courses, or during walks in the open air.

Information: Mobilization by availability

Information /availability: Political-administrative actors

It is virtually impossible for political administrative actors to conduct public policy without a minimum of current and/or historical information concerning phenomena as varied as the status and evolution of the public problem to be resolved as perceived by the future policy beneficiaries, the behaviour of the actors assumed to be at the root of this problem (causal hypotheses), the social composition and spatial distribution etc of these actors that are possibly to be defined as target groups of the policy in question, and institutional or social factors that determine their behaviour, for example. With a view to avoiding errors in the construction of the causality model of the policy in question, the political–administrative actors should compile solid dossiers before proposing the creation of new public policies or projects for the revision of existing ones, in this case, based on the evaluative statements. This also applies to the development of action plans and outputs at cantonal level.

The use of this information is regulated to a greater extent in the case of administrative procedures for the production of outputs and to a lesser extent in the case of the production of legislation. The political-administrative actors are required, in particular, to document the data and sources and not to divulge the protected data (data protection), and to provide a 'cautious' interpretation of these data by contextualizing them adequately.

These data are frequently challenged, in particular at the level of policy implementation. Whether they relate, for example, to the environmental impacts of major infrastructure projects, the estimation of the market value of a plot of land, the extent of an individual's invalidity, the safety of a workplace, or the flood risk of a plot of land, according to the rule of law, the state must 'prove' with the help of reliable indicators that the current state of the phenomenon in question does not correspond to that postulated by the political–administrative programme. This often very local information is increasingly available today in the form of geocoded data (geographical information systems, GIS). Thanks to the resolution of such data improving from one year to the next, such databases enable the very rapid mobilization of the Information. Hence the cantonal administrations have access to information today that is geocoded at plot level for the collection of all the data necessary for the granting of planning permission (for example, is the plot located in a protected zone, a zone at risk from flooding or avalanches, near a contaminated site?).

With the aim of increasing the coherence of public policies, automatic systems for the exchange of information exist, in particular in relation to (international and intercantonal) fiscal policy, the prevention of criminality (Interpol), health policies (automatic exchange of information on an individual's state of health) and social policies (coordination between unemployment, invalidity and social welfare policies). Any exchange of information between sectoral policies raises the problem regarding the protection of the private data of individuals.

The non-use of Information on the part of political-administrative actors may be imposed by law in areas defined as 'sensitive' (for example, protection of data in the areas of public health, safety, professional confidentiality and in the context of fiscal policies). Likewise, the penal courts are obliged to disregard evidence that is obtained fraudulently. The political-administrative actors may also use Information as a threat or indeed refrain from its use if this appears expedient for the pursuit of their strategic objectives.

Examples of such threats include the use of information that is protected in principle if it is not revealed voluntarily by a member of the target group. This situation can arise in areas as varied as fiscal policy, social policy (access to personal medical information), security policy (exchange of information within Interpol), the policy for monitoring chemical products, and particularly in the context of often highly regulated implementation procedures. The second case is one that affects the entire generation of public policy products and involves the strategic use of confidential information or the intentional withholding of information (for example, attribution of confidential status to documents). Such strategies, which contravene legislation on federal and cantonal administrative transparency in principle and have become considerably more common in recent times, may enable the political-administrative actors to gain sometimes important advantages in their negotiations with other political-administrative actors and/or the target groups or beneficiaries of the public policies in question. Examples of this can be found in all public policies at critical stages in which they risk losing their Political Support due to 'scandals' that attract extensive media coverage ('confessions' made in instalments as public pressure increases).

The situation involving the lack of detailed information on the part of the political-administrative actors involved in the programming, implementation and/or evaluation of public policies is a recurrent phenomenon. If they do not succeed in obtaining useful and sufficiently reliable information themselves, the state actors are supposed to obtain it through an exchange of resources, in particular with the target groups and NGOs that both hold this information, sometimes complementarily (see below). This kind of situation shows the dependency that exists between public actors and civil society and, in particular, policy target groups.

In this context, some observers even refer to a veritable lack of autonomy on the part of the state, which is 'captured' by target groups. This lack manifests among other things in this dependence in relation to information. Accordingly, environmental policy cannot be well managed without detailed information about the emissions of atmospheric pollutants and greenhouse gases generated by the different companies involved; an economic policy is crucially dependent on the availability of data on the order books of industry, trade and services; agricultural policy cannot be implemented without access to the data on the actual state of ecological compensation areas on the level of the individual farms; and again, the imminent implementation of the policy to prevent the construction of secondary residences is only possible if the property owners provide credible information about the use they will make of their newly constructed houses.

Information/availability: Target groups

It should be noted, first, that the information necessary for the good functioning of many public policies is in the hands of the target groups. Hence it is crucial that both the individual members of target groups (in particular those in the context of implementation procedures) and the organizations that protect their interests provide access to this information in the course of the interaction with the relevant authorities and policy beneficiaries. Depending on the circumstances, the owners make defensive or offensive, permanent or sporadic use of this information (release of information in stages). An example here is the publication of all kinds of economic data that are crucial for economic policies like labour market policy, the Swiss National Bank's interest rate policy (in particular, the order book data surveyed regularly by the national business organization, economiesuisse), the publication of data used to obtain supplementary spending in the context of anticyclical economic policies (offensive use) and conversely, to demonstrate the harmful impacts of a given measure on the development of the economy (defensive use).

Such strategies for the use of Information are also found in the microcosms of policy implementation processes, at both cantonal and federal levels: for example, the authorization of arms exports, placement of chemical products on the market. They can be observed in relation to the development of action plans (for example, the use of data on the emissions of atmospheric pollutants to obtain a plan with measures for the prevention of atmospheric pollution to the advantage of a specific economic sector) and obviously, the development of administrative decisions (for example, patchy information in a planning application file, environmental impact studies that minimize the effects of a project, fraudulent tax declarations, manipulation of accounting data). It should be noted that such information also plays a role in the development of evaluative statements, for which similar strategies can be found on the part of target groups that are aimed at obtaining an evaluation that is favourable to their interests, for example, to 'prove' that a policy implementation process is too schematic, bureaucratic or detrimental to economic development.

In general the portfolios of target groups are quite well stocked with technical, economic and legal information (including the standards produced by private standardization bodies). This applies, in particular, to the data necessary for the programming of public policies. Two examples involving a lack of information that assumed a certain importance in the past are worthy of mention here. The first involves the geocoded data on the (often not very transparent) property markets, which are indispensible to the management of properties and the eventual granting of planning permission by the communal or cantonal administration. It will come as no surprise to learn that the property sector, which was previously opposed to any transparency in relation to the property market, eventually welcomed the Federal Act on Geoinformation, which was enacted in the first decade of this century and contains provisions for the creation of a record, similar to the land registry, containing the limitations under public law affecting every plot of land in Switzerland. The collection of these data for the purpose of completing a property transaction remains a tedious task today: the data in question are documented within a number of administrative services. Another example is that of public tendering policy whereby the cantonal and communal administrations often withhold information about the companies that win the contracts from the losing competitors. This situation, which also arises in other areas, can lead to internal conflict between competitors within one and the same target group.

Given that the target groups have to take medium- and long-term investment decisions, these groups sometimes find themselves lacking information about possible changes in the legislative framework (for example, eventual bans on chemical products, changes in interest rates, changes in the classification of plots of land that are of interest to them) that will have either direct repercussions on their decisions or on the implementation practices that are liable to change in the future (such as the content of planning permission, an airline operating licences, licences for the withdrawal of water, new obligations in relation to rehabilitation measures for minimum flow rates in streams located downstream of mountain dams).

Information /availability: Beneficiary groups

As mentioned in the Introduction to this book, from the 1980s, the organizations protecting the interests of public policy beneficiaries became the systematic observers of public policy outcomes. As a result, they have assumed an increasingly prominent role at the level of policy implementation activities, particularly in relation to cantonal policies: they track at close range the production of outputs and changes in the behaviour of target groups in the different sectors of public action (collection of monitoring data that can demonstrate the evolution of the public problems targeted by the sectoral policies).

According to the strategic objectives pursued by the organizations in question, the use of this information presents similarities to the use made of it by the target groups and/or political administrative actors (see above). Based on their objectives, which differ from those of the target groups, the information used by the NGOs in question often assumes a character that is considered 'polemical', particularly by the target groups. In effect, the proportion of information agreed by common accord on the part of the two groups is often far smaller than the proportion that is contested in terms of the actual content or that of the interpretation of statistical data (which are not contested in themselves), A simple glance at the daily newspapers demonstrates the breadth of the strategies adopted by NGOs in relation to the use of 'counter-information' in the programming, implementation and evaluation of public policies as varied as those governing the exportation of arms, the remediation of contaminated sites, disability (invalidity insurance), social welfare (financial status) and public health (closure of regional hospitals).

Like the beneficiaries, the target groups have a large portfolio of informational resources today. However, they can encounter situations at the level of policy implementation processes involving the blocking of information relating to action plans or the locations of future infrastructure, in particular, controversial installations (nuclear waste disposal sites, extension of airport runways, locations planned for the accommodation of asylum-seekers), which the political-administrative actors withhold intentionally so as to prevent the mobilization of opposition on the part of these groups. Similarly, these groups sometimes decry the lack of transparency around mass layoffs planned by major public and private companies, which are of crucial importance to the state of the local or regional labour market, and thus prevent the adoption of preventive measures at the level of regional labour market policies.

The strategies adopted to overcome this lack of information consist mainly in the homogenous or heterogeneous exchange of resources that vary in terms of their legality: for example, the mobilization of Law by demanding the publication of data to which the public has a right of access according to the legislation governing the transparency of public administrations, and the use of Force in the form of the theft of data on the financial situation of foreign taxpayers by a bank employee who deems the banking secrecy that protects rich taxpayers at the expense of all other 'respectable' tax payers as unjust.

Information: Mobilization by stage

Information/ stage: Political-administrative actors

The political-administrative actors must have access to the aforementioned information to prepare the legislative decisions to be taken during the policy programming stage. Thus the public authorities must acquire this information in advance of the decision-making, either by producing it themselves or through the exchange of resources. To obtain these data they are sometimes obliged to modify the content of the legislation to the advantage of the suppliers of the information in question. If this information is not reliable, complete and correct, the risk arises that the proposed public action will not conform to reality at implementation level and the policy will fail. However, it is also highly likely that the suppliers of information, particularly the target groups, have no interest in providing biased information to the administration as such misinformation can have negative impacts for them, too.

The public authority would be ill-advised to stop availing of information resources when making legislative decisions or implementing policies or, even worse, to discard the information that forms the basis of its decision-making, for example, when a public representative leaves office, an administrative body moves premises or during other 'storage' operations. All public policies need a 'memory' that exceeds that of the physical actors that participated directly in the creation of its products. Archives make all of the historical data available that was considered important during the different policy production processes. A good archiving system requires effective record management that tracks documents with a public interest from their creation. This has become indispensable for making documentary public information 'memorizable' (principle of written rather than oral record), for deciding on whether or not to archive information, and finally, for the proper management of the memorized stocks of information (in physical or electronic archives) with the help of a reliable meta-information system (catalogue) that makes these documents accessible to all in the future. This mobilization of Information for historic data is supplemented by the collection of new information. This information documents the development of data stored in the form of tracking that is often necessary due to the simple fact that time passes between the production of the different products of the public policy cycle and that these data can evolve rapidly.

Similarly, it is recommended that the political-administrative actors involved in policy implementation adopt tracking mechanisms in the form of the regular monitoring of the behaviour of target groups, for example, the need for a residence permit or operating licence after the granting of planning permission, the inspection of buildings, the issuing of automatic requests for information about production volumes, the evolution of jobs, for example, in relation to regional economic policy. In addition, the implementing authorities will establish the monitoring of the local and/or regional evolution of the problem to be resolved by the policy in question, for example, spatial planning observatories, regular measurement of the state of the air, soil, water and so on, collection of data on road traffic accidents, the state of the health of risk groups. When carried out on a long-term basis, this kind of monitoring greatly facilitates the development of future evaluative statements, which are increasingly required by modern legislation.

Information /stage: Target groups

Due to the cyclical structure of public policy processes, the target groups also have an interest in mobilizing their Information resources well in advance of the decision-making about the programme so that it is taken into account in good time by the decision-makers. Along with the organizations for the protection of the interests of beneficiaries, the umbrella organizations of the business world criticize the often very tight deadlines set for federal and cantonal legislative projects. This concerns very technical draft ordinances in particular, as the formulation of advance notice about them often requires the mobilization of large volumes of technical and legal data.

The target groups also develop a policy of archiving and record management of varying degrees of sophistication, and are sometimes even obliged to do this under specialized legislation, for example, legislation on chemical products and limited companies. This facilitates, for example, the tracing of the process of the development of pharmaceutical products or the different stages in the construction of major technical installations that present varying degrees of vulnerability to the impacts of technical or natural disasters. This accumulation of historical data does not primarily serve the interests of historians, but those of insurers and the courts that must decide in cases involving litigation about civil responsibility in the event of an accident. These data are also used to establish the composition of the construction materials used in 'end-of-life' buildings with a view to recycling these materials. In general, the interest of the target groups in the monitoring of these data coincides with that of the beneficiary groups and political-administrative actors, and such monitoring centres are often jointly managed as a result (see above).

Information /stage: Beneficiary groups

Although they are primarily interested in the provision of data about policy implementation, the organizations that protect the interests of beneficiaries are also interested in mobilizing their informational resources during the development stage of public policies. For example, these groups gained the confidence of their peers among environmental policy actors (Consensus) by carrying out serious, scientifically based work on atmospheric pollution (forest death), deterioration in soil quality (polluted sites) and more recently, the green economy and climate warming. Moreover, the results of various popular votes on environmental questions also demonstrate their capacity to mobilize Political Support through the consistent mobilization of Information. Credit for similar successes is due to NGOs working in the areas of health (battles against cancer, smoking and alcoholism), road safety (reckless driving) and the situation of women, in which they have become experts.

For different reasons, the beneficiary groups probably have a greater interest than the other two groups in using Information during the policy implementation stage. This may be due to their sometimes relatively precarious position in the decision-making processes relating to policy programming in which they can easily be placed in the minority. Their interest is simply based on the fact that they are the first actors affected by the policies in question as they are, by definition, the actors that suffer from the existence of the problem to be resolved. As a result, complex administrative procedures feature a proliferation of second opinions, references to the results of scientific research that challenge the base data of the administration or target groups, and the mobilization of scientists who are willing to represent the beneficiary groups on advisory committees for local, cantonal and federal projects.

Information: Exchange

Information /exchange: Political-administrative actors

What applies to all public policies is particularly applicable to the political-administrative actors: the homogenous exchange of Information probably accounts for over half of the resource exchanges that can be observed in reality. Even the processes of exchange involving other resources discussed in this book are accompanied by intensive exchanges of information that announce, threaten or recall such exchanges. Provided that the use of physical force does not arise, the exchange of insults and violent or mendacious words constitutes a homogenous exchange of information. Obviously, like the other exchanges of resources, since time immemorial such exchanges have been regulated by means of rules of different types as varied as linguistic rules (spelling, grammar), codes prohibiting the declaration of information considered insulting or mendacious, for example, and behavioural codes rooted in societal mores.

Hence the debates engaged in parliamentary commissions, the plenary sessions in the chambers, the submission of reports to the political-administrative actors, the statement of opposition during a public enquiry procedure and the debate of an appeal in an administrative court are considered as homogenous exchanges of Information. These examples demonstrate the obvious need to structure the process of exchange in detail depending on the location and function of the exchange so as to avoid imbalances of power between the participants (the right to speak) and to maintain what Habermas refers to as the 'discursivity' of the debate.

The spaces or platforms for the exchange of Information are regulated for each of the six public policy products to a greater (administrative procedure, legislative procedure) or lesser (procedure for defining the problem to be resolved and today, evaluation procedure) extent. The example of non-litigious administrative procedure is a prime example that is drawn, moreover, from the ancestral rules of civil litigation (Roman law). Its rules structure the procedure in different stages and thus guarantee the predictability of the progression of the decision-making process for all of the parties involved. This example shows, moreover, that the exchange of Information is also a process of resource exchange between the state and civil society actors (and not merely an exchange of information within the state itself).

The structure of these exchanges may derive from questions and answers prompted by the political-administrative actors (the latter initiate the exchange by submitting reports, draft legislation, decision proposals and so on to the other two groups) or questions and answers prompted by the target groups and/or beneficiaries (questions regarding the technical requirements of a company and response to the question by a cantonal administrative service). However, the exchange can also be triggered by the unilateral spreading of information, of which the other actor takes note. In this case, the act of exchange by the recipient consists in the reference to this information − or not − in the form of its integration into the brief of the political-administrative actor in question.

Despite the aforementioned observation that all heterogeneous exchanges of Information and other resources are accompanied by a homogenous exchange of Information, it makes sense to refer to heterogeneous exchanges when the information in question is of real value to each of the two actors involved. In effect, one actor (the giver) has a certain interest in considering this resource as an asset and the other (the recipient) cannot act reasonably without receiving it. It is important to remember, moreover, that these conditions of exchange are necessary for all heterogeneous exchanges of all categories of resources.

Information /exchange: Target groups

The target groups are increasingly at the origin of homogenous exchanges of Information in that they strongly influence the policy agenda through the exploitation of events that receive a lot of media exposure. The political-administrative actors cannot fail to respond to this information or at least take it into consideration.

The target groups, in particular, are often behind such exchanges if they believe that the use of the information by the political-administrative actors will have a positive influence on the legislative (programming) or administrative (outputs) decision-making. In such specific cases, they gain Political Support in return for their proposals – Political Support in the sense that their proposals become capable of obtaining majority support (*mehrheitsfähig*) – and/or they obtain Consensus from the other two actor groups involved in the implementation process, for example, through the renunciation of an appeal by the beneficiary groups or other political-administrative actors.

Moreover, it is possible to observe an increase in the exchange of Information for payment (co-financing of pharmaceutical research carried out in a company through technology promotion policy) and exchanges of the same resources, also for payment or in exchange for other favours, in that the target groups are willing to disclose confidential information in their possession to accelerate the programming or implementation of a specific public policy: for example, the renunciation of patent secrecy before the expiry date for drugs required for development aid policy. In the latter case, the company in question often aims to gain good will by acquiring Consensus from the political-administrative actors and/or beneficiaries.

Information /exchange: Beneficiary groups

The heterogeneous exchange initiated by the beneficiary groups (primarily with the political administrative actors but sometimes also with the target groups) probably arises in relation to the same resources as the exchange initiated by the target groups. It should be noted that the value of this information (held by organizations that protect the interests of beneficiaries) only exists if there is a real interest in the existence and extent of the public problem that is considered as a serious, urgent and dangerous matter for society, for example, acts of vandalism and violence among young people. The beneficiaries expect the mobilization of Law and/or Political Support on the part of the political-administrative actors in return.

Recommended further reading

Textbooks and specialist literature

Calenge, B. (2008) *Bibliothèques et politiques documentaires à l'heure d'internet*, Paris: Editions du cercle de la librairie.

Glassey, O. (2013) 'Administration en ligne: Quand les utilisateurs deviennent des agents publics', in A. Ladner, J.-L. Chappelet, Y. Emery, P. Knoepfel, L. Mader, N. Soguel and F. Varone (eds) *Manuel d'administration publique suisse*, Lausanne: PPUR, pp 423-42.

Hess, C. and Ostrom, E. (2005) 'A framework for analyzing the knowledge commons: A chapter from "Understanding knowledge as a commons: From theory to practice"', *Libraries' and Librarians' Publications*, 21.

ISO 22310 (2006) *Informations et documentations – Lignes directrices pour les redacteurs de normes pour les exigences de 'records management' dans les normes*.

Lochard, Y. and Simonet-Cusset, M. (2003) 'Entre science et politique: Les politiques du savoir dans le monde associatif', *Lien social et politiques*, 50: 127-34.

Mettler, T., Rohner, P. and Winter, R. (2010) 'Towards a classification of maturing models in information systems', in A. D'Atri, M. de Marco, A. Braccini and F. Cabiddu (eds) *Management of the interconnected world*, Physica-Verlag HD, pp 333-40.

Padioleau, J.-G. (1999) 'L'action publique post-moderne: Le gouvernement politique des risques', *Politiques et management public*, 17(4): 85-127.

Pasquier, M. (ed) (2013a) *Le principe de la transparence en Suisse et dans le monde*, Lausanne: PPUR.

Pasquier, M. (2013b) 'Communication de l'administration et des organisations publiques', in A. Ladner, J.-L. Chappelet, Y. Emery, P. Knoepfel, L. Mader, N. Soguel and F. Varone (eds) *Manuel d'administration publique suisse*, Lausanne: PPUR, pp 401-22.

Radaelli, C. (2000) 'Logiques de pouvoir et *récits* dans les politiques publiques de l'Union Européenne', *Revue française de science politique*, 50(2): 255-75.

'In-house' applications

Kissling-Näf, I. (1996) *Lernprozesse und Umweltverträglichkeitsprüfung: Staatliche Steuerung über Verfahren und Netzwerkbildung in der Abfallpolitik*, Basel and Frankfurt am Main: Helbing & Lichtenhahn.

Knoepfel, P. and Wey, B. (2006) *Öffentlich-rechtliche Eigentumsbeschränkungen (ÖREB): Bestand nach Bundesgesetzgebung und ausgewählten Detailuntersuchungen*, Working Paper from l'IDHEAP no 7/2006, Chavannes-près-Renens: IDHEAP.

Olgiati Pelet, M. (2011) *Nouveau regard sur l'information documentaire publique – Régulation d'une ressource en émergence dans l'univers des archives, des bibliothèques et de l'administration suisse*, Zürich and Chur: Rüegger.

Weidner, H., Knoepfel, P. and Zieschank, R. (1992) *Umwelt-Information. Berichterstattung und Informationssysteme in zwölf Ländern*, Berlin: Edition Sigma.

12

Organization

Definition

This resource involves two partly complementary dimensions: first, the internal organizational characteristics of the different actors and, second, the quality of the network that links the different actors within a policy configuration or network. Thus the organizational resources available to actors vary according to the actors' characteristics (relevance of the organization of an actor's administrative structures) as does the quality of the network that keeps them in contact with the world outside the organization. Therefore the capacity of an actor to bring together or link other actors involved in a given public policy space in a network that links them to each other and in which they occupy a central position is a good example of the mobilization of this interactive resource. There is no doubt that this resource is also fundamental to the organizations that represent the interests of policy beneficiaries and target groups.

An organization that is functionally adapted to its institutional, physical, political and social environment makes it possible to improve the quality of the services provided while reducing the use of some resources (for example, personnel and time) or increasing the use of others (for example, consensus and information). Thus a strongly hierarchized structure tends to undermine the accountability of officials working in direct contact with the administered citizens or "clients". Moreover this kind of organization tends to fragment the processes for the management of dossiers and this, in turn, can alter the quality of administrative services. Nor does it allow the introduction of transverse coordination and monitoring functions which ensure the coherence of public policy programming and implementation, for example, in the conduct of environmental impact studies. According to the new wording of the Federal Act on the Organization of the Government and Administration Organization Act (GAOA),[1] in terms of federal public actors, organizational competency for the creation and modification of federal offices and their allocations reverts to the Federal Council. (Knoepfel et al, 2010: 64–5)

Specifics

For a public policy's political–administrative actors and its two groups of social actors, the mobilization of Organization means involving other actors that, based on their mission, are part of the same public policy structure. This may even consist in referring to superior actors that do not usually become involved – or only sporadically – in the everyday production of the policy product in question. This is particularly true of 'controversial' cases, such as the production of supplementary reports on controversial aspects of a federal legislative procedure; such reports are subject to the exceptional approval of the Federal Council (and not only the head of the federal department responsible for their compilation) prior to being submitted to the parliamentary advisory committee that commissioned them. Another example is the exceptional involvement of a councillor of state (member of the cantonal government) in a simple planning permission procedure at cantonal level.

This recourse to other actors, either belonging to the policy in question or external actors that may or may not belong to the political–administrative system, is only possible if the organizational environment of the actor in question is adequately 'structured', that is, actors exist that, based on their mission and professional profile, are eligible to give advice, and that this environment is 'accessible' thanks to well-oiled procedures that enable them to be consulted.

Figure 12.1 presents two possible models for the circulation of a planning application file within the 'involved' administrations. In this particular case, the dossier concerns a request for planning permission for the construction of a large shopping centre (with or without a residential district land-use plan). The different actors (black circles) express their positions through (binding or non-binding) advance notices. This work is generally done by the smallest specialized units within the different administrations (that is, federal administration: sections; cantonal and communal administrations: services). Their advance notices are usually signed by the head of the service or section heads within the services. The communal structures can differ considerably depending on the size of the commune in question. Today, all average-sized communes have specialized services; however, dossiers

Figure 12.1: Simple and complex modes of circulation of identical planning applications

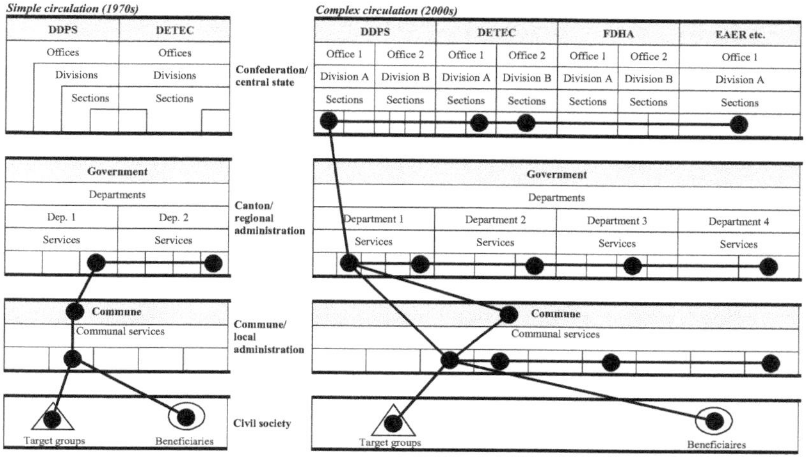

Notes: DDPS: Federal Department of Defence, Civil Protection and Sport (aspects of national security in the broadest sense)

DETEC: Federal Department of the Environment, Transport Energy and Communication (environment, energy and public transport)

FDHA: Federal Department of Home Affairs (aspects of public health)

EAER: Federal Department of Economic Affairs, Education and Research (aspects of economic promotion policy)

are generally signed (or countersigned) by the city council in charge of the local government division in question or by the communal president. The target groups are the parties requesting the planning permission and the beneficiaries are the citizens who participate in the public inquiry procedure.

The simple circulation process (left) shows how such dossiers were processed in the 1970s when the number of public policies of a spatial nature was still very limited (spatial planning in particular); this is why the number of political-administrative actors involved in the process is low. The right-hand part of the diagram presents the outline of the process that the same kind of dossier is subject to in the early 21st century. The number of public policies of a spatial nature has increased significantly and, depending on the size of the project in question, the dossier must also go through specialized services of the Confederation for advance notice. Accordingly, the number of actors involved in the administrative procedure has increased exponentially.

The two parts of Figures 12.1 and 12.2 represent two different political-administrative arrangements (PAA) for one and the same category of outputs: in this example, the granting of planning permission for large shopping centres that will generate considerable road traffic. For example, the expansion of these arrangements (right-hand side of Figure 12.2) will have strong repercussions on the duration of the processing of the dossiers, and this will be condemned as excessive in the cantonal public debate. It should be noted that the structure of simple or complex PAAs will depend, in part at least, on political decisions regarding the importance attributed by these political instances to territorial development and the environmental impacts of such projects. The principle of the formal concentration of procedures (a single procedure for a complex building on one and the same site), which was introduced at federal level in 2000, boosts the trend towards the increasing complexity of procedures.

Figure 12.2: The dilemma of divided loyalties

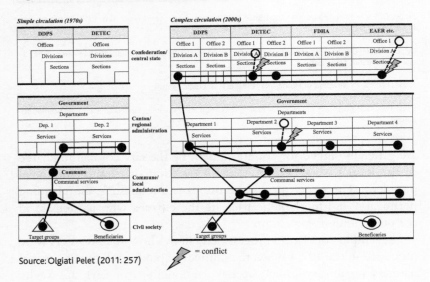

Source: Olgiati Pelet (2011: 257)

Figure 12.2, which is almost identical to Figure 12.1, demonstrates how the PAAs are rendered fragile by the multiple interdependencies between the different hierarchical lines within the federal, cantonal and communal administrations. Each of the actors involved may find themselves exposed to two potentially contradictory loyalties: first, loyalty to all of the other (federal, cantonal and communal) political-administrative actors that together constitute the network of the defined implementation arrangement for each of the output groups through the mechanism of the circulation of dossiers; and second, to the decisions of a more or less political nature taken by their superior. Thus it is possible that in the case of highly politicized dossiers, an implementation process will be blocked by the head of a cantonal department despite the agreement of all of the specialist actors of the PAA in question, who confirm that the project in question is compliant with the legal requirements for which they are responsible. Figure 12.2 demonstrates such a case (dotted line).

Organization: Mobilization by availability

Organization/availability: Political-administrative actors

As mentioned in Chapter 1, all federal political-administrative actors involved in public policies are usually based in an administrative and political environment that is structured hierarchically in sections (smallest units), divisions, federal offices and federal departments (ministries). Based on their mission, they occupy a position that gives them the right and obligation to fulfil a certain function within the policy in question (mobilization of Law).

This position is defined both by their membership of the entire group of political-administrative actors that are supposed to contribute to the production of a specific public policy product (structural component: structural organization) and by the temporal modalities of their intervention (procedural organization). Through their qualification as a political-administrative actor, the actor in question can mobilize the 'hierarchy'[2] if necessary. This also applies to the other social actors who, in important cases, will invoke a 'general assembly' or mobilize their members, for example, in the case of a referendum campaign. This organizational environment also structures the interactions between the political-administrative actors of a public policy and the two other social actors (external interaction as opposed to the aforementioned internal interaction).

A political-administrative actor has access to Organization under the condition that it is integrated into its environment through the procedures provided for by the 'cultural mores' or, increasingly, the explicit provisions of the public policy in question (specific institutional rules) and legislative documents dealing with the organization of the entire federal, cantonal and communal public administration. These documents are generally governmental in nature and based on parliamentary laws.[3]

For the political-administrative actors involved in sectoral policies, making use of Organization means including actors from their environment to a greater or lesser extent in the programming and/or implementation of the policy in question (inter-policy coordination). The recourse to this resource enables them, among other things, to increase their portfolio of Personnel, Time, Consensus and Political Support. This recourse is increasingly advisable or rendered obligatory by legislation on the organization of the public administration, in particular, in relation to cantonal policy implementation – the obligation of formal and material coordination. However, the political-administrative actors still enjoy a certain freedom of choice in their use of this resource today.

For example, the groundwater section of the Water Division of the Federal Office for the Environment – the political-administrative actor with responsibility for the federal programming of the protection of water catchments for the supply of drinking water from groundwater – should not always mobilize its Organization so as to avoid antagonizing its sister sections with responsibility for surface water bodies and water quality, which are merely peripheral political-administrative actors in relation to 'its' water catchment protection policy. Thus the latter will only be included in dossiers dealing with problems on the interface between groundwater and surface water, for example, the renaturation of watercourses. Similarly, the cantonal spatial planning services responsible for granting planning permission will not involve the different sections of the environmental protection service in every planning permission procedure. They will only involve them in cases where the structure in question could have significant environmental impacts. Nonetheless, these actors can mobilize their Organization resources if necessary, as they are freely available.

The renunciation of access to Organization may well produce effects that may be positive or negative depending on the point of view of the target groups and/or beneficiaries, in that the regulation of the public problem will take aspects into account – or not – that may have a significant political impact, for example, in the aforementioned case, the interaction between groundwater and surface waters. If necessary the political-administrative actors can also threaten to make more direct use of Organization by stating that another administrative service may become involved if the applicant does not alter their plans. Accordingly, the implementation of an environmental impact assessment, which, by its nature, considerably increases the number of services involved in a planning permission procedure, constitutes a real threat that usually results in the modification of the project in question by the applicant.

For this reason, the reorganization of administrations, which varies in scope and is aimed at making public action more efficient and/or effective, is a common occurrence. The issue of effectiveness is often behind structural and/or procedural changes that facilitate the accommodation of 'lateral' public policies. The omission of this phenomenon in the past often resulted in the production of incoherent policy outputs compared to the inputs developed by other public policies.

The political-administrative actors carry out changes to their Organization when they have to set up a new administrative structure to accommodate new tasks. Such situations are common at federal level but also at the level of cantonal policy implementation structures, in particular, since the 1970s, with the mass emergence of new sectoral policies. At the time, such structures were built more or less from scratch in the area of energy policy (energy saving in buildings), social policy (regional employment offices), environmental policy (for example, expansion of old water protection services to include the 'new environmental policies' on air, noise, hazardous substances), aliens policy (reception centres for asylum-seekers) and economic promotion policy (regional policies).

Later on these modifications consisted in the introduction of new horizontal or vertical coordination procedures, for example, environmental policies: environmental impact assessment; cantonal and federal sustainability policies: sustainability assessment; social policies: coordination procedures between policies relating to unemployment, disability and social welfare; agricultural policy: 'ecologization' of agriculture; spatial planning policy: formal and material coordination of procedures.

Situations can be observed today involving the extreme exploitation of Organization with the objective of saving on other public action resources such as Personnel, Money and Force. This practice has often led to the creation of veritable building sites for administrative reorganization, processes that have been implemented in the public sector with increasing rapidity from the 1990s. This need for reorganization was – and still is – often an expression of the desire on the part of specific public policies to overcome the administrative compartmentalization of their environment, through which they acknowledge a certain degree of interconnectivity (procedural reorganization). These reorganization processes can involve, in particular, the amalgamation of services, for example, the successive amalgamations of the Federal Office for the Environment with, first, the Swiss Agency for Forests and Landscapes and then with the old Office for Hydrology. These processes unfolded simultaneously with the emerging recognition of the interconnectivity of different ecological systems. Similar processes also arose on the level of the cantonal administrations, for example, environmental policy: integration of forest, water and so-called grey environmental policies; and education policy: integration of special education, standard education and professional training of people with disabilities.

Due to these amalgamations public authorities in Switzerland today include fewer federal offices and cantonal services than in the 1990s. The latest major shift at federal level involved the amalgamation of policies relating to professional training policies and technological promotion (previously the Federal Office for Professional Education and Technology) with third-level education policies (universities of applied sciences, research universities) within the new State Secretariat for Education, Research and Innovation (SERI). This state secretariat was allotted to the Department of Public Economics. This development is also an expression of the desire to move education and third-level research closer to the world of business (see below).

If, despite the creation of new services and/or the reorganization of existing ones, the political-administrative actors do not succeed in consolidating their interactional resources, they can then deploy the organizational resources of the target groups and/or beneficiary groups (see below).

Organization/availability: Target groups

The interests of target groups are often represented by major organizations with the legal structure of an association or sometimes, of a company or foundation. Specific decisional structures, which differentiate between the competencies of the general assembly, its committee, its board and presidency, are provided for each type of body under civil law. Regarding so-called 'policy' dossiers, structures also exist that allocate decision-making competencies to people holding posts dedicated to these areas and, moreover, procedures to be followed in the production of decisions. These structures can be cumbersome and rigid or conversely, relatively flexible and light. They dictate the rhythm of decision-making in relation to the use of the available action resources, which is often imposed on the decision-makers by the political-administrative agenda. For example, an excessively cumbersome organization that requires the frequent 'democratic' involvement of the general assembly (for example, with a minimum deadline for the convocation of the assembly and mandatory definition of the agenda in the convocation) may affect the rapid use of available public action resources, in particular, in emergency situations that may be encountered by a public policy.

In general, these structures and the decisional procedures that define the Organization held by the target groups are, however, 'lighter' than those found in public administration. They often involve ad hoc 'working groups', teleconferences and cooperation between different associations with a shared interest in a particular issue. They also appear to have a greater capacity to mobilize public action resources with the help of access to organizational, flexible resources. This does not preclude the respect of (civil law) rules that make it possible, for example, to avoid the circumvention of the views of members of the secretariat or management by the presidency. The 'lightest' structure of this type is probably that of the simple partnership (*société simple*), as exemplified by the group representing the Basel chemical industry in the first stage of the negotiations on the remediation of the Bonfol chemical landfill in the canton of Jura.

The more similar or identical the interests of the represented target groups and the fewer they are in number, the easier it is to convene meetings of the target groups in question. This is one of the most important differences between the representation of the interests of target groups and that of the interests of beneficiaries or 'public' interest itself.

When Organization fails to function correctly, the umbrella organizations representing the interests of the target groups will embark on similar reorganization processes to those described in the public administration. This process can include the establishment of greater internal differentiation (creation of new units in the context of personnel policy), simplification of procedures (amalgamation of units considered as having operated too autonomously in the past giving rise to mutual blockages), and increasing membership or increasing the number of ad hoc working groups. One of the problems specific to these organizations is that of the 'representativity' of their 'representatives' in governmental consultative committees located on the interface between political-administrative actors and social actors. The organizational remedy for such weaknesses consists in strengthening the links between these delegates and the body they are supposed to represent (greater obligation to 'report', formulation of clearer strategic mandates, establishment of internal consultation procedures for dossiers of major interest for the members). With a view to improving the organizational conditions for the exchange of resources (in particular, with political-administrative actors but also with public policy beneficiary groups), these organizations may create new units responsible for 'external relations' with the task of maintaining more or less informal regular contact (routine procedure) with the political–administrative actors responsible for the policies that concern them (for example, meeting for drinks during parliamentary sessions, scientific meetings, other forms of lobbying) and, if necessary, with the beneficiary groups.

Organization/availability: Beneficiary groups

The resource Organization is one of the most important public action resources available to actors that represents the interests of public policy beneficiaries. It provides rapid access to Information, Law (right of appeal of members of these associations), Personnel (voluntary workers) and Force (demonstrations). It can be confirmed that their address book and, more recently, their access to social networks is their key resource, and is often essential for producing and/or using the other resources available to them. It should be noted that this access to other partners and beyond them, society as a whole, is a crucial factor for these groups: in effect, they are frequently challenged in relation to their representativity regarding the individuals whose interests they are supposed to represent.

These organizations are almost all associations in accordance with Article 60ff of the Swiss Civil Code. They are generally financed through membership contributions (see above), and maintain a permanent, sporadic or intensive cooperation network with other groups. In addition they are often based on regional sections with identical or similar objectives to the national organizations. This 'federalist' structure may give rise to conflicts of competency between national bodies and cantonal associations (see above). A good example to be found among the environmental protection organizations concerns competency for the launch of appeals against planning permission or the licensing of important national projects. In such cases, decision-making at national level is required (for example, Association Transports et Environnement [ATE], Pro Natura and WWF Switzerland).

Similarly, the large organizations representing the interests of public policy beneficiaries in the different areas of state intervention maintain their resource Organization meticulously and undoubtedly more systematically than the target groups. They can draw from a large pool of members to create ad hoc working groups composed of people from different professional circles, and rely on an often very solid structure of cantonal sections or again, create special bodies for the monitoring of particular developments arising in the area of intervention in question.

In the case of the lack of a suitable structure, strategies will be sought for the pooling of action resources with other bodies with similar objectives or political parties closely aligned with their interests. Finally, the sharing of dossiers based on specific areas within a coordination commission (Swiss environmental NGOs, for example) also provides a possible solution to this problem.

Organization: Mobilization by stage

Organization/stage: Political-administrative actors

The structures and procedures linking the political-administrative actors vary on the basis of the different stages in the public policy cycle. During the 'birth', emergence, formulation of causality models and initial legislation plans, these actors are linked with each other through a flexible and multipolar network that is dominated, however, by actors of the 'public entrepreneur' type (spatial planning delegate, environment delegate, sustainable development delegate etc) who originate in most cases from political circles (for example, former councillors of state, WWF secretaries) or scientific ones (for example, Swiss Academy of Sciences, Federal Offices of Hydrology, Nature Conservation, Environmental Monitoring). These actors maintain sporadic and informal interaction with a large number of other political-administrative and social actors. The strength of these 'units' lies precisely in their extremely dynamic, multi-actorial and informal organizational resources (public policy 'activists').

It is only after the establishment of a consolidated political-administrative programme (laws and decrees) that the federal or cantonal government will set about establishing a more solid administrative structure, which is well rooted in the general administration and will maintain far more structured and regulated interaction with its administrative and social environment. This applies to the programming administration at federal level and even more so to the policy implementation administration at cantonal level. The one-time activists become functionaries that administer the public policy in question. Thus Organization changes its characteristics, relinquishing its structures and dynamic processes to acquire more stable structures and procedures. The old pioneers are suddenly no longer needed; 'productive chaos' is no longer required but instead, the predictable, stable and accordingly, ordered management of public policy resources. This transformation will enable each of the political-administrative actors of the newly created structure to maintain structured or routine exchanges with their administrative and social environment within clearly delineated perimeters of action.

Organization/stage: Target groups

While the administrative structures associated with a public policy undergo this structural and procedural process of differentiation, the organizations representing the interests of the target groups are probably going through a similar though less visible process. Nonetheless, it is possible to observe processes involving the pooling of organizational resources with the political-administrative actors (see 'homogenous exchange', discussed below).

The following hypothesis may also be suggested: the establishment of specialized structures and procedures arises sooner among the target groups than at state level, as such structures often have the aim of avoiding public interventions through mechanisms of self-regulation, particularly in the sectors in question. By way of example, we can refer here to the stages preceding the creation of administrative structures for environmental policy, particularly in the area of chemical products, waste and technical norms relating to work safety and energy.

Organization/stage: Beneficiary groups

While thanks to their significant portfolio of Organization as a resource, the target groups generally succeed in responding to the change initiated by the political-administrative actors involving the resource Organization, this kind of adaptation appears to be far more difficult to achieve for actors that defend the interests of beneficiaries. In effect, their political staff is often composed of militants who are less disposed to operating in differentiated structures than the personnel of the target group organizations or political-administrative actors. The structure and procedures that govern the interactions of the political-administrative actors prior to the legislative decision-making, that is, 'chaotic', very dynamic and not systemic, are more suited to them. This is probably one of the reasons why these groups do not favour the creation of a completely new administrative entity in social fields that they formally considered as 'theirs'. Such entities have sometimes been condemned as too 'bureaucratic', 'reductive' and unsuitable for accommodating the dynamics of the problem to be resolved.

Organization: Exchange

Organization/exchange: Political-administrative actors

If the political-administrative actors consider that their stock of Organization is insufficient, they embark on homogenous exchanges between themselves. For example, the administration of environmental policies, in other words, their programming and particularly their implementation, avails of the Organization arising from agricultural policies to gain better access to a considerable proportion of their target groups, that is, farmers. Similarly, like other policies elsewhere, the policy to combat climate change, which does not have a suitable administrative structure for collecting the taxes on CO_2, avails of customs policies. As another example, the incentive policy for combating volatile organic compounds (VOCs) distributes the revenue from the tax levied on target groups by making use of health insurance policy.[4] On closer examination such exchanges show that they are not automatic, as public policy political-administrative actors tend to consider 'their' administrative structures and procedures, which are sometimes co-constructed with 'their' target groups or 'their' beneficiaries, as 'their' property.

The political-administrative actors also sometimes initiate attempts to exchange organizational resources with actors belonging to the target groups or beneficiary groups. This exchange may take the form of the creation of a joint structure or that of recourse to organizations belonging to the target group for the implementation of public tasks (professional training policies: attribution of teaching function to professional organizations; CO_2 reduction policies: recourse to the energy agency established by the business association economiesuisse; agricultural policy: availing of cantonal chambers of agriculture for direct payments or for the training of farmers; public health policies: availing of the Swiss Medical Association [FMH]; environmental policies in the vehicle testing sector: availing of services of garage owners). In the latter case, the exchange of the Organization is sometimes accompanied by an exchange of Property (installation of areas in garages made available to the state for carrying out environmental tests on vehicles), and it is highly likely that the counter-service will take the form of Money (if only due to the monopoly of garage owners increasing their business capital). The latter case involves a heterogeneous exchange of resources.

Swiss executive federalism is based on the idea that the cantonal political-administrative actors make the procedural structures and arrangements of their cantonal administrations available to the Confederation – generally free of charge – for the implementation of federal policies. This can be described as the provision of Organization freely created by the cantons (autonomy of organization, Federal Constitution, Articles 44 and 46). However, this rule is increasingly being challenged, and the cantons would like an at least sporadic subsidy in return for the services they provide, such as the compilation of all kinds of reports and analyses required by the Confederation and the compilation of spatial planning master plans. This could then be described as a heterogeneous exchange of the resource Organization for that of Money within the political-administrative system.

With the establishment of the Conference of Cantonal Governments in 1993 and the political strengthening of the role of the cantons as a horizontal power located between the individual cantons and the Confederation (fourth level), new political-administrative structures emerged on the interface between the cantonal and federal political-administrative actors; the Maison des cantons in Bern hosts the secretariats of these Conferences. By definition these cantonal actors mainly deal with questions concerning the implementation of federal public policies that have already been dealt with in detail – or not – on the level of future federal legislation, particularly decrees. These Conferences of Cantonal Directors definitely constitute the priority interlocutors of the Confederation in relation to questions concerning heterogeneous and homogenous exchanges of Organization between 'federal Bern' and the cantonal capitals.

The political-administrative actors of the Confederation, cantons and communes may spearhead heterogeneous exchanges of Organization by proposing the establishment of new mixed organizations, as described below, co-financing this resource with a view to reinforcing the implementation of their policies (Money). The currency of the exchange on the part of the Confederation may also involve Consensus ('less control'), Property (provision of access to federal buildings to the cantonal administrations) and Time (extension of deadlines for the implementation of federal policies).

Finally, it should be noted that such heterogeneous exchanges initiated by the political-administrative actors can also take place between the latter and the organizations representing the interests of target groups and beneficiary groups. As explained above, the counter-services of exchange with the target groups can involve Law (delegation of competency for the formulation of a law), Money (structural subsidies or piece-rate implementation acts, for example, in the context of service mandates) or Consensus (indications of trust, attribution of credibility). In the case of the beneficiary groups, the resources exchanged include, for example, Consensus (recognition of credibility) and Money (structural subsidies for policy implementation projects).

Organization/exchange: Target groups

The initiative for this (homogenous) exchange of Organization with political–administrative actors can also come from one or more organizations representing the interests of target groups. These organizations then propose the pooling of these resources by creating a new agency (limited company, partnership or association) whose members are composed equally of political–administrative actors and private citizens (individual companies or umbrella organizations). An example of this is the Agence Suisse de l'énergie pour l'économie (Swiss Agency for Energy for the Economy) and the mixed associations for the implementation of environmental policies (Cercl'Air, Société Suisse de l'industrie du gaz et des eaux) and social policies (private social insurance companies). It is possible to observe an increase in the number of these organizations located 'between the state and business circles' today. Other classical examples include private foundations in bodies of which political–administrative actors are members who, in many cases, come from the administrative service responsible for subsidizing the foundations in question.[5]

The hypothesis may be advanced that this pooling of the resource Organization between political–administrative actors and representatives of target groups does not involve an entirely homogenous exchange. The two partners expect counter-services in the form of the transfer of other resources, for example, Money or Law, in the form of delegations of competency giving the bodies of these new organizations real powers – particularly in relation to policy implementation – or the transfer of Information or Consensus (building of values and beliefs shared by the community of actors from a specific public policy arena).

The initiative for a heterogeneous exchange may come from target groups that wish to 'monetize' the successful operation of their organizations by making them available to political–administrative actors (or beneficiary actors). One example would be the resumption by these organizations of the production of (part of) the outputs in exchange for payment (resource Money), for example, the issuing of certificates of origin for wood by the cantonal chambers of commerce, the issuing of certificates of federal capacity by recognized professional organizations etc. Once again, in these cases the act of recognition also signifies that the political–administrative actors give Consensus (credibility) to these organizations.

Organization/exchange: Beneficiary groups

Similar initiatives for homogenous exchanges, which initially appear to be of no interest in terms of a counter-service, may also originate from the organizations representing the interests of beneficiaries, which are sometimes also represented in the aforementioned new partnership organizations established between the state and civil society, for example, in the form of so-called 'tripartite' organizations.

If these organizations have large numbers of members or supporters, they can make their 'address books' available, which are of particular interest for political-administrative actors in the area of public policies that use persuasive instruments in the form of more or less targeted information campaigns. Examples of such exchanges can be found in the area of health (fight against AIDS: PINK Cross, umbrella organization for homosexuals; battle against cancer: Ligue contre le cancer), family policy (battle against alcoholism, Blue Cross), the promotion of women's employment (Pro Familia), agricultural policy (promotion of organic farming, Bio Suisse), environmental policies (energy sector: Touring Club Suisse – and Association transports et environnement, ATE), anti-smoking policy (campaigns targeting young people: Ligue Suisse contre le cancer) and child protection policy (sex education: Pro Familia, the churches).

This provision of access to the resource Organization, which is available to the organizations for the protection of the interests of beneficiary groups, is not always purely 'charitable' or 'idealistic'. As in the case of the target groups, the beneficiary NGOs also succeed sometimes in obtaining counter-services, which means that the exchange of resources is not purely homogenous but, in fact, heterogeneous. The counter-services expected of the political-administrative actors include, for example, Money (subsidies or service contracts), Consensus (acceptance of values or beliefs conveyed, for example, with information of a religious, ecological or health nature, as a recognized brand image) and Political Support. It should be noted that, to my knowledge, and probably in contrast to the case of the target groups, actual transfers of competency (Law) with these organizations are rare. One known case involves the transfer of Law in the area of environmental policy, work protection policy, consumer policy and patient policy: the right of appeal was granted to these organizations precisely because they 'provide' huge potential in the form of benevolent and well-organized observers.

Truly heterogeneous, sporadic or permanent exchanges based on specific contracts are often conditional and prohibit all 'abusive' use of the resource that is not compliant with the public mandate, for example, for purely lucrative ends for the benefit of members or for the spreading of ideological, religious or political messages.

Recommended further reading

Textbooks and specialist literature

Börzel, T. (1998) 'Organizing Babylon – On the different conceptions of policy networks', *Public Administration*, 76 (summer 1998): 253-73.

Bressers, H. (2009) 'From public administration to policy network: Contextual interaction analysis', in S. Nahrath and F. Varone (eds) *Rediscovering public law and public administration in comparative policy analysis: A tribute to Peter Knoepfel*, Lausanne: PPUR, pp 123-42.

Crozier, M. and Friedberg, E. (1981) *Actors and systems*, Chicago, IL: Chicago University Press.

Curien, N. (2005) *Économie des réseaux*, Paris: La Découverte.

Giauque, D. (2003) *La bureaucratie libérale: Nouvelle gestion publique et régulation organisationnelle*, Paris: Harmattan.

Knoke, D. and Kuklinski, J.H. (1982) *Network analysis*, Beverly Hills, CA: Sage Publications.

Knoke Levitt, B. and March, J.G. (1988) 'Organizational learning', *Annual Review of Sociology*, 14: 319-40.

Lundin, M. (2007) 'Explaining cooperation: How resource interdependence, goal congruence and trust affect joint actions in policy implementation', *Journal of Public Administration Research and Theory (GPART)*, 17(4): 651-72.

March, J.G. and Olsen, J.P. (1975) 'The uncertainty of the past. Organizational learning under ambiguity', *European Journal of Political Research*, 3(2): 147-71.

Marsh, D. and Smith, M. (2000) 'Understanding policy networks: Towards a dialectical approach', *Political Studies*, 48(1): 4-21.

Norbert, T. and Adrian, R. (2000) *Public management – Innovative Konzepte zur Führung im öffentlichen Sektor*, Wiesbaden: Gabler.

Ritz, A. and Sinelli, P. (2013) 'Management de la performance dans l'administration publique', in A. Ladner, J.-L. Chappelet, Y. Emery, P. Knoepfel, L. Mader, N. Soguel and F. Varone (eds) *Manuel d'administration publique suisse*, Lausanne: PPUR, pp 345-68.

Rose, R. (1993) *Lesson – Drawing in public policy. A guide to learning across time and space*, Chatham: Chatham House.

Sabatier, P. and Jenkins-Smith, H. (1993) 'The Advocacy Coalition Framework: Assessment, revisions and implications for scholars and practitioners', in P. Sabatier and H. Jenkins-Smith (eds) *Policy change and learning: An advocacy coalition approach*, Boulder, CO: Westview Press, pp 211-35.

Schedler, K. and Eichler, A. (2013) 'Rapport entre l'administration et la politique', in A. Ladner, J.-L. Chappelet, Y. Emery, P. Knoepfel, L. Mader, N. Soguel and F. Varone (eds) *Manuel d'administration publique suisse*, Lausanne: PPUR, pp 369-86.

Scott, J. (1991) *Social network analysis*, London: Sage.

Soparnot, R. (2012) *Organisation et gestion des entreprises*, Paris: Dunod.

Thom, N. and Ritz, A. (2000) *Innovative Konzepte zur Führung im öffentlichen Sektor*, Wiesbaden: Gabler.

van Dam, N. and Jos, M. (2007) *Organization and management: An international approach*, London: Routledge.

Vogel, S.K. (1996) *Freer markets. More rules. Regulatory reforms in advanced industrial countries*, Ithaca, NY: Cornell University Press, p 312.

Wasserman, S. and Faust, K. (1994) *Social network analysis. Methods and applications*, Cambridge: Cambridge University Press.

'In-house' applications

Baitsch, C., Knoepfel, P. and Eberle, A. (2000) 'Lernprozesse in Verwaltungen, Ueberlegungen zur Arbeitsteilung zwischen Internen und Externen', in Y. Emery (ed) *L'administration dans tous ses états, réalisations et conséquences/Grossbaustelle Verwaltung – Bilanzen und Ausblicke*, Lausanne: IDHEAP/PPUR, 259-77.

Clivaz, C. (1990) *Influence des réseaux d'action publique sur les changements politique – Le cas de l'écologisation du tourisme alpin en Suisse et dans le canton du Valais*, Bâle: Helbing & Lichtenhahn.

Kissling-Näf, I. (1996) *Lernprozesse und Umweltverträglichkeitsprüfung: Staatliche Steuerung über Verfahren und Netzwerkbildung in der Abfallpolitik*, Basel and Frankfurt am Main: Helbing & Lichtenhahn.

Knoepfel, P. (ed), in Auftrag der Schweizerischen Arbeitsgemeinschaft für Umweltfotrschung (SAGUF) (1990) *Landwirtschaftliche ökologische Beratung – Ein Modell für allgemeine Umweltberatung*, Basel: Helbing & Lichtenhahn.

Knoepfel, P. (1995) 'New institutional arrangements for the next generation of environmental policy instruments: Intra- and interpolicy cooperation', in B. Dente (ed) *Environmental policy in search of new instruments*, Dordrecht and Boston, MA: Kluwer, pp 197-233.

Knoepfel, P. (1995) 'Nouvelle gestion publique (NPM)', *Revue Suisse de science politique*, 1 (1): i–xv.

Knoepfel, P. (2011) *L'ancrage institutionnel du développement durable dans l'administration fédérale et dans trois cantons (VD, BE, AG)*, Working Paper from l'IDHEAP no 1a, Chavannes-près-Renens: IDHEAP.

Knoepfel, P. and Boisseaux, S. (2012) *Expertise sur l'effectivité du service valaisan de l'environnement en matière de préavis sur des projets de construction*, Chavannes-près-Renens: IDHEAP.

Knoepfel, P. and Zimmermann, W., with Sailer, G. and Matafora, E. (1993) *Evaluation des BUWAL. Expertenbericht zur Evaluation der Luftreinhaltung, des ländlichen Gewässerschutzes und der UVP des Bundes, Schlussbericht*, 18 November 1991, Bern: EDMZ.

Knoepfel, P., Baitsch, C. and Eberle, A. (1995) *Überprüfung der Aufbauorganisation des Amtes für Umweltschutz des Kantons St Gallen, Schlussbericht*, 1 February, Chavannes-près-Renens: IDHEAP, p 64.

Knoepfel, P., Kissling, I. and Marek, D. (1997) *Lernen in öffentlichen Politiken*, Basel: Helbing & Lichtenhahn.

Tretjak, T., Marusenko, R. and Knoepfel, P. (2017) *Transport related environmental policy implementation in four cities of Ukraine*, Final report of the project 'Environmental Policy Implementation Seminary', financed by the Swiss National Science Foundation, IZ74ZO_160473.

Notes

[1] Government and Administration Organization Act (GAOA) of 21 March 1997; RS 172.010.

[2] For example, to lend greater political weight (Political Support) to its contribution to the public policy in question.

[3] At federal level: Government and Administration Organization Act (GAOA) of 21 March 1997 with the formal delegation of organizational responsibility to the Federal Council; Canton of Jura: Décret sur l'organisation générale de l'Administration du 20 octobre 1990 (Decree on the General Organisation of the Administration of 20 October 1990), principle of organizational power of the parliament of Jura.

[4] Deduction of sum distributed to each citizen for health insurance premiums collected in December.

[5] This previously common practice is in the course of being abandoned due to eventual conflicts of interest on the part of the representatives of the Confederation.

13

Consensus

Definition

The implementation of a public policy requires at least minimal agreement between the actors of its basic triangle. Thus a certain level of consensus must exist between the political-administrative actors, the end beneficiaries and the target groups in relation to the modalities of production and content of the policy implementation acts. This enables the actors to establish the minimum trust necessary for all cooperation. From the point of view of the administration, it becomes very difficult to give concrete form to a public policy without the support of the social groups involved.

Consensus must not be confused with the resource political support.... The latter provides the primary legitimacy of sectoral policies through democratic decision-making mechanisms that operate outside the policy space. Consensus enables the conferring of a second kind of legitimacy referred to as "secondary" through the relationships between the actors belonging to the triangle of the policy in question. This other legitimacy depends on the perception by the actors of the quality of either the policy's implementation acts (administrative achievements – outputs) or the procedure.... In addition, trust assumes particular importance: if it happens to be lacking it can undermine the legitimacy of the state during concrete public intervention processes.

Consensus constitutes an increasingly important factor in the execution of public policies, for example, construction of new roads or power lines, storage of nuclear waste, education reform, public health, hospital closures etc. It would appear, therefore, that this resource is not only precious but also very fragile. The research carried out on participative approaches, in particular, teaches us that a "culture of consensus" requires a certain degree of continuity over time, an equal openness to all actors, standardized conflict-resolution methods, flexible political-administrative practice that enables adaptation to change, and, finally, an adequate routine for exchange between the bodies involved to avoid the structures being too dependent on the turnover of people. Recent examples of measures aimed at strengthening this resource include the establishment of conciliation groups in relation to energy policy (nuclear waste, hydropower, high voltage power lines) and the publication of recommendations by the Confederation for the negotiation of environmental conflicts (DETEC 2004). The ... group that has and avails of consensus most is that comprising the representatives of the interests of public policy beneficiaries. According to many surveys, they enjoy the greatest capital of trust among the public policy actors. (Knoepfel et al, 2010: 69-70)

Specifics

Although, like the other resources, it is the outcome of an interactive process that unfolds between the three groups of public policy actors, Consensus is not understood as a (more or less agreed) characteristic of the decision-making but as part of the portfolio of action resources at the disposal of each of the actors. Consensus as a resource characterizes the relations that an actor maintains with the other actors of the basic public policy triangle. The resource confers greater or lesser credibility, reliability and predictability on the actor. The actors keep their promises because they dispose of a stock of trust they have demonstrated in the past and on which people can rely in the future. If the actors have this capital, they created it themselves, although this capital only exists if the other actors consider it to be so. Hence Consensus enables an actor to gain the estimation of the other actors and, based on this, they are willing to exchange other action resources with the actor in question with complete confidence.

The resource Consensus is the relational public action resource *par excellence*. It only exists if the other actors attribute credibility to its holder. It may be considered as a fundamental resource in that its absence prevents the smooth functioning of the exchange of all resources within the triangle of public policy actors. And the distrust of the other actors vis-à-vis a group in which trust is lost – either thorough 'incorrect' or unpredictable behaviour on its part or through a change of perception in relation to it – will be reflected in alienation, denigration or an attempt to gain greater control over, marginalize or actually replace the actor in question by another actor. The interest of these actors in behaving in this way is to improve the atmosphere of mutual trust within the community of actors in their policy arena, which will enable them to establish the conditions necessary for the 'normal' mobilization of their resources through exchange.

Should we confirm, therefore, that the resource Consensus constitutes a common resource, the availability of which is an actual condition of the existence of a community of public policy actors? Would its decline destroy this community by definition and hence the public policy itself in that the latter would ultimately not produce any further products enabling the mutual exchange of resources?

In considering Consensus as a resource at the disposal of each of the public policy actors, we are obliged to respond in the negative to these questions. Despite its strongly relational character, the actor-based approach does not necessitate the consideration of this resource as a structure 'outside' the actors, but as a 'divisible' attribute that can be assigned to credible actors but is empirically lacking among 'non-credible' actors. This is confirmed by reality. In effect, a person or group of people can lose or gain their actual position as an actor or at least be temporarily delegated to the second rank because they have lost a certain degree of credibility in the eyes of one or other actor in the policy triangle, for example, due to deceitful behaviour involving the breaking of promises they made and thus violating the rules of the game (institutions).

Moreover, such situations show that cases of this kind affect not only the actor that loses their credibility but also the other actors that maintained trusting relations with this actor in the past and perhaps for too long.

The mobilization of Consensus can modify an existing relationship of trust either negatively (withdrawal of trust in a former companion) or positively (re-establishment or reinforcement of relationships of trust). It is a major operation that has repercussions on all of the processes of resource exchange that arise in a public policy space. This kind of mobilization can even result in the replacement of one actor by another and thus alter the actor constellation of a public policy community. It should be noted that this attribution of Consensus to specific actors is conveyed in everyday language. Actors speak of 'my' credibility, 'our' credibility and 'your' loss of credibility, and it is not unusual to hear statements such as 'I have lost my trust in the actor XY who has started failing to keep their promises, denigrating us in public.'

Due to its more relational character, it is more difficult to quantify the Consensus held by an actor empirically (see Chapter 17) than is the case with the other resources. Its loss and/or regain may be expressed in general surveys or it may also be expressed in the simple reduction of mutual exchanges of other resources undertaken with the actor in question. In general, more or less representative surveys about the credibility of the different groups of actors in 'civil society' can be useful but also misleading, as such surveys hardly take the relational character of the notion of trust into account. According to these surveys, credible actors can even be found among actors that display a very low level of mutual trust if their partners consider them credible; even in Mafia circles, actors exist that enjoy a high level of credibility within civil society.

It is important to remember that Consensus is not considered as a personal quality or characteristic of public policy actors. It exists independently of the personal traits of the actors. An honest person may – but does not necessary have to – gain the trust of other actors and conversely, a dishonest person may enjoy Consensus among other actors. Even if these two counterintuitive cases are rather rare, the simple fact that they are plausible demonstrates that Consensus is a resource that can be objectified, transferred and manoeuvred by the actors in the sense of our general definition (see Chapter 1), and is not simply an individual quality of the concrete actor.

Consensus: Mobilization by availability

Consensus/availability: Political-administrative actors

If the political-administrative actors have the trust of the target groups, the latter are likely to engage in homogenous or heterogeneous exchanges of public action resources. This availability may be increased with the help of so-called 'trust-building measures'. For example, the chemical industry may be willing to provide reliable data that are subject to professional confidentiality in its self-monitoring reports if the Swiss federal or European notification body (for example, REACH) formally undertakes not to divulge the data to their competitors. In the opposite case, possibly based on an institutional rule arising from administrative transparency policy, the state actors risk obtaining inaccurate or even false data. Another example could involve the actors responsible for the pursuit of criminal prosecutions making promises to obtain a reduction in custodial sentences to enable the recruitment of credible witnesses from the ranks of the offenders.

Similarly, based on their neutrality, political-administrative actors enjoy the trust of the representatives of the interests of the beneficiary groups, for example, groups representing patients, the environment, consumers. These organizations are thus willing to make less use of their right of appeal or to provide correct (and not exaggerated) monitoring information to the authority if the latter suspects that the information provided by the administrative services involved is biased, for example, due to their proximity to the target groups (see below).

If, due to their own blunders or as a result of systematic denigration on the part of the target groups and/or beneficiaries, the political-administrative actors no longer share Consensus with one or other of these groups, it follows that the latter are distrustful. This distrust may be expressed, for example, in the blocking of Information, the mobilization of Law (an increase in the number of appeals) or by a refusal to make their Property or Organization resources available (see below). In such situations, the political-administrative actors are obliged to make an effort to improve their image and instigate measures that generate trust; for example, in relation to policies for locating sites for the storage of radioactive material; public health prevention policies (campaigns considered as 'biased' or 'nudging'); or environmental and national defence policies, for example.

Consensus/availability: Target groups

If the target groups share Consensus with the political-administrative actors, the latter will demonstrate, in turn, a more understanding attitude towards their particular situations and also refrain from scrutinizing the information they provide during checks and monitoring or propose that they receive more generous subsidies. Typical examples of this from an everyday situation can be found in the practice of the cantonal inspectors of foodstuffs, building sites and the environment that often differentiate between the 'black sheep' on which they focus their attention and the 'trusted' companies. This clearly shows how there may be differences within one and the same group of the actor triangle in relation to the resource Consensus, and a subdivision may create a limited group that does not enjoy trust, and another, often much bigger group, that 'does not cause any problems'.

In situations involving the negotiation of solutions for policy implementation, a relationship of trust between target groups and beneficiaries may be crucial to enable a compromise to be reached. Just one inappropriate statement on the part of the target group's negotiators can damage the atmosphere of trust and permanently block further negotiations. Similarly, the organization of an unauthorized press conference in the middle of the negotiations, a tactic used mainly to put pressure on one or other of the participants of conciliation groups involved in a mediation process, may destroy any arrangements reached in the past. This shows how important it is for the participants of such mediation processes to make decisions about the 'rules of the game' in advance, generally with the support of mediation professionals.

In many public policies, due to the opposition they initially express against all public intervention – for example, during a popular vote on the main legislation relating to the policy in question – the target groups do not necessarily enjoy full credibility among the state actors and, moreover, the beneficiary groups. The situation of distrust with which these groups are faced is often reflected in the aforementioned surveys, for example, the poor 'credibility' of business, particularly in periods of crisis. Actual manuals and courses exist today on how to 'maintain' the image of a company or sectoral umbrella organization that instruct managers on the ways they can use the public action resources that are likely to enable them to (re-)gain credibility as a public policy actor involved in precarious situations.

Consensus/availability: Beneficiary groups

In general, the representatives of the beneficiary groups enjoy a relatively high level of credibility and trust among the 'population'. This positive perception may (but does not have to) be transformed into Consensus among political-administrative actors who are willing to embark on exchanges of resources with these groups themselves. However, this is not always the case on the side of the target groups. The latter often look unfavourably on the emergence of proximity that they consider as being too 'intimate' between political-administrative actors and beneficiaries, a proximity that is based precisely on what they see as 'excessive' mutual relationships of trust.

Despite this generally positive image, the organizations representing the interests of beneficiaries can themselves undergo difficult periods that involve a loss of credibility among political-administrative actors and target groups. The latter do not look favourably on these organizations, sometimes even as a matter of principle. Such situations arise quite often in the early days of new public policies. Examples can be found among the environmental policies of the 1980s, policies for the location of sites for the storage of nuclear waste, policies for the clean-up of contaminated sites, family policies (childcare) and policies for the free circulation of people (flanking measures against salary dumping in the context of contracts of work for foreign employees). This situation is explained primarily by the fact that, based on their objectives and the considerable demands of their members, these organizations often see themselves obliged to present the maximum possible demands and to challenge the credibility of the political-administrative actors and of their legislative and implementation measures.

Hence the gradual and temporary withdrawal of trust vis-à-vis the political-administrative actors and again, the target groups represents a deliberate strategy for the mobilization of Consensus (in the negative sense) among these groups. This mobilization is demonstrated in the shifting availabilities in relation to the exchange of other public action resources at the disposal of these groups (in particular, Information, Organization, Law and Force). Accordingly, these groups will tend to conceal 'their' information about issues of strategic importance, stage surprise actions (publication of confidential data), or simply refuse to participate in working groups, committees and media events.

Consensus: Mobilization by stage

Consensus/stage: Political-administrative actors

The political-administrative actors show their trust or distrust vis-à-vis the two other actor groups in the public policy formulation process by negotiating their involvement in or exclusion from the work carried out for the analysis and preparation of legislation. They may consider them – or not – in, for example, study groups and legislative preparation groups, take their suggestions into account – or not – in the process of such work, include them in or omit them from the list of interest groups to be consulted in the legislative consultation procedure, grant them the role of accredited lobbyists – or not – or include or exclude their suggestions in or from their legislative and policy programme.

The attribution of priority status in relation to trust in a legislative procedure constitutes a means of signalling recognition of the credibility of specific target groups and/or organizations representing the interests of beneficiaries (subsidies, recourse to their organizational resources, granting of a right of appeal in the legislation). Similarly during the policy implementation stage and the development of the evaluative statement, the public actors will refer more to trusted actors than those who played the game 'badly' in the past. For example, they will attempt to schedule the inspection of controversial construction projects during holiday periods when the 'adversary' is abroad, to adopt a selective communication policy, that is, failing to keep 'adversaries' fully informed, or to commission only 'friendly' consultancies for environmental impact studies while also excluding consultancies that are 'too green'.

Consensus/stage: Target groups

When the target groups distrust the political-administrative actors in charge of a legislative dossier, they contest their 'competency' in relation to the dossier in question and try to propose that they be replaced by other public actors. Hence it is possible to observe attempts on their part to bring about the intervention of federal offices or cantonal services that have already shown understanding in the past for the 'difficulties' facing a particular sector of business, agriculture or the transport sector. A well-known strategy involves prompting them to produce co-reports on the dossiers originating from other administrative bodies ('battle of the co-reports'). This may even prompt debates – both within and outside the administrations – about the real definition of the public problem to be resolved by a public policy that already exists or to be created (for example, the external trade policy of the Federal Department of Public Economics versus the European affairs policy of the Federal Department of Foreign Affairs; economic policy versus environmental policy; education policy versus economic policy). It should be noted that such games, often played in the opposite direction, can also be observed on the side of the beneficiary groups.

These uses of the resource Consensus by the target groups are repeated at policy implementation level and manifest in highly varied uses of other public action resources such as Time (making 'adversaries' in the administration wait until the last minute), Information (differentiated use of confidential information held by the target groups), Law (intensifying the threat of an appeal against distrusted political-administrative actors) and Property (actual use of property that is diametrically opposed to the will of the beneficiaries or political-administrative actors responsible for a dossier that concerns them).

Consensus/stage: Beneficiary groups

The behaviour of these groups vis-à-vis trusted or distrusted political-administrative actors – and also target groups – at the level of the legislative process scarcely differs from that of the target groups. In effect, they present as cooperative or oppositional in respect of their choice to participate or not in legislative committees and consultation procedures and in relation to the voting recommendations they make to 'their' representatives in parliament.

The same also applies to the policy implementation level, particularly in the small cantons where the use of resources also depends on the personal relations between the representatives of the beneficiaries and the different administrative services. Given the more dense nature of communal and cantonal networks, this personal factor will often carry greater weight in this context than at the level of federal policy programming. In addition, these relations are often more strongly coloured by the 'political' affiliation of the actors involved, a factor that often exceeds the concrete issues of specific public policies, particularly in relation to Consensus.

Consensus: Exchange

Consensus/exchange: Political-administrative actors

Given the very pronounced mutuality of the exchange of the resource Consensus arising from its strongly relational character, all exchanges of this resource in the form of the recognition of one actor's credibility by another actor or in the (negative) form of the refusal to grant such recognition due to a lack of credibility often constitutes a homogenous exchange. This exchange lays the foundations for homogenous and heterogeneous exchanges of the other public policy action resources dealt with in this book. Empirically, such exchanges present frequently during periods of rupture (withdrawal Consensus by one of the three actors). These ruptures can arise due to internal divisions, for example, the dissidence on the part of the small mountain farmers within the Swiss Farmers' Union in the 1970s, or external ones, for example, the stopping of the work of a commission, the withdrawal of a state representative from a foundation's board of trustees due to conflicts of interest between the state as subsidizer and the subsidized foundation and misappropriation of public funds by an association formerly selected for the implementation of public tasks.

As the existence of relations of trust between the two groups of actors is indispensible for the political-administrative actors, such periods of withdrawal of Consensus are usually followed by attempts at reconciliation or by the search for another beneficiary (sub-)group or target group. Such changes to the basic actor triangle risk leading to (slight) changes at the level of the definition of the public problem (new or other beneficiary groups) or the causal hypothesis (extension of the target group). The latter is more serious than the former, and the actors risk being unable to avoid the public policy being challenged in its entirety.

Consensus/exchange: Target groups

The target groups express their trust/distrust vis-à-vis the political-administrative actors through a greater willingness to exchange other public action resources in their possession. For example, they can change their behaviour (Property in their possession: case of reduction of polluting activities if the state undertakes to leave them 'in peace' in the future[1]), refrain from launching an appeal (Law) or promise the state officials to be 'generous' at the level of the implementation of other public policies (Force: refraining from regular inspections of work conditions if taxes are paid regularly or wastewater treatment is satisfactory).

The philosophy of target groups can be summarized as follows: it is better to accept precisely defined obligations and thus remain within the framework of the law than to live in a state of general uncertainty that does not allow security of planning and investment. Sometimes cases arise whereby these groups expressly request that their activities be subjected to an authorization regime that also enables them to defend themselves against potential attacks on the part of unpredictable beneficiary groups. Similarly, the target groups can signal the restoration of their trust through the respect of conditions of a amnesty (fiscal, for example) by cooperating in the development of conditions of such 'contracts' and showing a willingness to 'become legal again' in the future. A recent example of this (spring 2017) is the strange (to say the least) coalition formed between the Green Party of Switzerland and the road hauliers' association ASTAG in favour of more stringent emissions controls for trucks on Swiss roads.

Consensus/exchange: Beneficiary groups

Such 'declarations of peace' can also arise through the initiative of beneficiary groups and, moreover, in relation to political-administrative actors, for example, an agreement to (re-)join an official commission under the condition that the latter alters the (legal) mandate of the body in question, or the renunciation of an appeal against a decision on the location of future rail, road, aviation or energy infrastructure if the public actors state credibly that they will take the group's concerns into account in terms of concrete and definitive authorizations for the construction and operation of such works.

The same beneficiary groups can embark on such initiatives for (re-)establishing Consensus in relation to the target groups. For example, the creation of all kinds of bipartite or multipartite monitoring centres for tracking the – partly contested – impacts of future infrastructure or reforms that are introduced under their responsibility (for example, amalgamations of companies, the adoption of new practices for covering expenses by health insurance companies, codes of good conduct, gentlemen's agreements), and are explicitly responsible for proposing attenuating measures in the case of excessive or unpredicted impacts.

Recommended further reading

Textbooks and specialist literature

Fischer, F. and Forester, J. (eds) (1993) *The argumentative turn in policy analysis and planning*, Durham, NC and London: UCL Press.

Flückiger, A. (forthcoming) 'Gouverner par des coups de pouce (NUDGES). Instrumentaliser nos biais cognitifs au lieu de légiférer', *Actes du colloque internormativité*, 29 and 30 September 2016, Université Libre de Bruxelles.

Hall, P.A. (1993) 'Policy paradigms, social learning and the state', *Comparative Politics*, 25(3): 275-96.

Jänicke, M. and Weidner, H. (eds) (1995) *Successful environmental policy – A critical evaluation of 24 cases*, Berlin: Edition Sigma.

Lundin, M. (2007) 'Explaining cooperation: How resource interdependence, goal congruence and trust affect joint actions in policy implementation', *Journal of Public Administration Research and Theory (GPART)*, 17(4): 651-72.

Morand, C.-A. (ed) (1991) *L'Etat propulsive. Contribution à l'étude des instruments d'action de l'Etat*, Paris: Publisud.

Olsen, J.P. (1991) 'Modernizing programs in perspective: Institutional analysis of organisational change', *Governance*, 4(2): 125-49.

Weidner, H. (1993a) *Mediation as a policy instrument for resolving environmental disputes – With special reference to Germany*, WZB-Paper (FS II 93-301), Berlin: Wissenschaftszentrum Berlin für Sozialforschung.

Weidner, H. (1993b) 'Der verhandelnde Staat. Minderung von Vollzugskonflikten durch Mediationsverfahren', *Schweizerische Vereinigung für Politische Wissenschaft* (SVPW), 33: 225-44.

'In-house' applications

Kissling-Näf, I. (1996) *Lernprozesse und Umweltverträglichkeitsprüfung: Staatliche Steuerung über Verfahren und Netzwerkbildung in der Abfallpolitik*, Basel and Frankfurt am Main: Helbing & Lichtenhahn.

Knoepfel, P. (1995) *Die Lösung von Umweltkonflikten durch Verhandlungen*, Basel: Helbing & Lichtenhahn.

Knoepfel, P. (2001) 'Regulative Politik in föderativen Staaten – das Beispiel der Umweltpolitik', *Politische Viertelsjahresschrift* (PVS), Sonderheft 32/2001: 306-32.

Knoepfel, P. (2017) *Strengthening or weakening public policies' implementation by conscious games on actors' constellations*, Manuscript for publication.

Knoepfel, P. and Kissling-Näf, I. (1998) 'Social learning in policy networks', *Policy & Politics*, 26(3): 343-67.

Knoepfel, P., Müller-Yersin, H. and Pestalozzi, M. (2004) *Grundlagen zu den Verhandlungsempfehlungen UVEK: Fachbericht*, Bundesamt für Umwelt, Wald und Landschaft (BUWAL), Schriftenreihe Umwelt, 365.

Wälti, S. (2001) *Le fédéralisme d'exécution sous pression, la mise en œuvre des politiques à incidence spatiale dans le système fédéral suisse*, Genève and Bâle: Helbing & Lichtenhahn.

Note

[1] In this sense, an authorization or order of remediation gives the target groups a (relative) right to engage in an authorized activity even if this activity no longer meets very strict standards to the letter in the future (at least at the level of future legislation that often 'exempts' the holders of this right from applying the most stringent measures).

14

Time

Definition

This resource, whose stock is also limited, is indisputably necessary for all public policies. Policy participants always allocate a "time budget" that is clearly defined by the different types of institutional rules (constitutional, administrative or sectoral) governing the (temporal) space of the policy. The respecting of deadlines is, therefore, the essential object of numerous conflicts relating to policy implementation, for example ensuring the compliance of all kinds of installations. The controversial aspect of this case is less the obligation in itself but the time assigned to implement ... the changes in behaviour required under new legislation (for example, the remediation of polluted sites. The distribution of the resource time among the actors is usually unequal and the capacity to dominate the resource through control over the agenda constitutes a considerable power. The resource ... also depends in part on the mobilization of other resources which allow actors to gain or lose time (for example through the submission of a legal appeal).

Moreover, the public actors who, due to their function, have more time than the representatives of social groups, who often work on a voluntary basis, sometimes ... tend to over-estimate the importance of this resource in their projections and, as a result, block the participation of non-professionals. Ultimately, the public and private actors can ... play on time by indicating that they will only act if the other actors involved also act in anticipation, simultaneously or subsequently: the application of the principle of "symmetry of sacrifice" which aims to ensure that all actors contribute equally to the resolution of the problem, also includes the temporal dimension, for example the equal or unequal treatment of the different target groups from a temporal perspective. (Knoepfel et al, 2010: 65)

Specifics

As in everyday life, the notion of time is omnipresent in public action that can proceed accordingly 'on time' or 'behind schedule'. The indispensible delimitation of Time arising from this can result in the imposition of imprescriptible deadlines, for example, referendum deadlines (three months), appeal deadlines, enquiry submission deadlines and so on. In doing this, the political-administrative actors assign time budgets to other actors that try to gain it, avoid wasting it or have it 'stolen'. Time is also a universal unit of measure for public performance. For example, a common aim of administrative reorganization projects is that of 'speeding up' procedures that are considered too slow, hampering economic development and thus politically unacceptable: for example, the procedures for granting planning permission, authorizing the marketing of chemical products and for obtaining subsidies.

Everyday language makes frequent use of personal pronouns in association with time (for example, 'my time', 'I don't want to waste your time'), and refers to time as though it were an increasingly rare and precious resource (for example, 'time is money', saving time to gain an advantage over a competitor). Like Consensus, time is also a highly relational resource. A veritable fourth dimension (in addition to the three spatial dimensions) for assessing an actor's position, time is always evaluated in relation to the position of another actor (for example, being ahead of or behind another actor).

Common usage also makes frequent reference to the exchange of time using verbs like 'give', 'waste', 'offer' and 'allocate' time budgets. Moreover, a temporal institutional policy exists, that is, the 'agenda' or 'calendar' of public action that is supposed to coordinate, prioritize etc large groups of public policies at the level of federal, cantonal or communal corporation under public law.

Based on its universal scope, like other public action resources, Time is governed by a generally unknown policy that is both institutional and substantive. The policy in question is the very old metrology policy that sets out to avoid the advent of widespread chaos that could result in a damaging invasion of the entire social, economic and ecological relations of our societies that all function on the basis of more or less strict 'timetables'. Switzerland is a paradigmatic example of this. This 'time policy' operates in secret and only presents to the general public on very rare occasions, such as the twice-yearly switchover to daylight saving.[1]

Time: Mobilization by availability

Time/availability: Political-administrative actors

Hence, political-administrative actors who 'have the time' may wait for and oppose target or beneficiary groups that extol the urgency of legislative intervention or implementation. However, they cannot avail of this resource in a completely arbitrary fashion. Rules, sometimes very detailed ones, exist that these actors impose on themselves or that are imposed on them by general institutional policies. Although the political-administrative actors, particularly those involved in the formulation of public policies, are the holders of the temporal public agenda, the use of this resource may be imposed on them by actors that exploit an event (natural or technological disaster) or mobilize another resource (for example, Force, Law or Property), and in this way present the public actors with a *fait accompli* and oblige them to make changes to the planned schedule. In this way the action becomes 'urgent' and the creation of this urgency is clearly a process of social construction.[2]

Within the above-described limits, the political-administrative actors may have access to Time if the legislation authorizes them to allocate limited time budgets to the social actors; this probably constitutes an under-estimated expression of their power in terms of public policy management. In effect, these temporal budgets open and close windows of opportunity for the social actors in relation to making use of an entire series of resources available to them. Hence, in the context of the actors' game, these windows of opportunity represent both a resource and a rule of the game that applies for a limited period of time (deadlines for appeals and referendums: the right to mobilize Law and Political Support). These examples show the importance of access to Time in relation to stabilizing the mutual attempts of actors to make the future visible based on today's action, and in this way guarantee the future organization of economic and social life in a state based on the rule of law.

If the political-administrative actors consider the problem to be resolved through the formulation or implementation of a (new) public policy to be urgent, and deem that its production should be accelerated, they will attempt to gain time by imposing shorter time budgets on themselves (parliaments and government parties) and the target and beneficiary groups involved, for example, in the context of the procedure for legislative consultation or implementation. If necessary the public authorities will even attempt to eliminate a stage in the process, for example, by forgoing the implementation of a consultation procedure or enquiry, even if such a measure does not comply with the institutional rules governing such processes. For example, in the aftermath of a large-scale natural disaster, the reconstruction work to be carried out immediately after the event will be conducted without time-consuming planning permission processes (such as in the city of Port-au-Prince in Haiti). Similarly, a shortened procedure will be chosen for declaring a state of emergency and carrying out evacuations in the event of imminent natural risks, or immediate plenary meetings will be organized instead of the usual process of written consultation (in the case of Switzerland).

Of course, for the public and private actors involved, the time gained in this way represents a loss of the time required for calm and clear planning, and they will complain sooner or later if the government resorts to such extraordinary procedures too often. By necessity, their response will take the form of non-participation – mobilization of Force or other resources, for example, Law – to enable them to correct what they consider a wrongful procedure with reference to the institutional decisional rules that govern their activities.

Time /availability: Target groups

Unlike the above-described scenario, situations exist in which the target groups and/or the organizations representing them 'can wait'. By their nature these actors are often reticent when it comes to the initiation of new public actions or the implementation of public policies that have been decided on. In these situations, in their view, the initiative for a public action coming from the political-administrative actors (possibly under pressure from the beneficiary groups) should be delayed at most. This delay allows them to maintain the habitual behaviours that are most beneficial for them.

How can they gain time? Numerous possibilities are available here and consist in mobilizing other resources ranging from Force (refusing inspectors access to an industrial or agricultural operation, the 'shotgun' factor) and Property (mobilization of the right to refuse access to an official based on land ownership) to Personnel (contractual obligation of employees not to provide the information required by the political-administrative actors). Other action may be taken, such as recourse to the courts (with greater or lesser justification, 'up to the federal court') to exploit the suspensive effect of an appeal or again, the commitment of a sector for the establishment of self-regulation solutions, or the promise of a company to create additional jobs (Property).

The target groups often complain about a lack of time in the context of procedures for the implementation of new legislation, particularly in relation to remediation deadlines that are considered economically infeasible. Hence requests for the extension of remediation deadlines, transitional regimes and even moratoriums or amnesties in relation to sanctions for their delay are the order of the day. Such requests have considerable chances of success, as they are often accompanied by all kinds of threats involving the combined mobilization of other public action resources: for example, Law: right of appeal against clean-up orders; Property: threat of the closure or relocation of companies or of redundancies; and Consensus: more or less credible promises that the required change of behaviour will automatically arise after the upgrading of the machinery with more effective work safety or anti-pollution equipment. These threats can be considerable and credible, and sometimes include announcements posing serious risks to the economic development of the region involved.

A special case referred to below as an example of a homogenous exchange of Time involves the successful demonstration by the target groups that the granting of extra time will render the change in their behaviour more effective which, in turn, will enable the authority to gain time, for example, in terms of reducing the need for time-consuming and expensive monitoring procedures.

Time /availability: Beneficiary groups

By definition, these groups do not usually have 'the time to wait'. For them it is always preferable to resolve the problem affecting them sooner rather than later. Gaining time in this case usually means accelerating the public action by demonstrating the urgent need for public intervention. Such situations may also involve rapid public action that prevents a sudden deterioration in their situation. This deterioration will only be prevented through the intervention of the political-administrative actors aimed at the target groups and at the avoidance of a predictable change in behaviour: for example, the construction of a nuclear power station, extension of an airport, large-scale destruction of biotopes. Sometimes the urgency is expressed in the need to terminate an activity if the deterioration has already arisen: for example, halting the construction of secondary residences in tourist locations to protect the landscape. In the latter case, as in the case of the target groups, the aim of the action is to 'gain' time but, contrary to their case, it is achieved through the acceleration of public action.

For the beneficiary groups and the organizations that represent them, a lack of time on the part of the public actors is manifested in the prolonging of their affliction or the excessively rapid emergence of an additional risk that seriously and irreparably undermines their quality of life. They will do everything possible to ensure that the two other state and social actor groups act quickly. Hence they will request that their problems be put on the (usually already full) agenda, that a sufficient time budget be provided for the effective development and implementation of a less time-consuming legislative act than that proposed by the target groups etc. Given that these beneficiary groups cannot afford to wait, they are incapable of directly mobilizing Time, and will mobilize other significant resources in their portfolio instead, for example, Organization, Force and Information.

Time: Mobilization by stage

Time/stage: Political-administrative actors

Probably due to the very high degree of complexity of public policy programming processes that also necessitate the availability of Political Support, the time budgets allocated for the development of the problem definition and its causality model and the production of legislation (laws, decrees or directives) are generally more generous than those dedicated to the implementation processes following the entry into force of a political-administrative programme. Experience shows, in contrast, that the availability of Time is more limited among the cantonal administrations responsible for policy implementation. For this reason, they support processes that often originate among the target groups and are deemed unacceptable by the organizations representing the interests of the beneficiaries that request the extension of deadlines (see above).

One of the tools that the political-administrative actors avail of to manage their time budget better is the development of action plans (product four of the public policy cycle; see Chapter 16 later), which designate the categories of priority target groups. This temporal prioritization has the legal drawback that all of the actors involved are obliged to implicitly or explicitly accept the existence of temporal (and often spatial) implementation 'gaps' despite the fundamental requirement of the simultaneous implementation of the new legal provisions. Given their general nature, the action plans only rarely provide for an explicitly phased implementation in relation to time and space that would often be necessary for the cantonal implementation policies. Such situations are aggravated by a lack of qualified personnel capable of managing the public action in a professional manner.

During the two stages it is possible to observe the adoption of very different strategies in relation to the use of Time, primarily within the group of political-administrative actors: for example, delaying strategies on the part of parliaments (filibustering, requests for additional reports and commissions of enquiry) or attempts by parliaments to accelerate processes (requests for extraordinary meetings and sessions, placing of topics acknowledged as urgent on the parliamentary agenda). This is also evident in the strategies adopted within the programming administration (delaying of advance notices to be provided for other political-administrative actors, moving of meetings due to overbooking) and implementation at cantonal level (delayed arrival of advance notices, requests for additional information by other services).

The games played by political-administrative actors in relation to Time in their interaction with the target groups and/or the actors representing the interests of beneficiaries can also be observed during the two stages. The aforementioned acceleration strategies are developed at programming level (reduction of deadlines for consultation procedures, holding of plenary sessions instead of submission of written position statements and even the renunciation of a consultation procedure). Regarding the implementation processes, examples of time-related strategies include the organization of public enquiry procedures during the school holidays with a view to avoiding opposition thanks to the potential absence of opponents, the acceptance by a commune of the commencement of works prior to the arrival of cantonal advance notices ('provisional permission') and the implementation of measures for the compensation of opponents to make them withdraw their opposition/appeal with a view to gaining time.

Time /stage: Target groups

The target and beneficiary groups already enjoy a strong presence during the definition of the problem, causality model (which concerns them directly) and the legislative programming of public policies, and they will certainly make use of Time to delay the legislative process if they see it as constituting a threat (see above). At implementation level, these groups are also frequently behind process of delay (remediation) or acceleration (authorization or subvention) or administrative procedures that will result in obligations being imposed on them, or conversely, rights being granted to them (right to build, right to place chemical products on the market, to open restaurants, right to operate installations subject to authorization).

Time/stage: Beneficiary groups

Among organizations that protect the interests of beneficiaries, the interest in mobilizing public action resources, whatever their specific nature, is generally more prominent in the policy implementation stages than the programming stage. The imminence of a concrete public action that is likely to affect their quality of life and is well defined in spatial and temporal terms is often the trigger for their mobilization of resources.

The decisions that are challenged include, therefore, the authorization and/or promotion of target group activities that are likely to have a direct impact on the beneficiaries' social, economic or ecological living conditions, for example, the closure of a neighbourhood restaurant by health inspectors, the appointment of a teacher who is a suspected paedophile, the approval of a plan for the construction of a new section of motorway or the decision to withdraw the licence of a local television station. The beneficiary groups can also play the same role of instigators in the converse situations, that is, during decisions by the state not to intervene against target groups whose behaviour undermines their quality of life, for example, a refusal by the authority to proceed with the remediation of a site occupied by a company that generates pollution, refusal of the commune to increase the number of police officers in a neighbourhood affected by crime or anti-social behaviour, refusal by the authorities to subsidize the local football club. The beneficiary groups will initially do everything in their power to delay the decision by mobilizing an entire series of resources (Force: occupation of the building site; Law: appeal; Information: distribution of leaflets). In the second case, the use of these same resources will serve to present their 'grievances' for the purpose of triggering rapid public action.[3]

Time: Exchange

Time /exchange: Political-administrative actors

Situations involving homogenous exchanges of Time both among political-administrative actors and with one of the two social groups are rare. A conceivable case involving such a win-win configuration is that already mentioned, whereby one of the actors gives the other more time so that they can do their work better, thereby also enabling the 'donor' actor to gain time. This exchange is carried out in parallel to a homogenous exchange of Information (the extension of the deadline for the submission of an impact assessment improves the quality of the assessment and considerably facilitates the evaluation of the impact report by the authorities) or another exchange of heterogeneous resources (Money for Information: payment for the processing of a planning application with an impact assessment works better if the assessment is complete than if the cantonal service has to waste time obtaining the missing information). It is also possible to imagine a situation involving a negative exchange of time budgets in the case of disasters, for example, if the political–administrative actors agree with the target groups on the application of an accelerated procedure in the interest of rapidly reconstructing a damaged site. The two actors renounce the normal time budget by necessity. It is important to note that such agreements may run counter to the interests of the beneficiaries who may insist instead that the normal procedure be maintained, thereby protecting their interests with a view to avoiding the emergence of chaotic 'disaster urbanism'.

One way of achieving such homogenous exchanges of Time consists in the imposition of moratoriums whereby all of the actors of a public policy community agree on a waiting period, during which research is carried out separately by each of them or by scientists, and promise to respect their findings: for example, the moratorium on the landscape initiative, the 20-year freeze on development zones, and the moratorium on genetically modified organisms (GMO), specifically, agricultural seed.

The heterogeneous exchange of Time among the political-administrative actors and the two civil society groups is equally common: for example, the exchange of Time for Law and Property: renunciation by target groups of the submission of an appeal if the public actors grant them longer deadlines for the adaptation of their machinery (at the level of implementation acts); for Money and Property: the acceptance by public actors in the area of taxation of longer amortization periods; and Information: the acceptance by public officials of exceptional deadlines for the development of time-consuming studies with a view to obtaining the authorization of pharmaceutical products or environmental impact assessments.

Time/exchange: Target groups

The initiative for a homogenous exchange of the resource Time between political-administrative actors and target groups probably originates in most cases from the latter. They suggest such 'deals' in relation to major projects for which experience in relation to environmental or social impacts is lacking. In contrast, target groups rarely propose solutions involving a moratorium unless it enables them to continue the pursuit of their activities in the meantime.

The examples presented in the section on the exchanges proposed by the political-administrative actors also apply to such exchanges initiated by the target groups.

Time/exchange: Beneficiary groups

A homogenous exchange of Time between beneficiary groups and political-administrative actors (and/or target groups) may consist of an 'armistice' or 'truce' in which the latter, for example, the occupants of a site on which it is planned to construct public infrastructure, undertake to discontinue their mobilization of Force during a given period. This delay enables the other actors to gain an 'artificial' period of time with a view to reflecting on alternative solutions. These different actor groups suspend the battle but will resume it if necessary, if the disagreement remains unresolved.

It should be noted that the majority of the examples mentioned in the preceding sections involve heterogeneous exchanges. This applies irrespective of the actor that initiates the exchange. In all cases, the actors agree to refrain from mobilizing a resource at their disposal for a period of time. They admit, however, that this period of non-use enables the actor in question to take the measures necessary to enable the use of one of their other resources, the mobilization of which sometimes takes time ('mobilization work'). Like the omnipresent homogeneity of the exchanges involving Consensus, this omnipresent heterogeneity of the exchanges involving Time reflects the fundamental character of this resource that ultimately dictates the pace of the advancement of public policies in all their stages by drawing the line between the 'before' and 'after'.

Recommended further reading

Textbooks and specialist literature

Dussauge-Laguna, M.I. (2012) 'The neglected dimension: bringing time back into cross-national policy transfer studies', *Policy Studies*, 33(6): 567–85.

Fleischer, J. (2013) 'Time and crisis', *Public Management Review*, 15(3): 313–29.

Hewlett, M. and Goetz, K.H. (2014) 'Introduction: Time, temporality and Time scapes in administration and policy', *International Review of Administrative Sciences*, 80(3), 477–92.

Application in IDHEAP studies

Knoepfel, P. and Boisseaux, S. (2012) *Expertise sur l'effectivité du service valaisan de l'environnement en matière de préavis sur des projets de construction*, Chavannes-près-Renens: IDHEAP.

Notes

[1] This switchover was the object of a popular vote in Switzerland (28 May 1978) and was rejected by the Swiss people. Due to multiple incompatibilities at the level of international relations, the Federal Parliament eventually had to return to this decision in the context of a new federal act regulating time in Switzerland. Daylight saving was introduced in Europe in 1977 and confirmed in late 2007. See Yvette Estermann's motion no 10.3674 of 21 September 2010 demanding the abandonment of daylight saving time which, according to the text of the motion, did not have any positive impact in terms of energy consumption.

[2] For example, the imposition of deadlines by popular initiatives in Switzerland. See the case of acceptance in 2014 of the initiative against mass immigration that obliged the federal authorities to legislate before the end of February 2017. This deadline would have been difficult to comply with if the draft decree had necessitated a renegotiation of the agreement on the free circulation of people with the European Union.

[3] A typical example of an appeal against a 'non-decision': an appeal by a group of elderly Swiss women against measures to mitigate climate change that were considered insufficient to fulfil the objectives of the Paris Agreement (autumn 2016).

15

Political support

Definition

According to the democratic rules applicable under the rule of law, when any public policy is established or undergoes a major change to its content, it needs a legal basis that has been approved by a parliamentary majority (sometimes also the population and, possibly, the cantons). This approval gives it "primary" legitimation which differs from "secondary" legitimacy, which depends on the assessment of the policy services and implementation procedure by social groups (see … "resource Consensus"). Hence, while consensus is associated more with the implementation stage, this resource … refers to the capacity to produce legislation within the political-administrative programme (PAP). In particular, it is … the priority weapon of public actors and enables them to assert themselves through the legal resource that it legitimizes vis-à-vis minority social groups.

However, even in the case of legislation supported by a comfortable majority of the executive, the implementation of a public policy can experience periods of crisis, during which this majority support can fluctuate. For example, a public policy can lose its legitimacy and acceptability in the eyes of the majority if the measures are challenged due to adverse affects or impacts that run contrary to the policy objectives (for example, in the absence of accompanying measures, a policy for the restriction of parking in a town or city centre can lead to the transfer of the problem to peripheral communes), or due to conflicting interpretations of the effects of certain provisions (for example, challenging of the right of appeal for organizations by the political right, which see it as a source of unhelpful blockages, while the left consider this right indispensable for the protection of the environment). Indications of the weakening of this resource are reflected in the submission of an increasing number of parliamentary intervention demanding changes to the legislation.

The resource ... makes it possible to save on the use of other resources, or in the case of its absence it can lead to their use or, indeed, abuse. Public policy actors that enjoy extensive political support can temporarily dispense with other resources, for example consensus (for example, nuclear policy in France in the 1970s), law (defence policy), time (acceleration and simplification of an intervention while short-circuiting procedures considered as too costly) and the cognitive resource.... All of these substitutions demonstrate the primordial importance of "political support", particularly during the stage consisting of the redefinition of the public problem to be defined and the identification of the causes.

Reference ... to symbolic values shared by the majority of actors (decision-makers) and/or the population appears to be a common means of producing and reproducing this resource: for example, political support for the conservation of agricultural areas may be re-established by referring to the contribution made by agriculture in "supplying the country in periods of crisis" and, based on this, the national defence. Hence there is a very close link between the "construction of the meaning"[1] of a policy ..., and the support it enjoys (linked with such symbolic values) ... would also appear to be an indispensible means in the production of the resource "political support".

In fact, in many cases, the symbols used transmit implicit hypotheses about the causes of the problem to be resolved. Given that they are widely shared by the political majority, there is little or no need to relate the latter to a specific rationale.[2] Thus it is not necessary, for example, to prove that all things "ecological" are 'good' or that all those who contribute to the national defence contribute to the well-being of the country, because ecology and the national defence are among the values commonly accepted by the majority of the (Swiss) population. (Knoepfel et al, 2010: 67-9)

Specifics

In the context of public policy analysis, Political Support is a resource that is required for the creation or modification of the resource Law. However, it is also a precarious resource. More than Law, it evades the control of the specific communities of public policy actors. In effect, these communities must take very particular account of the influence of the negatively and positively affected third parties (third party winners and losers) who are crucial to the general support of the policy in question, as these groups link the specific space of the public policy and that of the general political environment. Thus it is possible for this community of actors to lose its Political Support due to a coalition of opponents formed by third party losers and a large number of actor communities originating from other substantive public policies. The management, use, procurement and loss of this resource, which is essentially managed by the institutional policy of democracy – semi-direct in the case of Switzerland – mainly takes place outside the specific community in parliamentary commissions, the parliament itself, the executive and increasingly, the intercantonal conferences of specialized cantonal directors.

For this reason, the availability of Political Support is always precarious, and providing proof of its availability is an almost daily task. This is done not only to convince the beneficiary groups but also, and above all, public opinion throughout society, with which the third party winners and losers act as intermediaries. To be able to do this it is in the interests of these actors to limit the number of third party losers, as these groups will be unlikely to support the policy in question. For this reason, all of the key actors of the public policy triangle must constantly describe and remind the external actors of the gravity of the social problem that the policy in question sets out to resolve and, moreover, directly target these external actors.

This is the point at which, in our model, the political parties get involved as conveyors of the opinions, views, interests and so on of these third parties who, as we recall, generally represent a far larger number of people than the political-administrative actors, the target groups and beneficiary groups of the actual community of the substantive public policies in question (see Chapter 1). As some French colleagues in the field of political sociology (Bruno Jobert and Pierre Muller in particular) say, what is involved here is an attempt to bring the specific *référentiel* (cognitive framework) produced in the community of actors of a public policy into line with the general *référentiel* that underpins all public policies on a cross-cutting basis.

Through their general programmatic orientation, the political parties are more or less closely aligned with the target groups or beneficiaries of a public policy and are, in effect, responsible for establishing links between the two types of *référentiels*. This work is facilitated by the fact that each of the three groups of actors involved in a substantive public policy includes representatives from their ranks (groups of actors representing the interests of the target groups or the beneficiary groups; political-administrative actors, the so-called 'political' actors).

Figure 15.1[3] shows that at the level of the Swiss federal chambers, this role is played by the members of the seven most important political parties in Switzerland. They represent associations of target groups and beneficiaries from almost all of the areas covered by sectoral policies in Switzerland.[4]

Figure 15.1: Ten important federal sectoral policy areas and their representation by members of the federal chambers belonging to the seven most important political parties in Switzerland

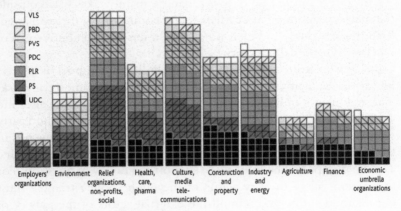

Source: Lobby register, state 4th of February 2016
Inspired by the figure published in the newspaper NZZ, 14th of March 2016, page 12.

There is no guarantee that this work will always succeed, however. It is possible that, despite the fact that its legal basis remains intact due to the simple fact that there is no clear majority in favour of its complete dismantling (an explicit decision to put its political-administrative programme out of play and thus withdraw the resource Law) or modification (for example, by removing a specific part of the legal basis through partial revision), a policy would not, in case of an explicit vote, achieve the support of a solid parliamentary political majority, for a period of time at least.

From the point of view of the community of public policy actors, this means that each must contribute to this task in its own way while taking into account the shared interests of the three actor groups in the survival of 'their' policy, despite diverging interests, values and strategic objectives. This work obviously requires the investment of action resources on the part of each of the three partners who must thus actively engage in the veritable 'external politics' of their policy. Moreover, it is important to stress that, even if they must 'change behaviour' by definition (a restriction), the target groups participate in the measures to support 'their' policy. It should also be remembered that the target group is not always as homogenous as one might think, and that it comprises a majority and a minority in itself.

In my experience, there is a serious risk that this work will fail if a policy's community of actors does not succeed in reaching an agreement on the basic components of 'their' policy, that is, its causality model – including the hypotheses relating to the causes and interventions – or if the language developed jointly by this community is so technical that it becomes incomprehensible and hence incommunicable to the rest of the world. Similar risks arise if the problem to be resolved is considered more as a private problem or 'non-existent' in the eyes of the world (for example, the national defence policy in the years following the end of the Cold War, climate policies in the mid-1970s), or if the adopted modes of intervention run counter to approved modalities of intervention according to a 'mega-trend' for all other public policies (for example, in contrast to incentive policies based on economic instruments, regulatory policies are considered quasi-universal today, although the opposite was the case in the 1960s and 1970s when such economic instruments appeared to be at odds with the rule of law). Other situations of discord can arise if the application of these modalities of intervention is accompanied by social and/or public costs that are considered disproportionate in terms of the benefits that can be obtained at the same cost in other public policies. In the history of Switzerland, agricultural policies (before the reform of 1992), the national defence policy and (consistent) anti-cartel policy were candidates for such failures.

This being the case, a systematic analysis based on the model used for the other nine public action resources does not make much sense in the case of Political Support. Despite confirmation that a policy has unfailing Political Support at a given moment, it does not appear appropriate to refer to some kind of use right available to the community of actors associated with this policy that they may dispose of or deploy, as is the case for the nine other resources. Ultimately nobody can hold any ownership of Political Support, at least in a democracy, as this support can collapse from one day to the next due to events or decisions that have nothing to do with the policy in question or the exchange of resources between its actors. Despite the dark clouds hanging over the general political landscape, this process can even continue to unfold peacefully thanks to a climate of mutual trust in this space.

For the same reason, it does not appear wise to try to identify the exchange of this resource among public policy actors as it is the community in itself that is its depositary and not one or other of its members. Nevertheless it is true that the relationships that the target groups, the beneficiaries and their organizations and the political-administrative actors maintain with their 'political parties' or with the country's large organizations representing, for example, economic, social and ecological interests are characterized by all kinds of exchanges of public action resources, to which each of these actors has collective or individual access. But none of these umbrella organizations and no political party can play a role in a representative democracy, even a semi-direct one, by relying on just one community of actors involved in a substantive public policy. These organizations must invest in the construction of general *référentiels*, which are, in fact, different, precisely because they aim to be general, because they are more encompassing, universal, cross-cutting and necessarily more reductionist than the sectoral *référentiels* of the substantive public policies in question.

If one or other of the public policy actors claims to mobilize Political Support in practice, what is involved in reality is an attempt to constrain the political-administrative actors that govern the substantive policy in question at federal, cantonal or communal level through decisions relating to policy programming or implementation. Hence these strategies aim to improve the position of the actor in question in relation to the other actor groups of the basic policy triangle. In this sense, it is possible to refer effectively to a Political Support enjoyed by the three actor groups that strongly resembles the unequal distribution of Consensus.[5] They attempt to influence them through the mobilization of one of the other nine public action resources presented here.

In practice, Political Support reveals its crucial importance during situations of change, be they 'internal' (changes of position among the three key actors of the substantive policy in question) or external (changes of position among the third party winners and losers, political parties etc). For this reason, the presentation here is structured in a slightly different way to that of the other resources. In effect, these changes manifest in situations in which the resource risks disappearing, leading to a veritable loss of political legitimacy for the public action in the area involved. In the 'mobilization' section I present, first, specific situations involving the loss of Political Support and second, observable strategies of the three actor groups aiming to regain this vital resource for the smooth functioning of 'their' sectoral public policies. In the 'mobilization by stage' section, I present the strategies observable at implementation level that is threatened by a loss of legitimacy on the part of the policy in question. For reasons already explained, I omit to present a specific section on the exchange of Political Support, as this is almost ubiquitous in concordance systems like the Swiss political system (compromise solutions).

Political Support: Mobilization

Situations involving a risk of the loss of Political Support

From the perspective of all of the dominant actors of substantive public policies, but particularly that of the beneficiary and political-administrative actors, it is possible to differentiate between two situations involving the risk of the loss of Political Support:

- *Collapse of the triangular structure of the internal actors:* this situation arises when one of the three actors loses the trust of one of the two other main actors and the loss is irrevocable. This may be due to simple disinterest, voluntary departure or exclusion by the two remaining actors. The policy risks 'collapsing' and 'losing its meaning' as a result. The remaining actors, who no longer succeed in establishing the basic Consensus on the causality model, lose their credibility. Such a situation may arise if the dissenting actor group challenges the problem definition and, accordingly, the hypotheses on the causes and/or constitutive interventions. What is involved here is an existential crisis at the epicentre of the policy itself that risks prompting a general questioning of the legitimacy of the policy in question. This situation gives rise, first, to a quest for internal reorganization strategies, for example, by seeking a new definition of the public problem while attempting to maintain the basic actor configuration, or seeking a new actor to replace the dissenting actor. Examples of this can be found in the different sectoral agricultural policies – cheese, dairy, viticulture – fluctuations between the function of providing an adequate food supply and the other social functions of agriculture, for example, spatial planning and sustainable development.
- *The loss of external Political Support:* in this situation, the substantive policy in question loses its Political Support among a majority of

public and private actors in its environment. This loss manifests, primarily, among the third party winners and/or losers (positively or negatively affected third party groups), and ultimately spreads in the form of a political attempt to bring about radical change or a complete dismantling of the sectoral policy in question. This situation arises in particular in the context of successive parliamentary interventions or popular initiatives relating to it. In the eyes of a parliamentary majority and/or the executive, the sectoral policy in question loses primary legitimacy and, if necessary, in opposition to the intact consensus of the three constitutive actor groups that will do everything in their power to maintain it. Such cases are very common among energy policies, for example, the abandonment of nuclear power and petrol.

Actor strategies for recovering Political Support

Strategies adopted by political-administrative actors

The two above-described situations (internal collapse and loss of external support) challenge the very existence of the administrative units responsible for the policy in question. It is obvious that these units do everything in their power to ensure their own survival; the inventory of observable defence strategies deployed in reality is thus extensive and includes the following:

- *New definition of the problem:* intensified presentation of the public problem that the policy threatened with collapse aims to resolve, and demonstration of the harmful consequences of its disappearance. In some cases it is possible to observe an actual change in the definition of the problem ('solutions in search of a problem'). I would claim that this strategy is very common and is also adopted when there is no actual threat of a loss of Political Support. Such modification of the problem definition also constitutes an opportunity to expand the beneficiary groups and guarantee a broader basis, for example, the shifting of the definition of climate policy in the direction of adaptation measures and away from the focus in the initial definition on the reduction of greenhouse gas emissions – 'living with irreversible change'.
- *Modification of the causality model* through a modification (restriction or extension) of the target groups (causal hypotheses) and/or changes in the main intervention instrument (attenuation or strengthening, depending on criticisms made by the target groups or beneficiaries).

It should nonetheless be recalled that any extension of the target groups risks creating new third party losers and thus calling into question the general political support enjoyed by the old policy. By way of example, we can mention here the extension of the number of target groups of the policy for the elimination of money laundering (traditional bankers and others, for example, trustees, hoteliers), environmental policies (inclusion of drivers and/or farmers as a group of greenhouse gas emitters that were initially excluded), and policies relating to the international battle against drug consumption (extension of target groups to include farmers who cultivate basic products for the production of drugs).

- *Reduction of the third party losers group:* this strategy consists in transforming losers into winners by proposing new lucrative areas of activity to them. An example can be found in the new renewable energies policy that attempts to transform the economic sectors that are currently reliant on oil into companies that can benefit from renewable energies.

Any repositioning of a substantive policy whose existence is under threat from the outside requires a minimum level of internal coherence (thus consensus on the part of the target and beneficiary groups) and the support of the decision-makers (parliament or the executive). Moreover, this kind of repositioning can be accompanied by a change in the policy's administrative context, for example, a change in the department responsible for the policy.

Strategies adopted by target groups

In the case of a threat to the Consensus on the part of beneficiary groups and/or (less common) the political-administrative actors that risks disturbing the equilibrium within the basic actor triangle, thus leading to a loss of external Political Support, the target groups find themselves faced with a choice between saving the policy through a (more or less consistent) change in their behaviour in the direction of adherence with the public action in question or seeking external support with a view to reinforcing their internal position and risking the total collapse of the policy in question. Given that the existence of an established policy can strengthen the predictability of the general economic situation, the risk associated with the second option is not negligible. Hence the target groups will have an interest in maintaining the pre-existing policy, as a 'break everything' strategy can also have an unfavourable impact on their Political Support. So it is reasonable to assume that in the case of external threats, the target groups will tend to maintain the policy in question and fight side-by-side with the political-administrative actors and the beneficiaries to regain Political Support of the political actors.

Strategies adopted by the beneficiary groups

The strategies adopted by the beneficiary groups are very similar to those of the target groups. Given that the disappearance of the policy in question risks challenging their position as beneficiaries, they will fight even harder to maintain the status quo (including regarding the definition of the problem) as they risk having to share this privileged status with the arrival of new beneficiary groups. Hence they will be good allies for the political-administrative actors in mounting a defence in response to threats from the external actors. This also applies in cases where the political-administrative actors succeed in transforming third party losers into winners who, if necessary, risk diluting their benefits, in the short term at least, due to the additional costs generated for the provision of services relating to the new 'policy business' (for example, increase in health insurance costs, exposure to new competitors in the labour market). It should be noted that cases where the beneficiaries of a substantive public policy form a political majority at parliamentary or executive level are rare.

Specifics of the mobilization of Political Support in the context of policy implementation

The collapse of Political Support for a substantive public policy can originate in the context of the implementation of policies that are particularly controversial and have a high media profile. This arises in particular since the emergence of powerful social networks that are capable of consuming an entire substantive public policy starting from purely local acts of dissent. A high media profile often has the effect of decontextualizing these cases and generalizing them. Having been decoupled from its content, the case lends itself to the dissent of target groups and/or beneficiaries that succeed in getting it onto the front page of the major daily national newspapers. Moreover, there are always parliamentarians who attempt to raise their profile by demanding 'drastic reforms'.

This real risk generates, among other things, the need for the local actors that are unaccustomed to being involved in such matters of national importance to engage teams of public communicators who have the task of recontextualizing the case in question, and do so with varying degrees of success. The challenges demonstrated above proliferate throughout the space between policy implementation at local level and policy programming at national level. For the actors of the basic policy triangle, it is a question of 'keeping things in proportion', 'setting the record straight' and avoiding the political exploitation of individual cases by political actors on all sides.

Recommended further reading

Textbooks and specialist literature

Jobert, B. and Muller, P. (1987) *L'Etat en action. Politiques publiques et corporatismes*, Paris: Presses universitaires de France.

Knoepfel, P., Papadopoulos, Y., Sciarini, P., Vatter, A. and Häusermann, S. (2014) *Handbuch der Schweizer Politik/Manuel de la politique Suisse*, 5th edn, Zürich: NZZ Verlag. In particular, Chapter 5 on federalism (Adrian Vatter), 6 on direct democracy (Wolf Linder, Rolf Wirz), 14 on the political parties (Andreas Ladner), 15 on social movements (Marco Giugni) and 16 on the interest groups (André Mach). Also recommended are Chapters 18 on elections (Georg Lutz, Peter Selb) and 19 on popular votations (Pascal Sciarini, Anke Tresch).

Such textbooks exist for almost all European countries. All kinds of contributions on the relation between politics and public policies are strongly recommended.

'In-house' applications

Dupuis, J. and Knoepfel, P. (2013) 'The adaptation policy paradox: The implementation deficit of policies framed as climate change adaptation', *Ecology and Society*, 18(4): 31.

Savary, J. (2007) 'Mise en œuvre des politiques de la mobilité urbaine: Analyse comparée de processus de régulation des usages des voies publiques et de l'air dans quatre villes suisses', Thèse à l'Université de Lausanne.

Notes

[1] See the *référentiels* (cognitive framework) approach in Jobert and Muller (1987) and Muller (1995). For a discussion of the translation of *référentiel*, see Barbier (2015).

[2] Refer to Jobert and Muller's (1987) notion of 'image'.

[3] *Neue Zürcher Zeitung*, 14 March 2016: 12 (translated and slightly adapted by the author in terms of presentation).

[4] Employees: 21 members, almost exclusively from the left; Environment: 56 members, mostly left; Social support, non-profit sector: 115 members, mainly centre-left; Health, care, pharma: 71, mainly centre-left; Culture, media, telecommunications: 108 members, no obvious partisan affiliation; Construction, property: 80 members, mainly centre-left; Industry and energy: 86 members, mainly centre-right; Agriculture: 35 members, mainly centre-right; Finance: 42 members, mainly right; Economy umbrella organizations: 36 members, almost exclusively right.

[5] However, at the level of implementation (which is of primary interest here), this equation only works if the political-administrative actors in some way represent a position close or identical to that held by the majority of political parties (at national and cantonal levels). Experience shows that this is far from always the case, even when the councillor of state with responsibility for the case in question is a member of a strong party at national or cantonal level. The positions adopted by the latter even differ frequently from those of their own party (at cantonal level).

Part IV
Outlook and advice for practical application

In this final part of the book I begin by examining a practical application of crucial importance for public policy management, that of involving the targeted allocation of public action resources to the political-administrative actors on the basis of action plans or, more specifically, the instrument generally referred to in Switzerland as 'service-level agreements' (see Chapter 16).

Chapter 17 presents some practical advice for researching portfolios of public action resources, and carrying out explanatory analyses that relate the results of decision-making processes and the activities of different actor groups to the mobilization of resources. This should facilitate the evaluation of power relations between actors and the outcomes of public action in specific areas.

Public policy management by actors' endowment

The focus of this chapter is limited to the use of public action resources by the political–administrative actors. It is inspired by the widespread emergence of action plans that arise in connection with almost every public policy today. We have already identified action plans as a separate product of the public policy cycle located between the programming and production of individual and concrete outputs. It should be remembered, nonetheless, that such plans can also be used to manage public policy interventions carried out by large organizations of target groups or beneficiaries. They play a primordial role in public policy implementation processes.

This chapter begins with some reflections on the fundamental premise concerning the efficient and effective use of resources in the conduct of public policies, particularly in the context of their implementation. It then revisits our definition of action plans as a product whose objective is to allocate public action resources in a more targeted way than was the case prior to their – relatively recent – emergence, and demonstrates the key role they assume in the management of public policy implementation. The chapter concludes with some reflections on service-level agreements, a form of contract I consider a category of action plan.

Basic premise for policy implementation: the efficient and effective use of public action resources[1]

The analysis of public action resources facilitates a rational debate on the relationship between the premise of efficiency and that of effectiveness. Efficiency is generally defined as the measurement of the comparative costs of the production of outputs by unit. The measurement is usually limited to traditional resources like Time, Personnel, Money and Property. In contrast, the measurement of effectiveness also includes the impacts (changes in the behaviour of the target groups) and the outcomes of the public action (the contribution of the policy implementation activities, which incur a certain cost, to the resolution of the public problem the policy sets out to resolve).[2]

An efficient administration is not necessarily an effective administration. Of course, economies made at the level of the production of outputs – for example, by means of an acceleration in production (Time), the rationalization of production (Personnel through alteration of the adopted procedures) or not taking the position of opposing actors into account (Consensus) – can reduce the cost of their production. However, this production process will ultimately prove more costly if it triggers the mobilization of resources by the target groups and/or beneficiaries aimed at opposing inappropriate outputs, for example, because they are produced under 'authoritarian', non-participative conditions that contravene the general or specific institutional rules, or because the outputs become notoriously inadequate when it comes to actually resolving the problem in question. In effect, such outputs risk lacking secondary legitimation and undermine the effectiveness of the policy implementation, and the administration risks losing the very precious resource Consensus as a result. This situation often leads to an increase in the set of resources mobilized for contesting and appealing procedures and ultimately, not only for the political-administrative actors, but also, and above all, for the two other target groups.

'Good' public policy implementation requires public actors to be able to anticipate this kind of opposition through greater knowledge of the status of the resources at the disposal of the crucial social groups in the sector of intervention in question. The art of public management necessitates the measured limitation of economies in relation to the public resources invested by the public actors, and the instinctive identification of the 'tipping point' between an outcome that appears positive at initial glance and a mitigated result to be identified in the medium to long term. Given the presence of particular actor groups in several policy fields, such opposition movements can easily extend to related and even unrelated policies, which makes this economizing on resources even more debatable.

For this reason, in the case of budget cuts that are generally considered indispensible, it is in the interest of public managers to propose the limitation of the actual production of outputs to a smaller number of groups that are nonetheless crucial to the success of a public policy rather than simultaneously applying 'mitigation' or 'simplification' procedures to all implementation activities. It is known that in order to simplify administrative procedures, the directors of public administrations frequently commission committees of external experts to limit the number of administrative actors to be included in procedures for the circulation of dossiers that provide advance notice of a project (see above), to reduce the duration of the production of such advance notices or, even worse again, to reduce the duration of public enquiry procedures or even entrust the actual production of the dossiers to external actors (that are often close to the target group circles). Unfortunately, consultants still exist today who simply transpose revenue from the private sector to the public sector so that they can play this game of miraculous savings, and they still feign innocence when the above-described consequences arise: in some cases something they sold as an administrative reform that will generate savings proves to be something that generates enormous additional costs.

In summary, the consideration of the resources mobilized by all (public and private) actors strongly relativizes the putative positive impacts of budgetary cuts on the effectiveness of public policy implementation. These monetary restrictions almost always lead to the greater than expected mobilization of other resources by the political bodies, and ultimately result in the generation of greater monetary costs.

Action plans

In our basic textbook we define:

> ... APs [action plans], which are not necessarily observable as distinct formal elements in all policies, as the set of planning decisions considered as necessary for the coordinated and targeted production of administrative services (outputs).... Thus, APs define priorities for the production of concrete measures and for the allocation of resources necessary to implement administrative decisions and activities. As an intermediate stage in the policy execution process between the PAP and the sometimes unplanned appearance of implementation acts, APs are increasingly being adopted in policy processes as real management instruments.
>
> ... the AP should be interpreted as an individual product that makes it possible to establish a link between the general and abstract norms of the PAP and the individual and concrete implementation acts. Such plans may be distinguished from the intermediate implementation acts of certain policies (in particular those concerning land) that are defined as general and concrete products (but sometimes have the same name, such as a land-use plan).

Qualification of the public policy products PAP, AP and implementation acts according to the type of legal dimension

Legal dimension	General	Individual
Abstract	PPA norms	Action plans
Concrete	Intermediary implementation acts (for example, land-use plans)	(Formal) implementation acts (outputs)[a]

Note: [a] Formal administrative acts: decisions (in accordance with Article 6 of the Federal Act on Administrative Procedure of 20 December 1968 (LPA); 'material acts' (*Realakte*) in accordance with Article 25a of the LPA.

... This definition of priorities and lesser concerns may be undertaken from a functional (according to the type of activities subject to state intervention), temporal (according to the short, medium or long term), spatial (according to geographical zones) or social (according to the boundaries of socioeconomic groups) perspective. The definition of priorities, in the case of regulatory policies, in particular, is often associated with the decision to accept partial implementation deficits among certain target groups for a certain period. (Knoepfel et al, 2006: 218–21 [2011: 206–8])

According to the same text, these action plans can be explicit or implicit, and may be accompanied by the far-reaching or minor restructuring of the political–administrative arrangement (administration based on the 'project' model outside of the normal hierarchical line). In addition, a distinction is made between open and closed action plans, with and without the allocation of specific resources, and action plans that discriminate to varying degrees.

Based on this conception, these action plans are instruments for managing the implementation of valued public policies. In theory, these plans include concrete objects, a precise definition of those affected by the future implementation acts and statements regarding the impacts and, above all, the outcomes to be attained in the targeted areas. What is considered crucial is the contribution of public intervention to the (partial) resolution of the public problem in certain spaces, sub-sectors and so on that are prioritized in relation to other spaces or sub-sectors that are subject to explicit secondary treatment. However, an entirely different picture emerges from examining current public policy management practice. The focus of attention of parliamentarians and governments in relation to this management is not aimed at the level of outcomes but that of outputs (which are often still unknown at the time of the definition of the action plans as they depend on its concrete objectives and the reactions of target groups or the administrative cost of their processing). The result of this is the creation of a veritable bureaucracy dedicated to the management of 'service' indicators and, in my view, this is highly misleading; it can, moreover, lead to the blocking of all innovative initiatives on the part of the services concerned with the social problems that the public policies aim to resolve.

However, action plans are supposed to enable the correlation of public action resources with policy outcomes. Hence they present as a robust, simple and manageable alternative to the management based on outputs. It is necessary, however, for these plans to be sufficiently discriminating and for them to make the public action predictable for spaces that are not temporally covered due to being treated only during a second or a third round. The regulations defined under the rule of law require that action be taken through the instrument of waiting lists that can balance the expectations of the target groups and beneficiaries in the future. The legal nature of these action plans is not always clear beyond the observation that they involve individualized but not always sufficiently concrete decisions (in terms of outputs). In view of their importance as a legal safeguard and their recent large-scale emergence in almost all public policies today, it is high time for these plans to be clarified by the legal experts.[3]

It remains to be specified that action plans are not simply 'to do' lists in which the authority notes everything that should be accomplished in the future. In other words, the value of action plans consists essentially in their capacity to identify the areas covered by a policy and the gaps that exist in the targeted implementation activities. In view of the importance of these discriminatory decisions, on no account can these plans be considered as internal administrative documents or simple directives. In effect, these plans create inequalities of treatment and thus require a clear legal basis that stipulates, in particular, precise criteria for this discrimination that the administration can use to easily identify the boundary between the 'ins' and the 'outs'.[4] Once decided on and published, these plans create legitimate interests and rights to the public action in question. It is imperative that their – indispensible – evaluation clauses suggest a functional link between the public actors' endowment with resources and the policy impacts and even the outcomes, and on no account should they be limited to serving as indicators of outputs.

Service-level agreements[5]

Since the dawn of time, public sovereigns (monarchs, parliaments, constituents and populations) have tried to manage public action through the allocation of public action resource budgets to both public and civil society actors. The objective was always the same: to avoid the reign of the arbitrary and make the future predictable by balancing the mutual expectations of public actors and civil society. An initial high point of this movement was undoubtedly the French Revolution, which led to the limitation of the Force, Money and Law allocated to the leaders of public actors by the parliaments. It is important to remember that at the time parliaments already allocated resource budgets to civil society actors, in particular, target groups, by granting them the fundamental rights and instruments of their legal defence (Law, Property and Time).

This regime was motivated by the attempt to limit the resource budgets of state actors so as to avoid the arbitrary and excessive production of norms and administrative acts associated with their execution. In our terms, this involved in particular avoiding the production of outputs that were unpredictable and undesirable from the perspective of the powerful target groups without the government having the indispensible resources of Political Support and Law available to it. These restrictions imposed on the liberal state essentially concerned the areas of taxation, penal law and freedom of business and trade. The implicit (and sometimes even explicit) equation at the root of this liberal philosophy is to attribute limited resource budgets to public actors to guarantee that the production of outputs is limited to a strictly necessary level. In short, this philosophy consisted in the management of public action through the limitation of the resource budgets available to public actors while guaranteeing the extensive portfolios of resources to the (powerful) civil society actors.

This conception was extended considerably during the period of the emergence of 'major' public policies (1960s), and once again in response to the public finance deficits of the 1980s when parliaments intentionally enlarged the number of (increasingly scarce) resources under their control by explicitly including them in their legislation. The main idea, again, was to control the quantity and quality of public policy products – in this instance, implementation in the form of outputs – through the increasingly targeted management of the resources made available to the executives and a particular focus on the efficiency of the public service. This was all the more important as the growth of the welfare state had considerably increased the quantity of resources in circulation.

By way of example, we can refer here to recent parliamentary decisions on Organization (parliamentary legislation on the government and administration that encompasses the organizational competence of the creation, modification and so on of new administrative units and their detailed terms and conditions – management through the endowment of the resource Organization), Time (for example, legislation provisions concerning all kinds of implementation deadlines), Personnel ('hiring freezes', requirements in relation to the qualifications held by personnel, particularly at cantonal level), Property (in particular, harmonization of accounting rules for the public sector) and Consensus (for example, limitation of communication budgets on the part of public actors). Similar attempts at management were also focused for a long time on Information (the creation of independent statistics services, archiving).

The rise of the movement formerly known as New Public Management (NPM) (Osborne and Gaebler, 1983) signalled the end of the validity of the equation to the effect that the management of public actors' resources alone would guarantee good public policy results. Even before the emergence of NPM, analysts and practitioners who found themselves facing increasing challenges in relation to the quality of public policy outputs had introduced the notion of 'secondary legitimization' or 'legitimization of public action through its quality'. Hence the focus of interest in relation to public management shifted, in part, in that the parliaments and later governments tried to introduce a link between the resource budgets and the results generated by the activities of the public service. This link came to be broadly accepted between the end of the 20th century and the present day.

In Switzerland and many other European countries, the main instrument adopted to achieve this objective was and remains the 'service mandate', later the 'service-level agreement' and later again, the 'reconciliation of objectives' agreed between parliaments or governments and specific entities within the administration or private bodies. For the last 20 years it has been possible to observe the considerable extension of these agreements at federal and cantonal levels in Switzerland with the aim of making public action more efficient and more effective.

However, critical scrutiny of these agreements[6] demonstrates an astonishing focus on the old philosophy of efficiency and far less emphasis on the effectiveness of public policies transformed in this way. The quantity and – sometimes – quality of the 'groups of products' to be supplied during a given period is agreed on without defining any objectives in terms of impacts (which changes should be attained in the behaviour of target groups?) and even more seriously, in terms of the results (outcomes) to be obtained at the level of civil society (to what extent should the public problem be resolved?). Moreover, it is possible to observe the extremely vague definition of 'groups of outputs' that have no real capacity for targeted management. The same applies to the service-level agreements used at cantonal level for the implementation activities of the services, offices and administrative units, although the level of concrete detail involved is usually slightly higher. Moreover, this coupling of public action resources and outputs remains flawed because it does not include all of the public action resources presented here, and does not take into account the resources mobilized (in a positive or negative sense) by the civil society actors (target groups and beneficiaries).

So what happened? Although it is too early to provide a detailed explanation of this 'twist in the tale', which is often denied by the public and private actors involved in the policies in question, the adoption of (easily quantifiable) (see Knoepfel and Varone, 1999) administrative outputs as the main dimension of reference for the attainment of objectives logically had to exclude the consideration of objectives in relation to impacts (effects) and/or outcomes (results). There is no reason to assume that a precise causal relation in the form of a miraculous algorithm exists between outcome and outputs, and moreover, due to the mobilization of resources on the part of social actors that remains practically unpredictable. Mathematics cannot replace 'the art of governing' that must leave the choice of the 'good output' to the 'good administrator' within the scope of the institutional rules in force (in particular for Switzerland, the rule of law and semi-direct democracy). It is precisely at the level of the choice of suitable outputs that the famous 'flexibility' of political-administrative actors as required (rightly or wrongly) by NPM resides.

Notes

[1] In relation to Switzerland, see Rieder et al (2014: 242).

[2] As I have a personal preference for the old terminology (modified in Knoepfel et al, 2010) – output = administrative achievement (*réalisation administrative*); impact = effect; outcome = result) – I ask my colleagues to excuse its use in this book.

[3] It should be noted that what is involved here are neither intermediate general and concrete acts (such as urban plans, for example) or material administrative acts (in the sense of Article 26a of the Administrative Procedure Act) that are individual and extremely concrete.

[4] The 'ins' are those who are particularly 'affected in their rights and obligations' (Act on Administrative Procedure, Article 25a) through the administrative activity in question; the 'outs' are the *quisquis ex populo* (anyone and everyone).

[5] French: *mandat/contrat de prestation*; German: *Leistungsvertrag*.

[6] Conseil fédéral, 20 novembre 2013. Message sur le développement de la gestion administrative axée sur les objectifs et les résultats; nouveau modèle de gestion de l'administration fédérale (NMG). 13.092: 741–856. See Ritz (2003); Schedler and Proeller (2006).

Advice for practical application

This final chapter is composed entirely of the results of my teaching activities, over the course of which my students carried out various empirical studies on public action resources in relation to freely selected, and therefore very wide-ranging, public policies with a view to analysing the relations of power between the policy actors. Between five and eight different federal or cantonal policies were analysed in the courses held over each year. Given the limited time available and the desirable comparability of the results, the proposed process necessitated a certain standardization of the empirical approach to facilitate the feasibility of the work. Obliged to choose between conceptual 'purity' and practical feasibility that would enable the students to experience the pleasure of discovering new issues, I opted for pragmatic guidance. This concerned the units of measurement used for qualifying the observed resources, a comparative model for the visualization of the actors' resource portfolios and a simple method for identifying exchanges of resources. This chapter ends with a checklist to enable the explanatory role of the actor games to be identified in terms of public policy results.

Units of measurement and indicators

Table 17.1 presents the units of measurement adopted, on the basis of our practical experience, for each of the 10 resources, specified, if required, for each of the three actor groups. It also presents a sample of particular indicators that may, however, vary considerably in reality.

The utility of the units of measurement suggested here is intentionally generic. The indicators also enable the analysis of power relations between public policy actors for descriptive purposes, for example, for discussing the relevance of strategies for changing these power relations with a view to instigating administrative or political reforms in a particular political system.

Identification of the resource portfolios of public policy actors

It is imperative that both the policy analyst and those who hold strategic positions within the actor groups are aware of all of the resources at

Table 17.1: Units of measurement and suggested choice of indicators for each of the 10 public action resources

Resource	Units of measurement	Choice of indicators for the political-administrative actors	Choice of indicators for the target groups	Choice of indicators for the beneficiary groups
Force	- Number of armed people - Security devices	- Security personnel workforce (policy, army, civil protection) - Capacity of installed security equipment (IT)	- Security personnel workforce available - Existence of data protection mechanisms - Capacity (offensive) for unlawful acquisition of secure data	- Number of people who can be mobilized and are available for direct action (occupation of public places, building sites etc) - Degree of compulsion of specialized objective law invoked
Law	- Clarity of legal basis that grants competency (authority) or rights of appeal (civil society groups)	- Degree of constraint of public interventions (mandatory or optional) - Degree of precision of legal basis for public intervention - Capacity for the control of monitoring of outputs	- Existence of rights of appeal - Degree of credibility of threats of recourse to legal action - Existence of internal control regimes (compliance)	- Existence of rights of appeal - Frequency of credible threats of recourse to legal action - Frequency of recourse to legal action and rate of success
Personnel	- Number, qualifications and political loyalties of contracted personnel	- Number of personnel at the competent administrative entity - Existence and quality of personnel qualification policy (initial and further education and training) - Recruitment policy (age, sex, language, political positions) - Rate of rotation of personnel - Competitiveness of salaries in the labour market context	- Number of personnel in unit responsible for the monitoring of public policies (legal services, senior policy staff) - Proximity to public service personnel ('revolving door')	- Number and qualifications of personnel in the secretariat responsible for policy and legal questions - Availability of volunteers - Capacity for consultation of external experts
Money	- Swiss francs - Parts of total budget dedicated to activities relating to a specific policy (%)	- Significant modification of financial resources dedicated to a specific policy (increase/decrease) - Degree of precision of the definition of the budget line in question (scope for manoeuvre)	- Amount and proportion of the budget dedicated to the 'policy' activity and/or defence of professional interests (increase, stability and/or decrease)	- Amount and proportion of the budget dedicated to the 'policy' activity and/or defence of professional interests (increase, stability and/or decrease) - Proportion of subsidies and proportion of fees from available general budgets

Resource	Units of measurement	Choice of indicators for the political-administrative actors	Choice of indicators for the target groups	Choice of indicators for the beneficiary groups
Property	- Balance sheet assets (assets and buildings; movable and immaterial assets)	- Available premises and IT equipment - Assets in public ownership - Access to communication networks - Status of progress in the digitization of specific information - Ownership of strategic plots	- Taxable wealth and income (tax declaration) - Property portfolio and strategic plots - Holding of use rights to natural, artificial, social and human resources	- Access to social networks and the media - Ownership of strategic plots of land - Holding of use rights to natural, artificial, social and human resources
Information	- Proportion of total necessary information that is confidential (inaccessible to the other actors) - Proportion of the information that is inaccessible (as held exclusively by one of the two other actors)	- Importance and use made of 'confidential' information - Availability of so-called 'independent' sources of information - Capacity for the processing of statistical information and databases (recourse to 'big data') - Policies for the consultation of external experts (commissioned reports) - Threats to make confidential information accessible	- Existence and use made of 'confidential' information - Capacity to contest the validity of the information produced for the political-administrative actors or by the beneficiaries - Utilization of confidential data obtained legally or illegally	- Utilization of confidential data obtained legally or illegally - Capacity for the control or validation of information originating from the target groups and/or political-administrative actors
Organization	- Number of partner organizations that can be mobilized to defend or contest a project (method: network analysis)	- Number of political-administrative, federal, cantonal and communal actors willing to cooperate	- Existence of communities of actors including representatives of other target groups and beneficiaries - Direct access to actors from the target groups and/or beneficiary group	- Number of active members of organizations for defending the interests of beneficiaries - Access to social networks - Presence of active members in the most important implementation processes (action plans and outputs)

Resource	Units of measurement	Choice of indicators for the political-administrative actors	Choice of indicators for the target groups	Choice of indicators for the beneficiary groups
Consensus	- Number of vetoes in decision-making processes, the use of which results in an existential threat to the decision in question - Number of rejections of such decisions with immediate effect in the form of the modification of the position of the other two actors - Absolute and relative number of proposals (ie, proportion of all proposals made by the actor) accepted by the two other actor groups - Importance of dissent in the eyes of the other actors	- Degree of recognition of proposals among target groups and beneficiaries - Control of an actorial space that is stabilized in terms of the control of its borders	- Capacity for challenging public policy space through the threat of mobilizing external allied actors (in particular, third party losers) - Support of representatives by all of the target group - Acquisition or loss of recognition on the part of the beneficiary groups and/or political-administrative actors	- Degree of recognition in public opinion (specialist media, scientific experience etc) - Number of credible threats to mobilize public opinion leading to a change in the position of the two other groups

Resource	Units of measurement	Choice of indicators for the political-administrative actors	Choice of indicators for the target groups	Choice of indicators for the beneficiary groups
Time	- Absolute (hour, day, month, years etc) - Relative (time budget available compared to that of the other actors)	- Imposed time budgets (deadlines defined in institutional rules) - Strategies for the acquisition of additional time through requests for the moving of deadlines for urgent topics - Extension of time: additional hours, stress activism etc	- Requests for the extension of deadlines for particularly 'difficult' dossiers - Recourse to legal procedures with a view to 'gaining time' - Requests for additional expertise with a view to 'gaining time' - Anticipatory behaviour through the creation of *faits accomplis* that reduce the availability of time for the two other actor groups (closure of companies, moves abroad etc)	- Requests for the extension of deadlines for particularly 'difficult' dossiers - Recourse to legal procedures with a view to 'gaining time' (request with suspensive effect) - Requests for additional expertise with a view to 'gaining time' - Anticipatory behaviour through the creation of *faits accomplis* that reduce the availability of time for the two other actor groups (occupation of building sites, organization of strikes etc)
Political Support	- Number of votes (popular, parliamentary votes, parliamentary commissions, extra-parliamentary commissions) - Proportion of administration's personnel that is 'political' (executive, senior public service) compared to all senior executives	- Holding of a real or possible parliamentary majority - Holding of majorities within federal, cantonal, intercantonal (Conferences of Cantonal Governments: Maison des cantons) and communal executives	- Referendum capacity (popular initiative and referendum) - Support of political parties and key personalities with varying degrees of independence	- Referendum capacity (popular initiative and referendum) - Support of political parties and key personalities with varying degrees of independence - Support of other associations that defend the interests of beneficiaries (associations for the protection of consumer interests, the environment, hospital patients, trade unions etc)

their own disposal and that of the two other groups. We refer to this as the portfolio of resources, for which an inventory may be carried out for a given moment in time using different tools. This process must take into account the fact that these portfolios can only be understood by means of a comparative process that can capture the strengths and weaknesses of each portfolio compared to those of the other two groups. Thus I suggest using the units of measurement and indicators provided in Table 17.1 and applying them on a comparative basis, that is, using the same unit of measurement for each resource and paying particular attention to the 'more' and 'less'.

Based on this approach, Table 17.2 aims at identifying specifically the resources that are badly lacking and those that are available in abundance – it is these resources that are likely to form the object of exchange of resources throughout the decision-making process.

Figure 17.1 presents a graphical representation in the form of a wheel of the findings of analyses carried on this basis, indicating a very low level (position at the centre of the wheel: 0) or very high level (position at the edge of the wheel: 6) on a scale of 0 to 6 for each resource.

This reproduction of the portfolio of public action resources is also intentionally generic and applicable outside any explanatory process based on the strict public policy analysis model. In addition, Figure 17.1 shows portfolios that are relatively close to reality in the case of all three actor groups.[1]

(Homogenous and heterogeneous) resource exchange

The (homogenous or heterogeneous) exchange of a given resource should become apparent through a comparison of resource portfolios before and after the exchange. Thus it makes sense to carry out an inventory of these portfolios at t_0 (start of decision-making process) and t_1 (end of decision-making process, immediately after the decision-making).

To facilitate the structuring of research on such exchanges, I propose a simple double-entry table (see Figure 17.2) to be applied to each of the relations along the three sides of the triangle, that is, the exchanges between the political-administrative actors and target groups, between the political-administrative actors and the beneficiary groups and, exceptionally – such cases being rare – between the target groups and beneficiary groups.

Figure 17.1: Inventory of public action resources

Political-administrative actors

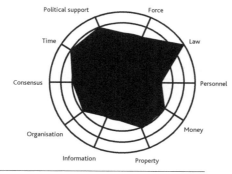

Target groups

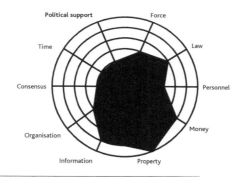

Beneficiary groups

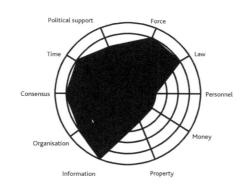

Figure 17.2: Template for identifying the exchange of resources between public policy actors

	Force	Law	Personnel	Money	Property	Information	Organiz-ation	Consensus	Time	Political Support
Force	■									
Law		■								
Personnel			■							
Money				■						
Property					■					
Information						■				
Organiz-ation							■			
Consensus								■		
Time									■	
Political Support										■

■ Homogenous exchanges   ☐ Heterogenous exchanges

This classical analysis enables the visualization of the exchange of resources between the three actor groups (to be carried out primarily between the political–administrative actors and target groups and between the political–administrative actors and beneficiary groups). In the case of emerging public policies in particular, it makes sense to also track the (direct) relations between target groups and beneficiary groups resulting in the rejection of the mounting of a given policy in favour of 'private' contractual solutions.

Seven-point checklist for analysing the effects of the mobilization of public action resources on public decision-making

This 'checklist' summarizes the approach proposed in this book (and in the basic textbook), and facilitates the testing of hypotheses concerning the power relations between public actors and public decision-making. A particular focus of interest here are the hypotheses of highly varied theoretical and/or ideological origins presented in the literature, and the partisan statements made in relation to the power available to a given actor at the level of public decision-making. The proposed approach is divided into seven analytical sequences that should produce a solid empirical basis for answering the age-old question regarding the power of the actors both in general and in a particular case. These results may be confirmed or rebutted with the help of comparative research simultaneously analysing several cases that differ particularly on the basis of the dependent variable as the result of the reconstructed decision-making process.[2] The checklist verifies the different explanatory variables adopted, and identifies their influence on the political decisions subject to explanation.

The approach encompasses the following seven operations:

1. Actors

> Before identifying the objects of the mobilization of public action resources, it makes sense to identify the constitutive actors of the basic policy triangle (political–administrative actors, target group actors, beneficiary group actors, third party winners and losers). This approach is tried-and-tested and can be implemented with the help of the traditional model of the actor triangle. (Knoepfel et al, 2006: 63 [2011: 57])

For explanations of the terms used in Figure 17.3, please refer to our basic textbook and some of the explanations provided in this book (see Chapter 1).

2. Decision(s)

> As a second step, it makes sense to identify the decision or decisions that are subject to the mobilization of resources by one or more actors. The distinction between the six products that emerge throughout the public policy cycle as presented in our basic textbook is reiterated here. (Knoepfel et al, 2006: 125f [2011: 119f])

Figure 17.3: (Classical) triangle of public policy actors

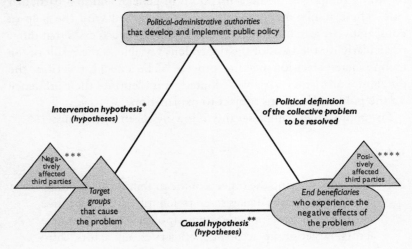

New terminology (since Knoepfel et al. 2011):
* hypothesis (hypotheses) on the intervention, ** hypothesis (hypotheses) on the causes,
*** third-party losers, **** third-party winners

Figure 17.4: The six public policy products

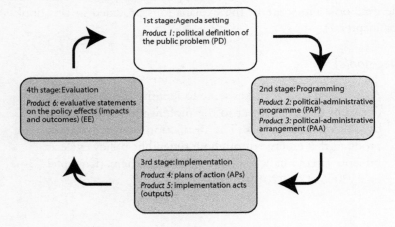

Thus, the analyst must try to identify the six types of products illustrated in Figure 17.4 for all policies based on the following characteristics:

– The political definition of the public problem (PD) not only includes the decision on political intervention but also, and above all, the delimitation of the perimeter of the public problem to be resolved, the identification of its probable causes by the public actors and the kinds of public intervention envisaged.

– The political-administrative programme (PAP) includes all of the legislative or regulatory decisions taken by both central state and public bodies and necessary to the implementation of the policy in question.

– The political-administrative arrangement (PAA) defines the competencies, responsibilities and main resources at the disposal of public actors for the execution of the political-administrative programme.

– The action plans (AP) establish the priorities for policy implementation in the context of geographical and social space and with respect to time.

– The implementation acts (administrative outputs/outcomes) cover all activities and administrative decisions involving the application of measures.

– The evaluative statements on the effects of a given policy objective aim to demonstrate the changes (that may have taken place) in the behaviour of target groups (effects/impacts) and the effects triggered among the end beneficiaries (outcomes, results) and to scientifically and/or politically appreciate the relevance, effectiveness, efficacy and efficiency of the applied policy. (Knoepfel et al, 2006: 125-6 [2011: 119f])

Experience shows that it is advisable to differentiate between these six products despite the observable overlaps between them. These overlaps prompted some analysts to abandon this fundamental differentiation – wrongly, in my view – and to even replace the term 'public policies' with 'public action' (see Chapter 1). In addition, and still in accordance with our basic textbook, it is possible to differentiate between different elements within each of these products according to whether they are substantive or institutional in nature. Hence some actor games can be identified that involve a mobilization of resources targeting the substantive elements of the policy decision in question, while others prefer to focus on the institutional elements that encompass the public action resources and their exchange. The results of the latter games are reflected at the level of the rules governing the production of the

Table 17.2: Substantive and institutional content of the six public policy products

Policy stage	Product to be explained	Generic definition of the product	Operational elements for analysis of the product	
			Predominantly substantive content	Predominantly institutional content
Agenda setting	Political definition of the public problem (PD)	Mandate formulated for the attention of the political authorities to formulate a policy aimed at resolving the public problem that has been placed on the political agenda (–> request for intervention and start of an initial solution)	• Degree of intensity (severity) • Perimeter (audience) • Degree of innovation	• Degree of urgency
Programming	Political-administrative programme (PAP)	All of the legislative norms and regulatory acts that define the substantive and procedural elements of the policy (–> definition of the normative content and primary legitimation)	• Substantiation of objectives • Evaluative criteria • Operational elements (or action instruments)	• Administrative authorities and resources • Procedural elements (including legal)
	Political-administrative arrangement (PAA)	Structured group of public and semi-public actors responsible for the implementation of the policy (–> definition of actors' competencies, intra- and interorganizational management and general allocation of resources)	• Number and type of actors • Context defined by other policies	• Degree of horizontal and vertical coordination • Degree of centrality • Degree of politicization • Degree of openness
Implementation	Action plans (AP)	All decisions of a planning nature that define the priorities in time, space and vis-à-vis social groups for implementation of the policy (–> specific allocation of resources for targeted production of outputs)	• Explicit (formal) vs absent • Degree of discrimination (in time, space and vis-à-vis social groups)	• Degree of structuring for implementing authorities • Associated resources vs non-associated resources • Degree of openness
	Implementation acts (outputs)	All end products of political-administrative processes that address the target groups at whom the policy measures are aimed (–> application, execution)	• Perimeter (complete vs incomplete) • Substantive, internal and external coherency	• Institutional content (eg creation of a target group) • Intermediary vs final • Formal vs informal
Evaluation	Evaluative statements on the policy effects (impacts and outputs)	All value judgements pertaining to changes in behaviour triggered among the target groups (impacts) and on the improvement of the situation observable among the end beneficiaries (outcomes) (–> secondary legitimation)	• Evaluative criteria applied • Recapitulative vs formative • Partial vs global	• Scientific vs ideological • *Ex-ante*, concomitant or *ex-post* • Formal vs informal • Consequences of statement

subsequent products, and are often played by actors that are too weak to affect the substantive elements of the decisions. To differentiate these elements within the different products, I suggest using the list provided at the end of the basic textbook (Knoepfel et al, 2006: 279 [2011: 264f]), and presented again in Table 17.2.

This process enables us to identify the contested objects precisely and for each actor and, by extension, the eventual mobilization of public action resources.

3. Strategic actor objectives

As described in Chapter 5, each of the actor groups pursues specific strategic objectives. These objectives are of particular interest specifically in cases in which they 'evade' prediction by researchers or managers, who risk deducing them too mechanically based on the simple positioning of the actors in the triangle. Thus it is essential to 'allow the actors to speak' and not to be content with abstract statements. 'Letting the actors speak' means collecting the written or oral statements of each actor while also realizing that these may be inaccessible for strategic reasons. To clarify:

- these statements must be identified for each of the five actor groups (thus including the third party winners and losers/positively and negatively affected third parties);
- if possible, they must relate to precise elements of the policy products in question (defined in stage 2 of the process).

4. Reconstructing the decision-making process

The development of each of the six products is divided into different stages, in a more or less precise and regulated way, starting with an initial plan for a decision (which is sometimes itself the result of an entire series of preparatory procedures), a consultation or enquiry procedure, a stage in which the relatively extensive mobilization of resources by actors may be expected, and a final stage from which the definitive decision emerges. Each of these stages is accompanied by draft projects that can be differentiated from each other on the basis of particular elements. It will be possible to identify the following elements, in particular:

- elements that undergo significant change through this production process;

- elements that remain unchanged (despite the fact that these may be the object of controversy and resource mobilization on the part of one or other actor).

At the end of this stage, the observer will have more detailed knowledge of the variable to be explained that consists precisely in the changes that have arisen in relation to one or other of the elements that compose the product in question.

5. Portfolios of public action resources by actor

This stage involves the reviewing of the strengths and weaknesses of the actors by comparing their portfolios of action resources based on the above-presented 'wheel' diagram (see Figure 17.1). It is advisable to use some of the units of measurement proposed at the beginning of this chapter for this.

As a general rule, and based on experience gained through the application of this approach by participants in my courses on public policy analysis, it is almost impossible to determine the resources used in an identifiable mobilization process, a step that would enable the identification of the portfolio of action resources available to each of the actors after mobilization. Thus I would advise that this should not be attempted. Furthermore, in practice, we content ourselves with focusing the analysis of these portfolios on the most important resources *in situ*. In this sense, it is important that the profiles of the 'wheels' clearly demonstrate the missing resources in contrast to those available in abundance: these two groups of resources should emerge quite clearly from this comparison. The missing resources, whose lack is felt and, if possibly, specifically referred to, are of particular interest because they are at the root of the mobilization process (supplementary production, substitution or exchange observable in reality). In these cases it is important to look for plausible empirical responses to the question as to why the actor in question cannot achieve their strategic objectives without having these missing resources at their disposal.

In some cases, we observe actors that pursue strategies for the acquisition of resources dedicated to the specific mobilization observable in a given area. Accordingly, a target group at which a future piece of legislation is aimed will collect funds to be reserved for a referendum campaign against the law, or beneficiary groups (for example, organizations representing patients, pensioners, consumers or protectors of the environment) accumulate money to finance the large number of planned appeals against implementation decisions in one of their priority areas. Such 'war chests' will regularly have a repercussion at the level of mobilization of public action resources during the development of a public policy product (final stage of legislation consisting of a referendum battle or final stage of implementation leading to the production of outputs [including court judgements]).

6. Mobilization – actor by actor[2]

This stage constitutes without doubt the *pièce de résistance* of the proposed approach as it should provide the ultimate proof of the existence of a link between the mobilization of action resources and the results of this mobilization. I suggest that the following seven points be dealt with actor by actor:

1. Existence or not of staggered mobilization plans (based on the stages and prioritizing the key element[s] contested by 'adversary' actors). Like the public action plans, these can identify the priority mobilization areas (in time and/or space) and also rule on the renunciation of mobilization in cases considered as minor.
2. Existence of indications of decisions regarding the substitution of missing resources with abundantly available resources, a situation that is sometimes expressed in the renunciation of the mobilization of resources X to the benefit of resources Y. This choice can even have repercussions on the choice of the contested element that will then be replaced by another.
3. Combination of resources with the aim of boosting the effect of the mobilization at the level of the decision-makers and/or that of the other social actors (for example, beneficiaries and/or third party losers).
4. Presence of (more or less credible) threats to mobilize resources and the effects of these threats on the decision-makers.
5. Explicit decisions to renounce the mobilization of an available resource (in exchange or not) for concessions at the level of the decision-making (political-administrative actors) or of one of the other two social actors (target group undertakes to change their behaviour voluntarily, beneficiary group refrains from launching an appeal, referendum etc).
6. Existence of real exchanges of resources (homogenous or heterogeneous): it should be noted that the mobilization of resources does not automatically lead to an explicit exchange of resources. Based on my experience, this kind of exchange should be empirically observable. In effect, we are not referring here to an exchange that

only takes place by mutual agreement between the actors involved. This presupposes the documentation of the counter-services. Nonetheless, it should be remembered that it is not necessarily in the actors' interest for all exchanges to be formalized. And it is also important to stress that similar mobilizations can also impact on the decisions of the political–administrative actors without there being any kind of formal contract. Figure 17.2 should be used for documenting such exchanges. As explained in the previous section, it is necessary to create three diagrams that document such homogenous and heterogeneous exchanges between (1) the target groups and political–administrative actors, (2) the beneficiaries and the political–administrative actors, and (3), if necessary, eventual exchanges between target groups and beneficiaries.

7. With a view to the discussion of the results, it helps to reconstruct and document the institutions activated by each of the actors during each act involving the mobilization of public action resources. The analyst or manager must never assess the legitimacy of the observed mobilization acts but should simply collect possible data on the institutions that are explicitly evoked – whether rightly or wrongly. It should be noted that any resource activation considered 'inappropriate' or 'illegal' may be subject to challenges that could explain the eventual mobilization of public action resources by other actors.

7. Assessment: Mobilization of public action resources and changes at the level of public policy products

It is only after conducting this empirical research that the researcher and manager will be able to answer the initial question concerning the winning and losing actors and their power relations. The proposed assessment will be based on a comparison of the changes observed in relation to the elements of the debated products and the resource mobilization activities of each of the actors involved. This process enables us to confirm or disprove the initially stated hypothesis on the power relations between public policy actors. However, it is essential that this assessment be itemized on the basis of the (institutional and/or substantive; see Table 17.2) elements of the public decision in question, which are identifiable for each of the actors involved. Such comparative analyses of a large number of cases can reveal similar models that indicate, for example, that, irrespective of the rules of the game activated, the winning actors are always the target groups (Marxist hypothesis), the beneficiaries (pluralist democracy hypothesis) or the political–administrative actors (hypothesis of the omnipotent state). Observations to the contrary will demonstrate the importance of institutional rules (in particular, behavioural and decisional ones) that systematically structure the decision-making processes in favour of actors who, based on the rules of possession, must be considered as weak actors, or conversely, in favour of actors that are already powerful by virtue of their portfolios of public action resources.

Notes

[1] Typical portfolios: political–administrative actors – abundant resources: Law and Political Support; scarce resources: Consensus and Personnel. Target groups – abundant resources: Property and Money; scarce resources: Consensus and Political Support. Beneficiary groups – abundant resources: Consensus and Force, scarce resources: Money and Property.

[2] For a more detailed analysis that is focused on resources (and not on the entire decision-making process), see Chapter 5 (on analytical dimensions of public action resources).

Conclusion: Strengths and weaknesses of the proposed approach

In order to evaluate the strengths and weaknesses of the approach presented in this book, which was written over the last four years with numerous interruptions and periods of doubt and reflection, let us return to its initial objectives. The aim was – and still is – to produce a textbook aimed at Master's and doctoral students and the heads of administrative services, private consultancies, NGOs and the staff of professional associations that protect the interests of target groups during public policy processes. The initial objective was to assemble and structure the experiences encountered in the context of their own activities as analysts and/or managers, and to process them in light of concepts already largely developed in our initial textbook of 2006 on public policy analysis and management (first version: 2001, English translation 2011).

What I did not intend initially was to attempt to combine the public action resources approach with that of institutional resource regimes (IRR), which was developed simultaneously on the basis of theoretical and practical research in the area of natural resources. This research initially concerned sustainable development in the area of natural resources (water, forests, landscape, climate and the genetic programme) and subsequently, in the areas of manufactured resources (for example, national memory, stock of rental buildings) and social resources. Today we can confirm that the latter development (presented, essentially, in Part II of this book) constitutes a real innovation that will, however, require future conceptual development.

Throughout the compilation of this book I battled with certain difficulties that I feel I have not quite succeeded in overcoming in this final version (see 'Weaknesses'). Other aspects of it have proved to be more successful (see 'Strengths'), at least in their application in the context of teaching and in the development of doctoral theses.

Strengths

Like several other authors who have addressed the topic of public action resources (see Chapter 3), my main preoccupation is to consider these resources as transferrable, objectifiable and in principle, dissociable from their actor-users. It was possible to sustain this conceptual belief throughout the book. This is not something that emerged in the course of my initial teaching or during the compilation of the basic textbook on policy analysis and management. The application of this principle posed a problem in particular in relation to the resources Law, Information and Consensus. In the case of Law, this distinction is not made in this book through the usual differentiation between objective and subjective law, but by the formula of competency (attributable or non-attributable) for the production and application of the law (legislation and administrative acts) on the one hand (public actors), and the (attributable or non-attributable) right of appeal which, in a given situation, enables the application of the objective law to a specific case of policy implementation (for the civil society actors). According to the version proposed in this book, in the case of Consensus, the distinction between the actor-holders and the social phenomenon (existence or absence of a consensus) is made by considering the esteem in which the actor-holder is held in the eyes of the other partner actors. In relation to Information, I distinguish between the informed actor as a characteristic of the actor and not the resource, on the one hand, and the object (information in itself), which is the cause of the holder being informed, on the other. It is up to the readers and users of this book to assess the practicability of these distinctions.

It would appear that I also succeeded in avoiding any hierarchization of the public action resources. While it is true that the principle of the substitutability or not of one or more resources with another may lead to the idea that the substituted resource enjoys a hierarchically superior position, this may on no account be taken as a general fact. The reason for this is that the substitution may not function in situ or yield the opposite results. Everything cannot be bought, even with a billionaire's fortune, and power of target groups residing in the resource Property is difficult to overcome, even with solid Political Support. This resource is extremely powerful on a material level and, moreover, is protected by a constitutional guarantee of private property. In addition, it is impossible to find any example of successful policy implementation in the absence of a minimum level of mutual trust between the three actor groups (Consensus).

This lack of a hierarchy means that the balancing of policy actors' resource portfolios is necessary on a permanent basis. In effect, it is not in the interest of any of the three groups for one of the other to be totally deprived of resources at a given point in time and thus incapable of acting and participating in the production of public decisions. Without peaceful re-balancing, they can quickly expect widespread processes of destabilization which, moreover, pose a threat to their own position of power.

This book also supports the key role played by institutional rules. Without them, there are no resources (except in situations of tyranny). Resources and rules are social products constructed by actors down through the centuries to make public life endurable in a way that is predictable and democratic. It was also possible to demonstrate the empirical existence of this conviction among the actors for each of the 10 resources dealt with in this book. In this sense, this text subscribes to a 'constructivist pragmatic' approach (Warin, 2009).

Although the examples presented in this book are largely drawn from cases relating to Switzerland, the concept of public action resources has also been applied to contexts with very different political systems such as France, Spain, Ukraine, the countries of Latin America and China. In the latter case, we experienced a significant failure, at least on the level of a course commissioned by the Chinese Communist Party: this party's ideology does not accept the idea of a structured civil society whose actors hold public action resources. For this reason, our concept of the actor triangle and the actors' game and the exchange of resources by the actors could not be applied logically.[1] A more detailed examination of Chinese public policies presented in the work of other Chinese students revealed, nonetheless, the existence of very powerful non-state actors within civil society there, and also the presence of empirically observable and very varied resource portfolios in the hands of these actors. How astonishing – actor games can be observed there involving the exchange of resources in accordance with institutional rules that may be very different to ours but are nonetheless attributable to the three categories of possession, behavioural and decisional rules.

Weaknesses

The fact that I did not succeed in establishing a truly productive dialogue between my concept of public action resources with other opposing or similar concepts is probably due, in part, to the limited status of the research in this area. On two occasions (2013 and 2015) my colleagues and I undertook research on the data available in the scientific literature in three languages (English, French and German). Despite this time-consuming effort, the results were rather weak (see Chapter 3). Although the term 'resource' is omnipresent in the social sciences today, it would appear that few researchers have tackled the phenomenon of public action resources in relation to the power of public policy actors in a truly systematic way. Obviously, the method we used to assemble these texts online can be criticized as being too simplistic, reductionist, and thus lacking in validity.

A second and more significant weakness arises from the lack of analysis of the capacity of actors to manage, manipulate, exchange etc public action resources. This is probably due to what I considered the strength of this book, that is, the strict distinction between actors and resources. This distinction resulted in a weaker focus on the actor side of this pair. However, it is known that individuals exist who, through their own characteristics, are capable of producing more powerful resource portfolios than other actors as they have extraordinary strategic and operational intelligence at their disposal. The very predominant attempt to 'depersonalize' public politics in this book results in the reduction of the 'human factor' to a residual status that it does not deserve. In fact, it is so important that it also merits an entire book of its own, which would probably sell better than this one. The reason for this is simple: who would not like to learn how to become an 'intelligent', Machiavellian or beneficial, egoistic or altruistic, nice or cunning etc actor? I personally would decline to write such a book. In this instance, even more than in the case of public action resources, there are few or no scientists or academics who can claim to be more intelligent than the actors of the real world.

A third series of weaknesses concerns my mode of presenting examples. By stylizing certain examples or grouping regularly observed facts into one ideal-typical example and also sometimes in referring allusively to widely known events, I did not engage in detailed and rigorous traceability, which is essential for transforming an example into formal proof in support of a scientific case. This is something I readily accept. Essentially, my intention was never to accuse, so there was no need for 'proof'. Moreover, the aim was to open up stimulating pathways for thinking about public action beyond how it is conceived today. It appeared to be more productive to view my examples as a rational synthesis of 40 years of experience as an observer of public policies.

I would like to conclude by recalling two weaknesses already mentioned in the book that represent invitations to researchers to take the efforts made here 'a step further'. The first concerns the disparities in the level of detail presented on the different resources. Time, Consensus and Organization, for example, await researchers who will be capable of tackling the considerable analytical interest they present with the necessary attention to detail. Second, the analytical potential developed in my colleagues' and my studies on institutional resource regimes, which is applied here to public action resources for the first time, is far from exhausted. The question of the overexploitation of public action resources, their maintenance and sustainability is an extremely promising prospect.

Note

[1]   A telling personal experience: after three hours of teaching on public policy, I received an email from the director of the programme (in Lausanne) stating that the Communist Party of China had sent him an email demanding 'urgently' that my course be cancelled. The course had been commissioned from the University of Lausanne and paid for by the Swiss Agency for Development and Cooperation. The reason given for the cancellation was that it was 'not compatible' with 'Chinese culture' (2015).

References

Athias, L. (2013) 'La contractualisation de services publics: une analyse économique', in A. Ladner, J.-L. Chappelet, Y. Emery, P. Knoepfel, L. Mader, N. Soguel and F. Varone (eds) *Manuel d'administration publique suisse*, Lausanne: PPUR, pp 679-98.

Baitsch, C., Knoepfel, P. and Eberle, A. (2000) 'Lernprozesse in Verwaltungen, Überlegungen zur Arbeitsteilung zwischen Internen und Externen', in Y. Emery (ed) *L'administration dans tous ses états, réalisations et conséquences/Grossbaustelle Verwaltung – Bilanzen und Ausblicke*, Lausanne: IDHEAP/PPUR, pp 259-77.

Barbier, J.-C. (2015) 'Languages of "social policy" at "the EU level"', in D. Béland and K. Peterson (eds) *Analysing social policy concepts and language: Comparative and transnational perspectives*, Bristol: Policy Press, pp 59-98.

Barrett, S. and Fudge, C. (1981) 'Reconstructing the field of analysis', in S. Barrett and C. Fudge (eds) *Policy and action: Essays on the implementation of public policy*, London/New York: Methuen, pp 249-78.

Baudepartements des Kantons St Gallen (1995) *Reorganisation des Amtes für Umweltschutz*.

Baumgartner, S. and de Montmollin, A. (2012) *Revision of the indicator system for the Federal Council and Parliament*, Swiss Federal Chancellery and the Federal Statistical Office.

Bellanger, F. and Roy, C. (2013) 'Evolution du cadre légal et réglementaire de la fonction publique suisse', in A. Ladner, J.-L. Chappelet, Y. Emery, P. Knoepfel, L. Mader, N. Soguel and F. Varone (eds) *Manuel d'administration publique suisse*, Lausanne: PPUR, pp 461-79.

Bergmann, A. (2009) *Public sector financial management*, Harlow: Pearson Education.

Berman, E.M., Bowman, J.S., West, J.P. and van Wart, M.R. (2015) *Human resource management in public service: Paradoxes, processes and problems*, Los Angeles, CA: Sage.

Boisseaux, S. (2012) *Les appellations d'origine et indications géographiques en Suisse, 1990 à 2006 – Politisation, institutionnalisation, nouveaux pouvoirs*, Zürich and Chur: Rüegger.

Bonoli, G. (2013) *The origins of active social policy. Labour market and childcare policies in a comparative perspective*, Oxford: Oxford University Press.

Bonoli, G. and Bertozzi F. (eds) (2008) *Les nouveaux défis de l'Etat social = Neue Herausforderungen für den Sozialstaat. Contributions à l'action publique*, Lausanne and Berne: PPUR, Haupt.

Börzel, T. (1998) 'Organizing Babylon – On the different conceptions of policy networks', *Public Administration*, 76 (summer): 253-73.

Bourdieu, P. (2006) 'Le capital social, notes provisoires', in A. Bevort, M. Lallement (eds) *Le capital social, performance, équité et réciprocité*, Paris: La Découverte, pp 29-34.

Blin, T. (2005) 'Ressources, stratégies et régulation d'un espace d'action collective: le cas des "réfugiés" de Saint-Ambroise', *L'Année sociologique*, 1(55): 171-96 (https://www.cairn.info/revue-l-annee-sociologique-2005-1-page-171.htmp).

Bressers, H. (2009) 'From public administration to policy network: Contextual interaction analysis', in S. Nahrath and F. Varone (eds) *Rediscovering public law and public administration in comparative policy analysis: A tribute to Peter Knoepfel*, Lausanne: PPUR, pp 123-42.

Bréthaud, C. and Nahrath, S. (2011) 'Entre imbrication, instrumentalisation et infusion', *Annales Valaisannes*, 2010-2011: 69-89.

Calenge, B. (2008) *Bibliothèques et politiques documentaires à l'heure d'internet*, Paris: Editions du cercle de la librairie.

Chappelet, J.-L. and Emery, Y. (2009) 'Discussion et recommandations: Le point de vue du management public', in P. Knoepfel (ed) *Réformes de politiques institutionnelles et action publique – Reformen institutioneller Politiken und Staatshandeln. Contributions à l'action publique*, Lausanne, Bern: PPUR, Haupt, pp 271-9.

Clapham, C. (1978) 'The requirements for explanation in comparative politics: Resources, rules and personality', *Government and Opposition. A Journal of Comparative Politics*, 13(3): 355-65.

Clivaz, C. (1990) *Influence des réseaux d'action publique sur les changements politique – Le cas de l'écologisation du tourisme alpin en Suisse et dans le canton du Valais*, Bâle: Helbing & Lichtenhahn.

Coleman, J.S. (1964) *Introduction to mathematical sociology*, New York: Free Press.

Commaille, J., Dumoulin, L. and Cécile, R. (2010) *La juridication du politique*, LGDJ – coll. 'droit et société'.

Compston, H. (2009) 'Networks, resources, political strategy and climate policy', *Environmental Policies*, 18(5): 727-46.

Condo Sales, V. (2017) 'Conflits dans la mise en œuvre de la politique de grands projets miniers et la stagnation de ceux-ci. Etude de cas autour de trois grands projets miniers au Pérou', Thèse, Lausanne: IDHEAP-UNIL.

Crozier, M. and Friedberg, E. (1981) *Actors and systems*, Chicago, IL: Chicago University Press.

Curien, N. (2005) *Économie des réseaux*, Paris: La Découverte.

Cusson, M. (ed) (2008) *Traité de sécurité intérieure*, Lausanne: PPUR.

Cusson, M. (2010) *L'art de la sécurité. Les enseignements de l'histoire et de la criminology*, Québec: Editions Hurtubise.

Dafflon, B. (1994) *La gestion financière des collectivités publiques locales*, Paris: Economica.

Dahl, R.A. (1957) 'The concept of power', *Behavioral Science*, 2(3): 201-15.

Dahl, R.A. (1961) *Who governs? Democracy and power in an American city*, New Haven, CT: Yale University Press.

Dahl, R.A. (1973) *L'analyse politique contemporaine*, Paris: R. Laffont.

Davern, M. (2001) 'Social networks and economic sociology: A proposed research agenda for a more complete social science', *American Journal of Economics and Sociology*, 287-302.

de Buren, G. (2015) *Understanding natural resource management – An introduction to Institutional Resource Regime (IRR) and a field-guide for empirical analysis*, Biel and Lausanne: Sanu durabilitas and IDHEAP, UNIL.

Dente, B. (2009) 'The law as a policy resource: Some scattered thoughts', in S. Nahrath and F. Varone (eds) *Rediscovering public law and public administration in comparative policy analysis: A tribute to Peter Knoepfel*, Lausanne: PPUR, pp 3-44.

Dente, B. (2014) *Understanding policy decisions*, Berlin and New York: Springer Briefs in Applied Sciences and Technologies.

DETEC (Federal Department of the Environment, Transport Energy and Communication) (2004) *Recommendations de la Confédération pour la négociation de conflits environnementaux*.

Deutsch, K.W. (1963) *The nerves of government*, New York: Macmillan Publishing Company.

Didry, C. (2001) 'La production juridique de la convention collective', *Annales. Histoire, sciences sociales*, 6: 1253.

Dowding, K. (2008) 'Power, capability and ableness: The fallacy of the vehicle fallacy', *Contemporary Political Theory*, 7: 238-58.

Dupuis, J. (2015) *S'adapter au changement climatique – Analyse critique des nouvelles politiques de gestion de l'environnement. Cas spécifiques de l'agriculture en Inde et du tourisme hivernal en Suisse*, Neuchâtel: Alphil.

Dupuis, J. and Knoepfel, P. (2013) 'The adaptation policy paradox: The implementation deficit of policies framed as climate change adaptation', *Ecology and Society*, 18(4): 31.

Dupuis, J. and Knoepfel, P. (2015) *The politics of contaminated sites management – Regime change and actors' mode of participation in the environmental management of the Bonfol chemical waste landfill in Switzerland*, Berlin and New York: Springer International.

Dupuis, J., Knoepfel, P., Schweizer, R., Marchesini, M., Du Pontavice, M. and Walter, L. (2016) *La politique suisse de reduction des émissions de gaz à effet de serre: Une analyye de la mise en oeuvre – Die Politik der Schweiz zur Reduktion der Treibhausgasemissionen: eine Vollzugsanalyse*, Rapport sur mandat de l'Office féderal de l'environnement (OFEV), Lausanne: IDHEAP.

Dussauge-Laguna, M.I. (2012) 'The neglected dimension: Bringing time back into cross-national policy transfer studies', *Policy Studies*, 33(6): 567–85.

Emerson, R.M. (1962) 'Power–dependence relations', *American Sociological Review*, 27(1): 31–41.

Emery, Y. (2013) 'Nouvelles politiques et processus de gestion publique des ressources humaines', in A. Ladner, J.-L. Chappelet, Y. Emery, P. Knoepfel, L. Mader, N. Soguel and F. Varone (eds) *Manuel d'administration publique suisse*, Lausanne: PPUR, pp 481–500.

Emery, Y. and Giauque, D. (2005) *Paradoxes de la gestion publique*, Paris: L'Harmattan.

Emery, Y. and Giauque, D. (2011) *Motivations et valeurs des agents publics à l'épreuve des réformes*, Laval: Les Presses de l'Université Laval.

Emery, Y. and Gonin, F. (2009) *Gérer les ressources humaines*, Lausanne: PPUR.

FDK-CDF, Conférence des directeurs cantonaux des finances (2008) *Manuel – Modèle comptable harmonisé pour les cantons et les communes – MCH2*, Bern: CDF.

Fischer, F. and Forester, J. (eds) (1993) *The argumentative turn in policy analysis and planning*, Durham, NC and London: UCL Press.

Fleischer, J. (2013) 'Time and crisis', *Public Management Review*, 15(3): 313–29.

Flückiger, A. (2018) 'Gouverner par des coups de pouce (*nudges*). Instrumentaliser nos biais cognitifs au lieu de légiférer', *Les Cahiers de Droit*, 59(1): 199–227.

Flückiger A. (2013) 'Les instruments de soft law en droit public', in A. Ladner, J.-L. Chappelet, Y. Emery, P. Knoepfel, L. Mader, N. Soguel and F. Varone (eds) *Manuel d'administration publique suisse*, Lausanne: PPUR, pp 299–313.

Flückiger, A., Morand, C.-A. and Tanquerelle, T. (2000) 'Evaluation du droit de recours des organisations de protection de l'environnement', *Cahier de l'environnement. Droit*, 314, Bern: Office fédéral de l'environnement, des forêts et du paysage.

Fredericksen, E.D., Witt, S.L., Patton, W.D. and Lovrich, N. (2016) *Human resource management: The public service perspective*, New York: Routledge.

Freeman, J. (1979) 'Resource mobilization and strategy: A model for analyzing social movement organization actions', in Z.N. Mayer and J.D. McCarthy (eds) *The dynamics of social movements*, Cambridge, MA: Winthrop Publishers, p 327.

Gamson, W.A. (1987) 'Introduction', in M.N. Zald and J.D. McCarthy (eds) *Social movements in an organizational society, Collected essays*, New Brunswick, NJ: Transaction Books.

Gerber, J.-D. (2006) *Structures de gestion des rivalités d'usage du paysage – Une analyse comparée de trois cas alpins*, Zürich and Chur: Rüegger.

Gerber, J.-D. (2012) 'The difficulty of integrating land trusts in land use planning', *Landscape & Urban Planning*, 104(2): 289-98.

Gerber, J.-D. (2016) 'The managerial turn and municipal land-use planning in Switzerland – Evidence from practice', *Planning Theory & Practice*, 17(2): 192-209.

Gerber, D. and Rissman, A.R. (2012) 'Land-conservation strategies: the dynamic relationship between acquisition and land use planning', *Environment and Planning A*, 44: 1836-55.

Gerber, J.-D., Knoepfel, P., Nahrath, S. and Varone, F. (2009) 'Institutional resource regimes: Towards sustainability through the combination of property-rights theory and policy analysis', *Ecological Economics*, 68(3): 798-809.

Giauque, D. (2003) *La bureaucratie libérale: Nouvelle gestion publique et régulation organisationnelle*, Paris: Harmattan.

Giauque, D. (2009) 'L'administration publique fédérale suisse en comparaison internationale: à la recherche d'une tradition administrative', in A. Ladner, J.-L. Chappelet, Y. Emery, P. Knoepfel, L. Mader, N. Soguel and F. Varone (eds) *Manuel d'administration publique suisse*, Lausanne: PPUR, pp 31-46.

Giauque, D. (2013) 'Motivation et identités des agents publics suisses', in A. Ladner, J.-L. Chappelet, Y. Emery, P. Knoepfel, L. Mader, N. Soguel and F. Varone (eds) *Manuel d'administration publique suisse*, Lausanne: PPUR, pp 523-40.

Giauque, D. and Emery, Y. (2016) *L'acteur et la bureaucratie au XXIe siècle*, Laval: Presses de l'Université de Laval.

Girad, N. and Knoepfel, P. (1997) *Cleuson-Dixence: Tout est bien qui finit bien?*, Etude de cas de l'IDHEAP, no 8, Chavannes-près-Renens: IDHEAP.

Glassey, O. (2013) 'Administration en ligne: Quand les utilisateurs deviennent des agents publics', in A. Ladner, J.-L. Chappelet, Y. Emery, P. Knoepfel, L. Mader, N. Soguel and F. Varone (eds) *Manuel d'administration publique suisse*, Lausanne: PPUR, pp 423-42.

Hall, P.A. (1993) 'Policy paradigms, social learning and the state', *Comparative Politics*, 25(3): 275-96.

Hendry, C. and Pettigrew, A. (1990) 'Human resource management: An agenda for the 1990s', *The International Journal of Human Resource Management*, 1(1): 17-43.

Hewlett, M. and Goetz, K.H. (2014) 'Introduction: Time, temporality and time scapes in administration and policy', *International Review of Administrative Sciences*, 80(3), 477-92.

Hess, C. and Ostrom, E. (2005) 'A framework for analyzing the knowledge commons: A chapter from "Understanding knowledge as a commons: From theory to practice"', *Libraries' and Librarians' Publications*, 21.

Hjern, B. and Hull, C. (1982) 'Implementation research as empirical constitutionalism', *European Journal of Political Research*, 10: 105-16.

Hood, C.C. and Margetts, H.Z. (2007) 'Exploring government's tool shed', in C.C. Hood and H.Z. Margetts (eds) *The tools of government in the digital age*, London: Palgrave Macmillan, pp 1-20.

Hugues, F., Hirczak, M. and Senil, N. (2006) 'Territoire et patrimoine: La co-construction d'une dynamique et de ses ressources', *Revue d'économie régionale & urbaine*, 5: 683-700.

Imbeau, L.M. (2009) 'Testing the "veil of ignorance" hypothesis in constitutional choice: A "walk-talk" approach', *Journal of Public Choice and Public Finance*, XXVI(1): 3-21.

Imbeau, L.M. and Couture, J. (2010) 'Pouvoir et politiques publiques', in S. Paquin, L. Bernier and G. Lachapelle (eds) *L'analyse des politiques publiques*, Montréal: Presses de l'Université de Montréal, pp 32–72.

ISO 22310 (2006) *Informations et documentations – Lignes directrices pour les redacteurs de normes pour les exigences de 'records management' dans les normes.*

Jänicke, M. and Weidner, H. (eds) (1995) *Successful environmental policy – A critical evaluation of 24 cases*, Berlin: Edition Sigma.

Jobert, B. and Muller, P. (1987) *L'Etat en action. Politiques publiques et corporatismes*, Paris: Presses universitaires de France.

Joerchel, B. (1999) 'Vugelles-La-Mothe /VD: Echos de tirs dans le vallon', in P. Knoepfel, A. Eberle, B. Joerchel Anhorn, M. Meyrat and F. Sager, *Militär und Umwelt im politischen Alltag, Vier Fallstudien für die Ausbildung/Militaire et environnement: la politique au quotidien. Quatre études de cas pour l'enseignement*, Sur mandat de l'Office fédéral du personnel, Bern: OCFIM, pp 168-324.

Kaluszynski, M. (2006) 'La judiciarisation de la société et du politique', *Colloque RIAD, Association internationale de l'assurance de protection juridique*, Paris, 21-22 September.

Kissling-Näf, I. (1996) *Lernprozesse und Umweltverträglichkeitsprüfung: Staatliche Steuerung über Verfahren und Netzwerkbildung in der Abfallpolitik*, Basel and Frankfurt am Main: Helbing & Lichtenhahn.

Kirchgässner, G. (2013) 'Economie politique de la dette et des déficits publics', in A. Ladner, J.-L. Chappelet, Y. Emery, P. Knoepfel, L. Mader, N. Soguel and F. Varone (eds) *Manuel d'administration publique suisse*, Lausanne: PPUR, pp 587-602.

Kiun, E.-H. (1996) 'Analyzing and managing policy processes in complex networks: A theoretical examination of the concept policy network and its problems', *Administration & Society*, 28: 90-119.

Klok, P.J. (1995) 'A classification of instruments for environmental policy', in B. Dente (ed) *Environmental policy in search of new instruments*, Dordrecht, Boston, MA and London: Kluwer Academic Publishers, pp 21-36.

Klüver, H. (2011) 'Informational lobbying in the European Union: Explaining information supply to the European Commission', *12th Biennial International Conference of the European Union Studies Association*, Boston, 3-5 March.

Knoepfel, P. (ed) (1990) in Auftrag der Schweizerischen Arbeitsgemeinschaft für Umweltforschung (SAGUF), *Landwirtschaftliche ökologische Beratung – Ein Modell für allgemeine Umweltberatung*, Basel: Helbing & Lichtenhahn.

Knoepfel, P. (1995a) 'Nouvelle gestion publique (NPM)', *Revue suisse de science politique*, 1(1): i-xv.

Knoepfel, P. (1995b) 'New institutional arrangements for the next generation of environmental policy instruments: Intra- and inter-policy cooperation', in B. Dente (ed) *Environmental policy in search of new instruments*, Dordrecht and Boston, MA: Kluwer, pp 197-233.

Knoepfel, P. (1995c) *Die Lösung von Umweltkonflikten durch Verhandlungen*, Basel: Helbing & Lichtenhahn.

Knoepfel, P. (2001) 'Regulative Politik in föderativen Staaten – das Beispiel der Umweltpolitik', *Politische Vierteljahresschrift* (PVS), Sonderheft 32/2001: 306-32.

Knoepfel, P. (2006) 'Der Staat als Eigentümer', in J.-L. Chappelet (ed) *Contributions à l'action publique = Beiträge zum öffentlichen Handeln*, Lausanne, Berne: PPUR.

Knoepfel, P. (2008) 'Positionsveränderungen der Akteure im sozialstaatlichen Leistungsgefüge: Ein politikanalytischer Essay', in G. Bonoli and F. Bertozzi (eds) *Les nouveaux défis de l'Etat social = Neue Herausforderungen für den Sozialstaat. Contributions à l'action publique*, Lausanne,Bern: PPUR, pp 223-34.

Knoepfel, P. (2011) *L'ancrage institutionnel du développement durable dans l'administration fédérale et dans trois cantons (VD, BE, AG)*, Working Paper from l'IDHEAP no 1a, Chavannes-près-Renens: IDHEAP.

Knoepfel, P. (2013) 'Institution killing policies – Policy killing institutions', Paper presented at the 1st International Conference on Public Policy, Grenoble.

Knoepfel, P. (2016) *Zur Gouvernanz des 'Lokalen': Anforderungen an eine nachhaltige Regulierung lokaler Mikrokosmen = On the governance of the 'local': Requirements for the sustainable regulation of local microcosms*, Cahier de l'IDHEAP 298, Chavannes-près-Renens: IDHEAP.

Knoepfel, P. (2017) *Strengthening or weakening public policies' implementation by conscious games on actors' constellations*, Manuscript for publication.

Knoepfel, P. and Boisseaux, S. (2012a) *Expertise sur l'effectivité du service valaisan de l'environnement en matière de préavis sur des projets de construction*, Chavannes-près-Renens: IDHEAP.

Knoepfel, P. and Descloux, M. (1988) *Valeurs limites d'immissions: Choix politiques ou déterminations scientifiques?*, Cahier de l'IDHEAP 48, Chavannes-près-Renens: IDHEAP.

Knoepfel, P. and Kissling-Näf, I. (1998) 'Social learning in policy networks', *Policy & Politics*, 26(3): 343-67.

Knoepfel, P. and Varone, F. (1999) 'Mesurer la performance publique: méfions-nous des terribles simplificateurs', *Politiques et management public*, 17(2): 123-45.

Knoepfel, P. and Varone, F. (2009) 'Politiques institutionnelles régulant les ressources des acteurs des politiques substantielles: un cadre d'analyse', in P. Knoepfel (ed) *Réformes de politiques institutionnelles et action publique*, Lausanne, Bern: PPUR, Haupt, pp 97-115.

Knoepfel, P. and Wey, B. (2006a) *Öffentlich-rechtliche Eigentumsbeschränkungen (ÖREB): Bestand nach Bundesgesetzgebung und ausgewählten Detailuntersuchungen*, Working Paper from l'IDHEAP no 7/2006, Chavannes-près-Renens: IDHEAP.

Knoepfel, P. and Zimmermann, W. (1986) 'Oekologisierung von Landwirtschaft', *Schweizerische Landwirtschaftliche Forschung/Recherche agronome en Suisse*, 25(2): 195-212.

Knoepfel, P. and Zimmermann, W., with von Sailer, G. and Matafora, E. (1993) *Evaluation des BUWAL. Expertenbericht zur Evaluation der Luftreinhaltung, des ländlichen Gewässerschutzes und der UVP des Bundes, Schlussbericht*, 18 November 1991, Bern: EDMZ.

Knoepfel, P., Baitsch, C. and Eberle, A. (1995) *Überprüfung der Aufbauorganisation des Amtes für Umweltschutz des Kantons St Gallen, Schlussbericht*, 1 February, Chavannes-près-Renens: IDHEAP, p 64.

Knoepfel, P., Kissling, I. and Marek, D. (1997) *Lernen in öffentlichen Politiken*, Basel: Helbing & Lichtenhahn.

Knoepfel, P., Kissling-Näf, I. and Varone, F. (eds) with Bisang, K., Mauch, C., Nahrath, S., Reynard, E. and Thorens, A. (2001) *Institutionelle Regime für natürliche Ressourcen: Boden, Wasser und Wald im Vergleich − Régimes institutionnels de ressources naturelles: Analyse comparée du sol, de l'eau et de la forêt*, Basel: Helbing & Lichtenhahn.

Knoepfel, P., Kissling-Näf, I. and Varone, F. (2003) *Institutionelle Regime natürlicher Ressourcen in Aktion/Régimes institutionnels de ressources naturelles en action*, Basel and Genf: Helbing & Lichtenhahn.

Knoepfel, P., Müller-Yersin, H. and Pestalozzi, M. (2004) *Grundlagen zu den Verhandlungsempfehlungen UVEK: Fachbericht*, Bundesamt für Umwelt, Wald und Landschaft (BUWAL), Schriftenreihe Umwelt, 365.

Knoepfel, P., Csikos, P., Gerber, J.-D. and Nahrath, S. (2012b) 'Transformation der Rolle des Staates und der Grundeigentümer', *PVS Politische Vierteljahresschrift*, 53(3): 414-43.

Knoepfel, P., Larrue, C. and Varone, F. (2006) *Analyse et pilotage des politiques publiques*, Zurich and Chur: Rüegger.

Knoepfel, P., Larrue, C., Varone, F. and Hill, M. (2011) *Public policy analysis*, Bristol: Policy Press.

Knoepfel, P., Nahrath, S., Csikos, P. and Gerber, J.-D. (2009) *Les stratégies politiques et foncières des grands propriétaires fonciers en action: Etudes de cas*, Cahier de l'IDHEAP 247, Chavannes-près-Renens: IDHEAP.

Knoepfel, P., Nahrath, S., Savary, J., Varone, F., with Dupuis, J. (2010) *Analyse des politiques suisses de l'environnement*, Zürich, Chur: Rüegger.

Knoepfel, P., Eberle, A., Joerchel Anhorn, B., Meyrat, M. and Sager, F. (1999) 'Cas de Neuchlen-Anschwilen. Conflit autour de l'extension de la place d'armes de Neuchlen-Anschwilen dans le canton de Saint-Galle', in P. Knoepfel et al (eds) *Militär und Umwelt im politischen Alltag: Vier Fallstudien für die Ausbildung/Militaire et environnement: la politique au quotidien: Quatre études de cas pour l'enseignement*, Bern: EPA, pp 33-168.

Knoepfel, P., Papadopoulos, Y., Sciarini, P., Vatter, A. and Häusermann, S. (2014) *Handbuch der Schweizer Politik/Manuel de la politique suisse*, 5th edn, Zürich: NZZ Verlag.

Knoke, D. and Kuklinski, J.H. (1982) *Network analysis*, Beverly Hills, CA: Sage Publications.

Knoke Levitt, B. and March, J.G. (1988) 'Organizational learning', *Annual Review of Sociology*, 14: 319-40.

Knoke, D. and Wood, J.R. (1981) *Organized for action: Commitment in voluntary associations*, New Brunswick, NJ: Rutgers University Press.

Koller, C. (2009) 'Profil du personnel de la function publique', in A. Ladner, J.-L. Chappelet, Y. Emery, P. Knoepfel, L. Mader, N. Soguel and F. Varone (eds) *Manuel d'administration publique suisse*, Lausanne: PPUR, pp 501-22.

Lacam, J.-P. (1988) 'Le politicien investisseur. Un modèle d'interprétation de la gestion des ressources politiques', *Revue française de sciences politiques*, 38(1): 23-47.

Ladner, A., Chappelet, J.-L., Emery, Y., Knoepfel, P., Mader, L., Soguel, N. and Varone, F. (2013) *Manuel d'administration publique suisse*, Lausanne: PPUR.

Laesslé, M. (2015) 'Valeurs, rivalités locales et créativité institutionnelle dans la vie de deux appellations de vin suisses', *Espaces et sociétés*, 162/3: 147-62.

Laesslé, M. (2016) 'Les appellations et la culture du vin: De la créativité institutionnelle pour exclure et pour inclure, en Suisse et en Nouvelle-Zélande', Thèse de l'IDHEAP.

Lajarge, R., Pecquert, B., Landel, P.-A. and Lardon, S. (2012) *Ressources territoriales: Gouvernance et politiques publiques* (https://halshs.archives-ouvertes.fr/halshs-00700760).

Lambelet, S. and Pflieger, G. (2016) 'Les ressources du pouvoir urbain', *Métropoles*, 18 (http://metropoles.revues.org/5329).

Lapeyronnie, D. (1988) 'Mouvements sociaux et action politique. Existe-t-il une théorie de la mobilisation des ressources?', *Revue française de sociologie*, 29-4: 593-619.

Lascoumes, P. and Le Galès, P. (2012) *Sociologie de l'action publique*, 2nd edn, Paris: Armand Colin.

Lasswell, H.D. and Kaplan, A. (1950) *Power and society: A framework for political enquiry*, New Haven, CT: Yale University Press.

Lemieux, V. (2002) *L'étude des politiques publiques. Les acteurs et leur pouvoir*, 2nd edn, Sainte-Foy: Les presses de l'Université Laval.

Lienhard, A. and Kettiger, D. (2016) *The judiciary between management and the rule of law*, Bern: Stämpfli Verlag.

Lochard, Y. and Simonet-Cusset, M. (2003) 'Entre science et politique: Les politiques du savoir dans le monde associatif', *Lien social et politiques*, 50: 127-34.

Lundin, M. (2007) 'Explaining cooperation: How resource interdependence, goal congruence and trust affect joint actions in policy implementation', *Journal of Public Administration Research and Theory (GPART)*, 17(4): 651-72.

Mader, L. (2013) 'Législation', in A. Ladner, J.-L. Chappelet, Y. Emery, P. Knoepfel, L. Mader, N. Soguel and F. Varone (eds) *Manuel d'administration publique suisse*, Lausanne: PPUR, pp 245-65.

March, J.G. and Olsen, J.P. (1975) 'The uncertainty of the past. Organizational learning under ambiguity', *European Journal of Political Research*, 3(2): 147-71.

Marsh, D. and Smith, M. (2000) 'Understanding policy networks: Towards a dialectical approach', *Political Studies*, 48(1): 4-21.

McCarthy, J.D. and Zald M.N. (1977) 'Resource mobilization and social movements: A partial theory', *American Journal of Sociology*, 82: 1212-41.

Meltsner, A.J. (1972) 'Political feasibility and policy analysis', *Public Administration Review*, 32(6): 859-67.

Mettler, T., Rohner, P. and Winter, R. (2010) 'Towards a classification of maturing models in information systems', in A. D'Atri, M. de Marco, A. Braccini and F. Cabiddu (eds) *Management of the interconnected world*, Physica-Verlag HD, pp 333-40.

Moor, P. (1997) 'Dire le droit', *Revue européenne de sciences sociales*, XXXV(105), Genève, Paris: Droz, 33-55.

Moor, P. (2010) *Dynamique du système juridique – Une théorie générale du droit*, Genève: Schulthess.

Moor, P. (2016) *Perméabilités du système juridique. Essais sur le droit de l'État de droit*, Québec: Presse de l'université de Laval.

Moor, P. with Poltier, E. (2011) *Droit administratif. Vol II: Les actes administratifs et leur contrôle*, 3rd edn, Bern: Stämpfli.

Moor, P. with Bellanger, F. and Tanquerel, F. (2016) *Droit administratif. Vol III: L'organisation des activités administratives. Les biens de l'Etat*, 2nd edn, Bern: Stämpfli.

Moor, P. with Flückiger, A. and Martenet, V. (2012) *Droit administratif. Vol I: Les fondements généraux*, 3rd edn, Bern: Stämpfli.

Morand, C.-A. (ed) (1991a) *L'Etat propulsive. Contribution à l'étude des instruments d'action de l'Etat*, Paris: Publisud.

Morand, C.-A. (1991b) 'Les nouveaux instruments d'action de l'Etat et le droit', in C.-A. Morand (ed) *Les instruments d'action de l'Etat*, Basel: Helbing & Lichtenhahn, pp 237-56.

Morriss, P. (2012) *Power: A philosophical analysis*, Manchester: Manchester University Press.

Muller, P. (1995) 'Les politiques publiques comme construction d'un rapport au monde', in A. Faure, G. Pollet and P. Warin (eds) *La construction de sens dans les politiques publiques. Débats autour de la notion de référentiel*, Paris: L'Harmattan, pp 153-79.

Nahrath, S. (2003) 'La mise en place du régime institutionnel de l'aménagement du territoire en Suisse entre 1960 et 1990', Thèse présentée à l'IDHEAP.

Nahrath, S. and Varone, F. (2009) 'Introduction. Peter Knoepfel's legacy to policy analysis', in S. Nahrath, S. and F. Varone (eds) *Rediscovering public law and public administration in comparative policy analysis. A tribute to Peter Knoepfel*, Lausanne: PPUR.

Nahrath, S., Pflieger, G. and Varone, F. (2011) 'Institutional network regimes: A new framework to better grasp the key role of infostructure', *Network Industry Quarterly*, 13(1): 23-6.

Nahrath, S., Knoepfel, P., Csikos, P. and Gerber, J.-D. (2009) *Les stratégies politiques et foncières des grands propriétaires fonciers au niveau national: Etude comparée*, Cahier de l'IDHEAP 246, Chavannes-près-Renens: IDHEAP.

Newig, J. (2005) 'Erleichtert Öffentlichkeitsbeteiligung die Umsetzung (umwelt-) politischer Maßnahmen? Ein Modellansatz zur Erklärung der Implementationseffektivität', in P.H. Feindt and J. Newig (eds) *Partizipation, Öffentlichkeitsbeteiligung, Nachhaltigkeit. Perspektiven der politischen Ökonomie*, Marburg: Metropolis, pp 1-19.

Norbert, T. and Adrian, R. (2000) *Public management – Innovative Konzepte zur Führung im öffentlichen Sektor*, Wiesbaden: Gabler.

Oberschall, A. (1973) *Social conflicts and social movements*, Prentice Hall, NJ: Pearson Education.

Olgiati Pelet, M. (2011) *Nouveau regard sur l'information documentaire publique – Régulation d'une ressource en émergence dans l'univers des archives, des bibliothèques et de l'administration suisse*, Zürich, Chur: Rüegger.

Olsen, J.P. (1991) 'Modernizing programs in perspective: Institutional analysis of organisational change', *Governance*, 4(2): 125-49.

Osborne, D. and Gaebler, T. (1983) *Reinventing government. How the entrepreneurial spirit is transforming the public sector*, New York: Penguin Books.

Ostrom, E. (1990) *Governing the commons. The evolution of institutions for collective actions*, Cambridge: Cambridge University Press.

Padioleau, J.-G. (1999) 'L'action publique post-moderne: Le gouvernement politique des risques', *Politiques et management public*, 17(4): 85-127.

Pasquier, M. (eds) (2013a) *Le principe de la transparence en Suisse et dans le monde*, Lausanne: PPUR.

Pasquier, M. (2013b) 'Communication de l'administration et des organisations publiques', in A. Ladner, J.-L. Chappelet, Y. Emery, P. Knoepfel, L. Mader, N. Soguel and F. Varone (eds) *Manuel d'administration publique suisse*, Lausanne: PPUR, pp 401-22.

Patton, D.W., Witt, S.L., Lovrich, N. and Fredericksen, P. (2016) *Human resource management: The public service perspective*, New York: Routledge.

Radaelli, C. (2000) 'Logiques de pouvoir et *récits* dans les politiques publiques de l'Union Européenne', *Revue française de science politique*, 50(2): 255-75.

Rieder, S., Balthasar, A. and Kissling-Näf, I. (2014) 'Vollzug und Wirkung öffentlicher Politiken', in P. Knoepfel, Y. Papadopoulos, P. Sciarini, A. Vatter and S. Häusermann (eds) *Handbuch der Schweizer Politik = Manuel de la politique suisse*, Zürich: NZZ Verlag, pp 563-98.

Ritz, A. (2003) *Evaluation von New public management – Grundlagen und empirische Ergebnisse der Bewertung von Verwaltungsreformen in der Schweizerischen Bundesverwaltung*, Bern: Haupt, p 570.

Ritz, A. and Sinelli, P. (2013) 'Management de la performance dans l'administration publique', in A. Ladner, J.-L. Chappelet, Y. Emery, P. Knoepfel, L. Mader, N. Soguel and F. Varone (eds) *Manuel d'administration publique suisse*, Lausanne: PPUR, pp 345-68.

Roads, R.A.W. (1985) 'Power dependence, policy communities and intergovernmental networks', *Public Administration Bulletin*, 49: 4-31.

Rodewald, R. and Knoepfel, P. (eds) (2005) *Institutionelle Regime für nachhaltige Landschaftsentwicklung – Régimes institutionnels pour le développement durable du paysage*, Zürich: Rüegger.

Rose, R. (1993) *Lesson – Drawing in public policy. A guide to learning across time and space*, Chatham: Chatham House.

Sabatier, P.A. and Jenkins-Smith, H. (1993) 'The Advocacy Coalition Framework: Assessment, revisions and implications for scholars and practitioners', in P. Sabatier and H. Jenkins-Smith (eds) *Policy change and learning: An advocacy coalition approach*, Boulder. CP: Westview Press, pp 211-35.

Sabatier, P.A. and Weible, C.M. (eds) (2007) 'The Advocacy Coalition Framework', in P.A Sabatier and C.M. Weible (eds) *Theories of the policy process*, Boulder, CO: Westview Press, pp 191-220.

Sager, F. (2013) 'Structures politico-administratives de la politique des transports', in A. Ladner, J.-L. Chappelet, Y. Emery, P. Knoepfel, L. Mader, N. Soguel and F. Varone (eds) *Manuel d'administration publique suisse*, Lausanne: PPUR, pp 811-34.

Savary, J. (2007) 'Mise en œuvre des politiques de la mobilité urbaine: Analyse comparée de processus de régulation des usages des voies publiques et de l'air dans quatre villes suisses', Thèse à l'Université de Lausanne.

Savary, J. (2008) *Poltiques publiques et mobilité urbaine, analyse de processus conflictuels dans quatre villes suisses*, Zürich and Chur: Rüegger.

Sauer, A. (2008) 'Conflict pattern analysis: Preparing the ground for participation in policy implementation', *Systemic Practice and Action Research*, 21: 497–515.

Schönenberger, A. (2013) 'Finances publiques en Suisse', in A. Ladner, J.-L. Chappelet, Y. Emery, P. Knoepfel, L. Mader, N. Soguel and F. Varone (eds) *Manuel d'administration publique suisse*, Lausanne: PPUR, pp 567–86.

Scharpf, F.W. (1970) *Die politischen Kosten des Rechtsstaats*, Tübingen: Mohr Siebeck.

Scharpf, F.W. (ed) (1997) *Games real actors play: Actor-centered institutionalism in policy research*, Boulder, CO: Westview Press.

Schedler, K. and Eichler, A. (2013) 'Rapport entre l'administration et la politique', in A. Ladner, J.-L. Chappelet, Y. Emery, P. Knoepfel, L. Mader, N. Soguel and F. Varone (eds) *Manuel d'administration publique suisse*, Lausanne: PPUR, pp 369–86.

Schedler, K. and Proeller, I. (2006) *New public management*, Bern: Haupt.

Schweizer, R. (2015) *Stratégies d'activation du droit dans les politiques environnementales – Cas autour des bis valaisans*, Zürich and Chur: Somedia, Rüegger.

Schweizer, R., Rodewald, R., Liechti, K. and Knoepfel, P. (2014) *Des systèmes d'irrigation alpins entre gouvernance communautaire et étatique – Alpine Bewässerungssysteme zwischen Genossenschaft und Staat*, Zürich and Chur: Rüegger.

Scott, J. (1991) *Social network analysis*, London: Sage.

Söderlund, P.J. (2005) 'Electoral success and federal-level influence of Russian regional executives', *Europe-Asia Studies*, 4(57): 521–41.

Soguel, N. (ed) (2011) *Des politiques au chevet de la conjoncture/Die Politiken als Retterinnen der Konjunktur*, Lausanne: PPUR.

Soguel, N. (2013) 'Présentation des états financiers publics', in A. Ladner, J.-L. Chappelet, Y. Emery, P. Knoepfel, L. Mader, N. Soguel and F. Varone (eds) *Manuel d'administration publique suisse*, Lausanne: PPUR, pp 623–44.

Soparnot, R. (2012) *Organisation et gestion des entreprises*, Paris: Dunod.

Thalmann, P. (2016) *Aspects économiques du développement durable – Bases pour l'évaluation de la durabilité de projets*, Bern: Office fédéral du développement territorial ARE.

Thom, N. and Ritz, A. (2000) *Innovative Konzepte zur Führung im öffentlichen Sektor*, Wiesbaden: Gabler.

Tilly, C. (1978) *From mobilization to revolution*, Reading, MA and Menlo Park, CA: Addison-Wesley Publishers.

Tippenhauer, L. (2014) *Evolution des usages et de la gestion d'un système ressourciel agroalimentaire fromager suisse: le cas du Gruyère (vol 3)*, l'IDHEAP 15m Chavannes–près–Renens: IDHEAP.

Travis, J., Chaiken, J. and Kaminski, R. (1999) *Use of force by the police*, Washington, DC: National Institute of Justice.

Tretjak, T., Marusenko, R. and Knoepfel, P. (2017) *Transport-related environmental policy implementation in four cities of Ukraine*, Final report of the project 'Environmental Policy Implementation Seminary', financed by the Swiss National Science Foundation, IZ74ZO_160473.

UN (United Nations) (2004) *United Nations handbook on practical anti-corruption measures for prosecutors and investigators*, Vienna, September.

van Dam, N. and Jos, M. (2007) *Organization and management: An international approach*, London: Routledge.

Varone, F. (2013) 'Administration fédérale', in A. Ladner, J.-L. Chappelet, Y. Emery, P. Knoepfel, L. Mader, N. Soguel and F. Varone (eds) *Manuel d'administration publique suisse*, Lausanne: PPUR, pp 103-18.

Vesan, P. and Graziano, P. (2008) *Local partnership as a new mode of governance: A framework for analysis*, Urge (Research Unit on European Governance), Working Paper, 1: 1-18.

Vogel, S.K. (1996) *Freer markets. More rules. Regulatory reforms in advanced industrial countries*, Ithaca, NY: Cornell University Press, p 312.

Walliser, B. (1977) *Systèmes et modèles: Introduction critique à l'analyse de systems*, Paris: Editions du seuil.

Wälti, S. (2001) *Le fédéralisme d'exécution sous pression, la mise en œuvre des politiques à incidence spatiale dans le système fédéral suisse*, Genève and Bâle: Helbing & Lichtenhahn.

Warin, P. (2009) 'A pragmatic constructivism', in S. Nahrath and F. Varone (eds) *Rediscovering public law and public administration in comparative policy analysis: A tribute to Peter Knoepfel*, Bern: Haupt, pp 319-32.

Warin, P. (2010) 'Les politiques publiques face à la non-demande sociale', in O. Borraz and V. Giraudon, *Politiques publiques 2. Changer la société*, Paris: Presses de Sciences Po, pp 287-312.

Wasserman, S. and Faust, K. (1994) *Social network analysis. Methods and applications*, Cambridge: Cambridge University Press.

Weber, M. (1978) in G. Roth and C. Wittich (eds) *Economy and society: An outline of interpretive sociology*, Berkeley, CA: University of California Press.

Weidner, H. (1989) 'Japanese environmental policy in an international perspective: Lessons for a preventive approach', in T. Shigeto and H. Weidner (eds) *Environmental policy in Japan*, Berlin: edition sigma, pp 479-552.

Weidner, H. (1993a) *Mediation as a policy instrument for resolving environmental disputes – With special reference to Germany*, WZB-Paper (FS II 93-301), Berlin: Wissenschaftszentrum Berlin für Sozialforschung.

Weidner, H. (1993b) 'Der verhandelnde Staat. Minderung von Vollzugskonflikten durch Mediationsverfahren', *Schweizerische Vereinigung für Politische Wissenschaft* (SVPW), 33: 225-44.

Weidner, H. (1995) 'Innovative Konfliktregelung in der Umweltpolitik durch Mediation: Anregungen aus dem Ausland für die Bundesrepublik Deutschland', in P. Knoepfel (ed) *Lösung von Umweltkonflikten durch Verhandlung – Beispiele aus dem In- und Ausland*, Basel and Frankfurt am Main: Helbing & Lichtenhahn, pp 105-25.

Weidner, H., Knoepfel, P. and Zieschank, R. (1992) *Umwelt-Information. Berichterstattung und Informationssysteme in zwölf Ländern*, Berlin: Edition Sigma.

World Bank, The (2006) *Where is the wealth of nations? Measuring capital for the 21st century*, Washington, DC: The World Bank.

World Bank, The (2011) *The changing wealth of nations? Measuring sustainable development in the new millennium*, Washington, DC: The World Bank.

World Bank, The (2014) *The little green databook*, Washington, DC: The World Bank.

Zuppinger, U. and Knoepfel, P. (1998) 'Swiss Border incident: A case study of the Ciba-Geigy special waste incineration plant in Basel, Switzerland', in B. Dente, P. Fareri and J. Ligteringen (eds) *The waste and the backyard: The creation of waste facilities: Success stories in six European countries*, Dordrecht: Kluwer Academic Publishers, pp 117-60.

Zwicker, J. (2007) 'Archivrecht 2006 – Andate ma non troppo', in G. Coutaz and R. Huber, *Archivpraxis in der Schweiz. Pratiques archivistiques en Suisse*, Baden: hier + jetzt, pp 164-94.

Index

Note: Page numbers for figures and tables appear in italics.

1960s, major policies of 27

A

abstract use of Property 164–5, 166
accounting rules 3, 168–9
action instruments 10
action logics, different 3
action plans (AP) 10, 12, 16–17, 29, 47,
    251, 253–5, 269, *270*
  and Information 183, 185
  and Time 230–1
action resources 58, 75
actio popularis 125
activation 39
actor games 13, 269, 271, 279
actor networks 67
actors
  definition 17–19
  objectives 271
  see also beneficiary groups; political-
    administrative actors; target groups
Actors and systems (Crozier and Friedberg)
    51
actor triangle 267, *268*, 279
  and Consensus 214, 217, 221
  and Political Support 239, 242, 245
actor-users 82–3, 86
addition, and use rights 180
address books 208
administrative decisions, and Information
    183
administrative entities 19
administrative property 166, 167, 169,
    171
'The Advocacy Coalition Framework'
    (ACF)/Sabatier and Weible 61
Agence Suisse de l'énergie pour
    l'économie 207
agenda setting *270*
agricultural policies 11–13, 93, 124, 138
  and Information 182
  and Organization 205, 208
  and Political Support 241, 243
agro-environmental programmes 11–13

aliens policy 199
amalgamation of services 199–200
amnesty 222
anti-cartel policy 241
anti-smoking policy 208
appeals 15, 125–6, 128, 129, 130, 208,
    273, 278
apprenticeships 138
archives 186, 187
armistice 234
army, Swiss 136–7
assessment 274–5
ASTAG 222
asylum policy 123, 128, 137
atheoretical inductivism 64
Authority 62, 63
availability
  and Consensus 216–19
  and Force 113–15
  and Information 180–5
  and Law 123–6
  and mobilization 105
  and Money 148–52
  and Organization 197–203
  and Personnel 136–40
  and Property 167–71
  and Time 227–30

B

banking 127, 138
Basel chemical industry 137, 201
basic triangle 14, 213
begging 122–3
behavioural rules 4, 33, *36*, 77, 84, 279
beneficiaries 2, 15, 22, 274, 275
  and Organization 208–9
  and political parties 29
  and production 95
  and Property 165
  and target groups 23
  and transport 21
beneficiary groups 16, 25–9, 272–3
  and Consensus 216–17, 218–19, 220–1,
    222–3

and exchange 206, 266
and Force 115, 116, 118–19
indicators 260–3
and Information 184–5, 188, 189, 191
and Law 125–6, 128–9, 130
and Money 151–2, 153, 155–6, 157–9
and Organization 195, 202–3, 204
and Personnel 139–40, 141–2, 143
and political parties 240
and Political Support 246
and Property 166, 170–1, 173, 175
and renunciation 98
and strategic objectives 92
and target groups 24, 217
and threats 97
and Time 227, 229–30, 231, 232, 234
Blin, Thierry 60–1, *73*
budgets 20, 41, 100, 256
  annuality 154
  flexibility 99
  non-use 149
  and target groups 150–1
building 129–30
business associations 143

C

cantons, and exchange with
    Confederation 205–6
capacity 63
cartels 77–8
causal hypotheses 11, 14–15, 30, 180,
    221
causality models 11, 14–15, 231, 241,
    244–5
Centre de Sociologie des Organisations
    (CSO) 51
change 242, 272
Chappelet, L. 78
chemical industry 137, 138, 201, 216
Chevallaz, André 148
China 279
Chinese Communist Party 279
civil society actors 48, 78, 110, 117, 122,
    189, 256
  see also beneficiary groups; target groups
civil society organizations 27–8
Clapham, Christopher 52–4, *73*
climate policy 205, 244
coalitions 152
coercive contextual resources 56
coercive personal resources 56
cognitive resources 71
coins 63
collective resources 59
combining resources 99–100
COMCO 77, 78
common pool resources 85

communal fiscal policy 172
communes owning land 22
company mergers 77–8
compensation 24–5, 93–4, 158
competency 48, 278
complex networks 57
Compston, Hugh 67–8, *74*, 75
concrete causality models 14–15
concrete use of Property 164, 165, 166,
    168, 172, 174
Confederation, as landowner 171
Conference of Cantonal Governments
    206
confidential information 182
'Conflict pattern analysis: Preparing the
    ground for participation in policy
    implementation' (Sauer) 65
confrontation, logics of 44
Consensus 24, 100, 107, 213–23, 252,
    257, *262*, 278, 280
  and beneficiary groups 152
  and civil society organizations 28
  and evaluative statement 17
  and farmers 93
  and Force 110
  and Law 123
  and Newig 59
  and Organization 206, 207, 208
  and Personnel 142, 143
  and political-administrative actors 156,
    198
  and production 95
  and Property 174
  and target groups 157, 190
  and Time 229
constructivist pragmatic approach 279
consultancy mandates 157
consumer policy 208
'contractual' arrangements 153
Control Committees 148
cooperation, logics of 44
co-reports 220
corruption 157, 158
counter-information 185
counter-services 208, 274
credibility 97, 216, 218, 219, 221, 243
crime, serious 128
Criminal Code, Swiss 111
criminality, prevention of 181
criminal prosecutions 216
Crozier, Michel 51, 57
customary law 33
customs 33
cybercrime 180

D

Dahl, Robert A. 52, 56, 59
dams 130
data management 179
data monitoring body 179
data protection 181
Davern, Michael 57–8, *73*, 75
deadlines 226, 229, 233
decisional rules 4, 33, *37*, 77, 279
decision-making 28–9, 200, 266, 271–2, 275
decisions 267–9, 271
definition of the problem 16
delaying strategies 231
demotivation 136
Dente, Bruno 69–71, *74*, 75
destabilization 279
DETEC (Federal Department of the Environment, Transport, Energy and Communication) 129
development stage, and Information 188
different action logics 3
disability 27, 137
dismissal 134
distrust 217, 218, 219, 222
donations 152
dossiers, sharing of 203, 252–3
do ut des 101–2, 106
Dowding, Keith 63–4, *74*
'dual' concept 138
dynamic component 57

E

economic action, and Force 110
economic data 183
economic development policies 171–2
economic policies 182, 183
economic promotion policy 199
economic resources 23–4, 30–1, 70, 78
education policies 127, 171, 200
effectiveness 251, 257
efficiency 251, 257–8
'Electoral success and federal-level influence of Russian regional executives' (Söderlund) 59–60
electricity generation utilities 22
Emery, Y. 78, 134
emissions controls 222
end beneficiaries 29
energy policies 199, 244
entrepreneur, public 203
environmental impact assessments 198, 220, 233
environmental policies
  and Consensus 217, 218
  and Information 179, 182, 188
  and Law 124, 128

and Organization 199, 204, 208
and Personnel 138
and Political Support 245
and pooling resources 207
environmental protection 130, 139, 166, 202
environmental resources 30–1
L'étude des politiques publiques. Les acteurs et leur pouvoir (Lemieux) 58
European Court of Justice 125
evaluation *270*
evaluative statement (ES) 10, 16, 17, 183, 219, 269, *270*
exchange 20, 93, 106, 264, 266, 273–4, 279
  and Consensus 221–3
  and Force 117–19
  of Information 188–91
  and Law 129–30
  and Money 156–9
  and Organization 204–9
  and Personnel 141–3
  and Property 174–5
  and target groups 24
  and Time 232–4
exchangeability 100–2
external actors 21, 94, 194, 239, 246, 253
external relations 201–2

F

faits accomplis 116
family policies 208, 218
farmers 12, 93, 138
Federal Act on Spatial Planning 126
Federal Act on the Organization of the Government and Administration Organization Act (GAOA) 193–4
Federal Council 152–3
Federal Office for the Protection of Water Bodies 138
Federal Police 137
federal spending 152–3
financial incentives 152
financial property 166, 171
financial resources 2, 59
fiscal policy 181
Flückiger et al 126
Force 12, 97, 109–19, *260*
  and action plan 17
  and beneficiary groups 159
  and Consensus 222
  and Information 185
  and Organization 202
  and substitution of resources 100
  and target groups 25
  and Time 228, 234
  and transport 21
foreign language teaching 127

forests 22
foundations 207
Freeman, J. 60
Friedberg, Erhard 51, 57
functionnariat 134

G

game of cards 32
*Games real actors play: Actor-centered
    institutionalism in public policy research*
    (Scharpf) 51
Gamson, W.A. 55
general institutional policies 40
general institutional rules 39–40, 41
general institutions *35, 36, 37*, 38,
    39–40, 42
geocoded data 181, 184
Giauque, D. 78, 134, 135
globalization 38
good faith rules 102
goods, public action resources 81–3
government tools 62–3
Graziano, Paolo 64–5, *74*
Green Party of Switzerland 222
Greenpeace 158, 171

H

Habermas, Jürgen 189
habitus 33
Hardturm football stadium 126
health 181, 188, 208
health insurance 205
heterogeneous exchanges 106, 264, 274
    and Consensus 221
    of Force 118
    of Information 185, 190, 191
    of Law 129, 130
    of Money 157, 158
    and Organization 205, 206, 207, 208–9
    of Personnel 136
    of Property 173, 175
    and Time 233, 234
hierarchy, lack of 278–9
historical data 187
homogenous exchanges 101, 106, 264,
    274
    and Consensus 221
    of Force 118
    of Information 188, 189, 190
    of Money 156
    of Personnel 142
    and political-administrative actors
        204–5
    of Time 229, 232–3, 234
Hood, Christopher 62–3, *74*, 75
horizontal coordination procedures 199
housing policies 172

human capital 24, 75
human resources 58, 75
    see also Personnel
hypotheses 14, 15

I

IDHEAP 107
Imbeau, Louis M. 66–7, *74*, 75
impact assessment 198, 199, 233
implementation stage 105, 251–3, *270*
    and beneficiary groups 155, 188
    and Consensus 219, 220, 221
    and Force 109, 111, 114, 115, 116
    and Information 181, 183, 185
    and Law 122, 124, 128
    and Money 151, 152
    and Organization 203
    and Personnel 140, 141
    and Political Support 246–7
    and Property 175
    and target groups 154
    and Time 231, 232
implicit hypotheses 40
improvements 26
indicators 260–3, 264
Information 12, 89, 98, 179–91, 257,
    261, 278
    and civil society organizations 28
    combining with Law 99
    and Consensus 217, 220
    damaging credibility of the resource 84
    and evaluative statement 17
    and Force 114, 115
    and manufactured capital resources 24
    and Organization 202
    and political-administrative actors 117,
        156
    and production 94
    and target groups 15, 25, 151, 157
    and Time 233
'Informational lobbying in the European
    Union: Explaining information supply
    to the European Commission' (Klüver)
    68–9
information campaign costs 153
information resources 58
    see also Information
infrastructure policies 20, 115, 171
infrastructure resources 96
institutional financial policies 20
institutional games 38
institutional policies 2, 3, 9, 40–1
    of sectoral policies 20
institutional policy actors 20
institutional policy products 20
institutional reforms 40

institutional resource regimes (IRR)
  44–5, 83, 277
institutional rules 31–41, 48, 77, 84, 102,
  228, 275, 279
  and Force 113
  and Personnel 134
  and resource mobilization 98
  and substitution of resources 100
  and use rights 96
institutions 5, 31–42, 53–4
insurance 23
intercantonal agreement 127
international comparisons 52–4
intervention hypotheses 10, 11, 14, 15

J

Jenkins, C.J. 60

K

Kaplan, Abraham 52
Kiun, Erik-Has 57, *73*
Klüver, Heike 68–9, *74*
Knoepfel et al 9, 19, 31, 32, 44, 51, 267,
  271
  on action plans 254
  on Consensus 214
  on definition of Law 121
  on evaluative statements 269
  on Information 180
  on institutions 31
  on Money 147
  on Organization 194
  on Personnel 133
  on Political Support 238
  on Property 162
  on Time 225
known action resources 1

L

labels, sale of false 158
Lacam, Jean-Patrice 55–7, *73*
lack of resources 99
land
  ownership 24
  taxation of 126
Lapeyronnie, Didier 54–5, *73*
Lasswell, Harold D. 52
Law 16, 71, 121–30, 256, *260*, 278
  and beneficiary groups 158, 191
  and civil society organizations 28
  combining 99–100
  and Consensus 217, 220, 222
  and evaluative statement 17
  and Force 115
  and Information 185
  and Organization 202, 206, 208
  and political-administrative actors 25,
    117, 175

and Political Support 239
and Property 172–3
and right of mobilization 47, 48
and target groups 151, 157
and threats 97
and Time 228, 229, 233
law, role of 46–9
legacies, taxation of 127–8
legal policies 20
legal resources 70–1
legislative consultation procedure 219
legislative decisions 12
legitimacy 213, 237, 242, 244, 274
legitimization 257
Lemieux, Vincent 58, *73*
Local partnership as a new mode of governance:
  A framework for analysis (Vesan and
  Graziano) 64–5
local regulatory arrangements (LRA) 39
logics of confrontation 44
logics of cooperation 44
loyalties 196–7

M

maintenance 96–7
majority support 190
management, and use rights 180
manufactured capital resources 24, 75
Margetts, Helen 62–3, *74*, 75
material resources 58, 68–9
McCarthy, J.D. 55
measurement, units of 260–3, 264
media profile 246–7
mediation processes 218
Meltsner, Arnold J. 52, *73*, 75
membership contributions 151
meta-information system 186
mobilization 11, 13–14, 17, 28–9, 30,
  47–8, 98, 273–5
  and availability 105
  and Consensus 216–21
  of Force 113–16
  and Information 180–8
  and Lapeyronnie 54
  of Law 122, 123–9
  and Money 148–56
  and Organization 197–204
  and Personnel 136–41
  and Political Support 243–4
  of Property 166, 167–73
  purpose 77
  by stage 105
  of Time 227–32
Money 15, 17, 147–59, *260*
  and civil society organizations 28
  exchange rights of use to 93
  and financial property 166
  and manufactured capital resources 24

and Organization 205, 206, 207, 208
and political-administrative actors 25, 117
and production 94
and Property 168, 172
relaxation of the rules 99
and resource mobilization 98
and substitution of resources 100
and Time 233
and transport 21
money laundering 137, 138, 245
monitoring 140–1, 150, 187–8
Moor, Pierre 96
moratoriums 233, 234
Morriss, Peter 64
Mouvements sociaux et action politique. Existe-t-il une théorie de la mobilisation des ressources?' ('Social movements and political action. Is there a theory of the mobilization of resources?')/Lapeyronnie 54
multi-annual financial frameworks 154
multiple interdependencies 196
mutual interests 106

N

national defence policies 217, 241
'NATO' 62–3
natural capital 24
natural lands 173
natural resources 23–4, 44–6, 75, 78, 82–3, 277
negotiations, internal 28
networks 57, 58, 67
'Networks, resources, political strategy and climate policy' (Compston) 67–8
Newig, Jens 59, 73
new information and communication technologies (NICT) 85
New Public Management (NPM) 99, 135, 257
NGOs
  and Information 185
  and Money 155, 158
  salaries 143
  see also beneficiary groups
nodality 62, 63
non-activation 39
non-litigious administrative procedure 189
non-mobilization 98
normative component 57
normative resources 58
nuclear waste 109, 115, 185, 213, 214, 218
nudging 110, 113, 116, 217

O

Oberschall, A. 54, 55
objective law 46–8, 49
oral exchange of information 180
Organization 12, 15, 62–3, 193–209, 256–7, 261, 280
  and action plan 17
  and beneficiary groups 152, 170
  and Consensus 217
  and Force 114, 115
  and maintenance 96
  and manufactured capital resources 24
  and production 95
  and substitution of resources 100
  and target groups 151
  and transport 21
organizational structures 69
outputs 14, 16, 29, 47, 252, 256, 258, 270
  and action plans 255
  and evaluative statement 17
  and Information 181
  see also implementation stage
outsourcing 137–8
over-exploitation of personnel 136
owner, the state 22, 23

P

pacta sunt servanda 101, 102
pantouflage 142
partnership, simple 201
paymasters 3
Pelet, Mirta Olgiati 85–9
penal courts 181
Personnel 133–43, 257, 260
  and civil society organizations 28
  and evaluative statement 17
  exchangeability of resources, limited 100–1
  and Force 114
  and manufactured capital resources 24
  and Organization 202
  and political-administrative actors 156, 175, 198
  and production 95
  and Time 228
persuasive contextual resources 56
persuasive institutional resources 56
planning applications 129, 194–5, 198, 202
planning policies 126, 171
Police, Federal 137
'policy' dossiers 200
policy personnel 141
political-administrative actors 2, 3, 251, 275
  and agricultural policy 93

and beneficiary groups 152, 222, 246
and civil society organizations 28
and Consensus 216–17, 218, 219–20, 221
description 19–22
and environmental policies 179
essential 29
and exchange 266
and Force 111, 114, 115–16, 117, 119
indicators 260–3
and Information 180–3, 185, 186–7, 188–90
and Law 122–4, 126–7, 129
and mobilization 274
and Money 148–50, 152–4, 156, 158
and Organization 197–200, 203, 204–6, 208
and Personnel 136–8, 140–1, 143
and Political Support 242, 244–5
and production 94–5
and Property 165–6, 167–9, 171–2, 174, 175
strategic objectives 91, 92
and target groups 15, 25, 201, 202, 207, 220
and Time 226, 227–8, 229, 230–1, 232–3, 234
political–administrative arrangements (PAA) 10, 13, 34, 47, 105, 195–7, 269, 270
political–administrative programmes (PAP) 10, 12, 16, 29, 34, 47, 105, 269, 270
political exchange 69
political parties 29–30, 152, 153, 239, 240
'political' personnel 142–3
political resources 70
Political Support 24, 213, 237–47, 256, 263, 278
and beneficiary groups 191
and Information 188
and Law 128
and maintenance 96
and Money 151
and Organization 208
and Personnel 142–3
and political–administrative actors 25, 156, 182, 198
and production 94
and Property 175
for target groups 151, 190
and Time 230
and transport 21
political work 151, 152
pollution 14–15, 24–5, 122, 124, 158
pooling 202–3, 204, 207
popular vote 157

possession rules 4, 33, 35, 47, 77, 110, 275, 279
poverty 30–1
power 46, 58, 63, 65–6, 67, 72
actorial 3–4
and actors 57
of economic, social and natural resources 24
of target groups 17, 23
'Power, capability and ableness: The fallacy of the vehicle fallacy' (Dowding) 63
power relations 15, 31, 259, 266–7
primary beneficiaries 26
priority target groups 230
private foundations 207
private sector, employment 134
problem definition (PD) 10
production 94–6, 150
professional bodies 138–9
professional training 138, 200
programming stage 105, 203, 270
and beneficiary groups 155
and Information 186
and Organization 203
and Property 175
and target groups 154
and Time 231, 232
Pro Natura 168, 170–1, 173
Property 12, 24, 147, 161–75, 257, 261, 278
and action plan 17
and beneficiary groups 159
and civil society organizations 28
and Consensus 217, 220, 222
and Force 112–13
and Law 129–30
and Newig 59
and NGOs 158
and Organization 205, 206
and political–administrative actors 25
and production 95
right of use to 93
and the state 22
and target groups 116, 151, 154, 156
and threats 97
and Time 228, 229, 233
and transport 21
valuation of 84
property sector 184
public action, definition 10
public action resources 2, 4, 15, 24, 81–4, 103–8
and action plans 255
definition 43–9
efficient and effective use 251–3
inventory 265
and resource-based approach 85–9

see also the individual resources
public action resources budgets 41
public actors 10, 15, 17, 21, 23, 25, 47,
    252, 255, 256, 257, 266, 269
  and Consensus 219, 220, 222
  and financial resources 2
  and Force 109, 110–11, 112, 118
  and Information 179, 180, 182
  and institutional policies 40–1
  and Law 48, 121
  and Organization 194
  and Political Support 237
  and Property 161, 163
  subsidies from 13
  and target groups 22
  and Time 225, 227, 230, 233
public authorities 23
public budgets 99, 100
public documentary information resource
    85–9
public entrepreneur 203
public finance policies 2
public health policies 124, 217
public interest organizations 139–40
public money, misappropriation of 149
public order 27
Public Policies and Sustainability Research
    Unit, IDHEAP 107
public policy actors 18, 40, 43, 44, 100,
    268
  and Consensus 214, 216
  and Dente 69
  and exchange 101
  and Force 109, 113
  and Lacam 56
  and Law 48, 49
  and Money 147
  and Personnel 133
  and Political Support 238, 239, 242
  and power 72
  and Property 161–2, 163, 164
  see also beneficiaries; beneficiary groups;
    political-administrative actors; target
    groups
public–private partnerships 64–5, 167–8
public problem (PD) 268–9, *270*
public registries 85
public sector
  and allocation of new tasks 137
  employment 134, 135, 137–8, 143
public service 134
public tendering 125, 184

R

railway policies 171
reconciliation of objectives 20
record management 186, 187

redistributive contextual resources 56
redistributive institutional resources 56
redundancy 134
referendum 128, 272, 273
référentiels 239, 240, 242
reforms, institutional 40
registries, public 85
remediation 229, 231
renewable energies policy 244
renunciation 97–8
reorganization
  need for 199
  and target groups 201
representativity 201–2
reputation 63–4
resource, definition 81, 82
resource-based approach 81–9
resource public documentary information
    85–9
resource-related institutional policies 41
resource wars 3
'Ressources, stratégies et régulation d'un
    espace d'action collective: Le cas
    des "réfugiés" de Saint-Ambroise'
    ('Resources, strategies and regulation
    of a collective action space: The case
    of the Saint-Ambroise "refugees"')/
    Blin 60
restrictive public action resources 15
retrenchment 150
right of appeal 15, 125–6, 128, 129, 130,
    278
rights of use to resources 92–4
rivalries, use 86–8
road hauliers 222
Roads, R.A.W. 67
road safety 188
rule of law 125, 135, 181, 227, 237, 241,
    255
  and Force 111, 117
rules 4, 48
  see also institutional rules
rules of the game 32, 33, 67, 98, 215,
    218

S

Sabatier, Paul 61–2, *74*
sampling activities 180
Sauer, Alexandra 65, *74*
Scharpf, Fritz 51, 57
Schweizer, R. 48, 122
secondary beneficiaries 26–7
secondary residences, ban on the
    construction of 172, 174, 182–3, 229
sections 19
sectoral policies 3, 41, 68, 181, 199, 240
sectoral *référentiels* 242

sectoral use rights 94
self-generated action resources 2, 3
self-regulation 127, 175, 204
serious crime 128
service-level agreements 20, 257
service mandate 257
services, and public action resources 81–3
shares 158–9
skills 52
social action, and Force 110
social actors 95, 197, 227
social capital 24, 59
social cohesion 59
social insurance 23
social networks, and Political Support
    246
'Social networks and economic sociology:
    A proposed research agenda for a more
    complete social science' (Davern) 57
social policies 14–15, 23, 27, 155–6, 181,
    199, 207
social resources 23–4, 30–1, 75, 78
social services 15
societal action resources 24
societal state, politically desirable 27
Söderlund, Peter J. 59–60, 73, 75
Spatial Planning Act 172, 173
special institutional rules 34, 39–40
spending, federal 152–3
stage mobilization 105
    and Consensus 219–21
    and Force 115–16
    and Information 186–8
    and Law 126–9
    and Money 152–6
    and Organization 203–4
    and Personnel 140–1
    and Property 171–3
    and Time 230–2
the state
    and civil society actors 189
    hypotheses on interventions of 15
    as owner 23
    and political-administrative actors 22
    and resources 2
State Secretariat for Education, Research
    and Innovation (SERI) 200
State Secretariat for Migration 137
statistical data 179
statistical databases 85
statutory resources 58
stress 135–6
strike, right to 134
structural component 57
subjective right 47, 48
subsidies 12, 13, 151–3, 158
substantive public policies 3, 9, 40, 41, 42
substantive rules 48

substantive sectoral policies 2
substitution 98–9, 100, 278
sustainability 98
sustainable development 277
Swiss army 136–7
Swiss Association of Property Owners
    126
Swiss Bankers Association 138
Swiss Civil Code 202
Swiss Criminal Code 111
Swiss Farmer's Union (SFU) 124
Swiss Federal Audit Office 148
Swiss federal chambers 240
Swiss Federal Office for Civil Protection
    136
Swiss Federal Office of Public Health 136
Swiss Federal Railways (SBB) 171
Swiss Federal Supreme Court 126
Swiss National Council 123–4
Swiss regional transport policy 21
symbolic values 238

T

tangible resources 60–1
target groups 2, 11, 14–15, 16, 21, 22–5,
    272, 275
    and beneficiary groups 158–9
    and Consensus 217–18, 219, 220, 222
    and environmental policies 179–80
    and evaluative statement 17
    and exchange 93, 205, 206, 266, 274
    and Force 112–13, 114–15, 116, 118
    indicators 260–3
    and Information 182, 183–4, 185,
        187–8, 189, 190
    and Law 124–5, 127–8, 129–30
    and Money 150–1, 152, 153, 154, 156,
        157
    and Organization 195, 200–2, 204, 207
    and Personnel 138–9, 140–1, 142–3
    and political-administrative actors
        216–19, 244–5
    and political parties 29, 240
    and Political Support 241, 245–6
    and political work 152
    and production 95
    and Property 165, 169–70, 172–3,
        174–5, 278
    and renunciation 98
    and the state 22
    strategic objectives 92
    and Time 227, 228–9, 230, 231–2,
        233, 234
taxation of legacies 127–8
tax competition 157
tax exemptions 156
technological promotion 200
teleconferences 201

temporary employees 140
tendering policy, public 184
'Testing the "veil of ignorance" hypothesis in constitutional choice: A "walk-talk" approach' (Imbeau) 66
theoretical conceptualizations 3
third-level education policies 200
third party losers 25, 29, 92, 97, 100, 153
   and Political Support 239, 244, 245, 246
third party winners 25, 27, 29, 92, 97, 100, 153
   and Political Support 239, 244, 246
threats 97, 112, 181–2, 198, 231, 246
Time 12, 25, 107, 225–34, 257, *263*, 280
   and Consensus 220
   and Newig 59
   and Organization 206
   and political-administrative actors 175, 198
   and production 95
   and resource mobilization 98
   and Söderlund 59
   and substitution of resources 100
   and target groups 157
tipping point 252
The tools of government in the digital age (Hood and Margetts) 62
traceability 279
tracking mechanisms 186–7
transparency 152, 180, 182, 185
transport policy, Swiss regional 21
Treasure 62, 63
triangle, basic 14, 213
truce 234
trust 216–17, 218, 219, 221, 222, 243, 278
trust-building measures 216

U

unemployment 27
units of measurement 260–3, 264
user-actors 45
use rights 92–4, 96, 180
use rivalries 86–8
users, definition 22

V

vertical coordination procedures 199
Vesan, Patrik 64–5, *74*
volatile organic compounds (VOCs) 205
volunteers 152

W

Warin, Philippe 72
waste processing 129
waters, protection of 12, 198

wealth 4, 30–1
Weber, Max 44
websites 170
Weible, Christopher 61–2, 74
welfare state 27
windows of opportunity 32, 227
wine producers 130
women
   as experts 188
   promotion of employment for 208
working groups 201, 202
work protection policy 208
World Bank 46, 75

Z

Zald, M.N. 55
Zwicker, Joseph 87–8